THE CANALS OF
YORKSHIRE AND NORTH EAST ENGLAND

Volume I

THE CANALS OF THE BRITISH ISLES

Edited by Charles Hadfield

British Canals. An illustrated history. By Charles Hadfield
The Canals of Eastern England. By J. H. Boyes
The Canals of the East Midlands (including part of London). By Charles Hadfield
The Canals of the North of Ireland. By W. A. McCutcheon
The Canals of North West England. By Charles Hadfield and Gordon Biddle
The Canals of Scotland. By Jean Lindsay
The Canals of the South of Ireland. By V. T. H. and D. R. Delany
The Canals of South and South East England. By Charles Hadfield
The Canals of South Wales and the Border. By Charles Hadfield
The Canals of South West England. By Charles Hadfield
The Canals of the West Midlands. By Charles Hadfield
The Canals of Yorkshire and North East England. By Charles Hadfield
Waterways to Stratford. By Charles Hadfield and John Norris

OTHER BOOKS BY CHARLES HADFIELD
Canals of the World
Holiday Cruising on Inland Waterways (with Michael Streat)
The Canal Age
Atmospheric Railways

THE CANALS OF YORKSHIRE AND NORTH EAST ENGLAND

by
Charles Hadfield

WITH PLATES AND MAPS

VOLUME I

DAVID & CHARLES: NEWTON ABBOT

ISBN 0 7153 5719 0

Printed in Great Britain by
Latimer Trend & Company Limited Plymouth
for David & Charles (Publishers) Limited
South Devon House   Newton Abbot   Devon

CONTENTS

VOLUME I

VOLUME II

PART TWO—1790-1845 *(continued)*

ILLUSTRATIONS

Volume I

PLATES

TEXT ILLUSTRATIONS AND MAPS

PREFACE

WHEN the second volume of this book appears in a few months'
time, accompanied by Mr John Boyes's study of *The Canals of
Eastern England*, the 'Canals of the British Isles' series will be
complete, in 13 titles and 15 volumes. The late Mr John Baker,
then at Phoenix House, published *British Canals* in 1950, after
three other firms had rejected it. The book was then intended to
stand by itself, but not long after it appeared, Mr R. R. Sellman
wrote to offer me the use of some material he had collected on
Sussex waterways. From that offer grew the idea of a regional
volume, the former *Canals of Southern England*, published also by
Phoenix House in 1955. From that book, in turn, grew the idea
of a British Isles series. In this series, *The Canals of Southern
England* was later rewritten and enlarged into two volumes as *The
Canals of South and South East England* and *The Canals of South
West England*.

It is difficult now to remember that before 1950 nothing
serious had been written on canal history since Jackman's great
Transportation in Modern England, published in 1914. British Transport Historical Records had only just been set up, and I have there
the reference number of S 1, or Student No. 1. Indeed, I began
researching during the war, in the library of the Institution of
Civil Engineers and the record room of the Great Western Railway. Very much was then unknown, and I set myself, in the
'Canals of the British Isles' series, a straightforward task: to write
down where the canals were and how they began, continued and
survived or died. The books were not meant as studies in economic
history, though they could provide some of the material for such
studies; nor were they to be definitive histories of each waterway:
that is a task other authors have undertaken in the 'Inland Waterways Histories' series.

I have, indeed, been fortunate that, over nearly thirty years, I
have been able to write nine of the thirteen books myself—two in
collaboration—and work closely with the authors of the others,

Dr McCutcheon and Mrs Delany for the Irish volumes, Dr Lindsay for *The Canals of Scotland*, and Mr John Boyes for *The Canals of Eastern England*. The series will soon be complete—perhaps the first of its kind in the field of transport. It falls to me therefore to thank all those who have contributed to its success. Many hundreds of names occur to me, but a few I must mention: my first publisher, John Baker, and my old friend, colleague and present publisher, David St J. Thomas of David & Charles, with whom I share the firm's name: the three archivists of British Transport Historical Records, Messrs Johnson, Atkinson and Fowkes; the members of the Railway & Canal Historical Society —it was I who in a fortunate moment suggested to the founders of a proposed Railway History Society that they should include canals; my children, three of whom have been or are members of the Society; and my wife. Thanks to one's wife are *de rigeur*. But my thanks are more than that. An author herself, she has encouraged, researched, typed for me and sustained me from that day when I read the first draft paragraphs of *British Canals* to her at the gas-stove, to now.

It is therefore fitting that this last book of mine in the series should mainly be about Yorkshire: for she was a Smyth, and her direct ancestor, John Smyth, was in 1699 a founder of the Aire & Calder Navigation. I have been fortunate while writing it to have the advice and help of such experts as J. E. Day, Baron F. Duckham, John Goodchild, Michael Lewis and W. N. Slatcher.

A last word of thanks to my secretaries, Mrs Tomlinson, Mrs Webb and Mrs Davis: I have the fun of research, the pleasures of friendship, the interest of exploration: they type and retype, check and recheck, for every chapter of this book, in some form or other, has been typed four times or more.

And so what was begun in 1947 is ended.

> 'I keep six honest serving men
>   (They taught me all I knew);
> Their names are What and Why and When
>   And How and Where and Who.
> I send them over land and sea,
>   I send them east and west;
> But after they have worked for me,
>   I give them all a rest.'

This series marks the end of an era in British inland waterway history. But another has begun, which promises full use of the smaller canals for public enjoyment, and, thanks to push-towing, barge-carrying ships, sea-going barges and startling progress in waterway engineering, the development of many British waterways as part of an international system.

'The world's great age begins anew,
The golden years return . . .'

I have no complaints of the time during which I have lived, but I confess I could wish for as much again.

CHARLES HADFIELD

PART ONE—TO 1790

CHAPTER I

The Old Navigation

✦✦✦

THE Aire & Calder[1] is perhaps the premier navigation of England, a line useful to the community and profitable to its owners from early in the eighteenth century to the present. The Act[2] of 4 May 1699 under which it was born enabled the undertakers to make the Calder navigable from Wakefield to its junction with the Aire at Castleford, and the latter from Leeds to Castleford and onwards from the confluence to Weeland, $3\frac{1}{2}$ miles above Snaith. Thence the river ran to Airmyn to join the Ouse about four miles above Goole, whence there was access to the Humber and so Hull.[3] The Aire was then navigable only to Knottingley, the tidal limit, and about thirty craft of up to 30 tons burthen traded on it.

Bills of 1621 and 1625 had come to nothing, as had William Pickering's efforts of 1679 for the Aire[4] when he was mayor of Leeds. From 1697 onwards, however, there was a general interest in making navigations: Bills were introduced for the Don in 1697, the Derbyshire Derwent in 1695 and 1698, and the Bristol Avon in 1699, and Acts passed for the upper Trent in 1699 and the Yorkshire Derwent in 1701, the latter after a Bill of 1700 had failed. It was in 1697 also that ideas of making the rivers Aire and Calder navigable were revived, at a time when trade was expanding and capital available.

A main motive was to make easier the export of west Yorkshire cloth, and in 1698 the clothiers of Leeds set out a typical situation in their petition supporting the Bill of that year:

'that the towns of Leeds and Wakefield are the principal markets in the north for woollen cloth . . . that it will be a great improvement of trade to all the trading towns of the north by reason of the conveniency of water carriage, for want of which the petitioners send their goods twenty-two miles by land carriage,*

---

* To Rawcliffe on the Aire about three miles from its junction with the Ouse at Goole; or perhaps Selby was meant.

the expence whereof is not only verey chargeable, but they are forced to stay two months sometimes while the roads are passable to market'.[5]

Other towns sent their cloth elsewhere for eventual carriage by sea, for instance to Knottingley, Tadcaster on the Wharfe, or Selby on the Ouse. Dr Pococke, visiting Selby in 1751, noted: 'Near the river is a large store house of hewn stone, which served for their cloth before the Aire was made navigable, when they brought it to this place by land to be ship'd of'.[6]

Allied with the desire for the easier export of cloth was the need to facilitate the import of wool. This came from east coast ports between King's Lynn and London, and some also by road transport from Lincolnshire and Leicestershire. Finally, the tax on seaborne coal imposed in 1695 potentially favoured the development of west Yorkshire collieries in competition with imports from the Tyne and Wear, or down the Trent from Nottinghamshire. The number of times coal from Newcastle had to be handled before it reached the consumer, and the distance it had to be brought, meant that York and other towns would use local coal as soon as it could be efficiently transported.

Two allied groups of promoters came forward, in Leeds and Wakefield. Those from Leeds were almost wholly cloth merchants, headed by the energetic mayor, William Milner; the Wakefield group a mixture of general traders, the landed interest and the law: woollen merchants there kept out or perhaps were kept out by those of Leeds. John Hadley[7] was employed to survey the Aire and 'questions not it being done, and with less charge than expected, affirming it the noblest river he ever saw not already navigable'.[8] With Samuel Shelton's help on the Calder, he made his survey for 15-ton boats, and early in 1698 a Bill was introduced. It was widely supported by petitions from West Riding towns, and from as far away as Lincoln, Manchester and Kendal, and opposed mainly by York. The York corporation claimed conservatorship of the tidal Aire to Knottingley, and feared that if the Bill passed the Ouse would

'be so drained by such Navigation, that no Boat or Vessels will be able to pass thereon, whereby the Trade of the City of York, carried on by the said River Ouse, will be quite carried into other remote Parts, and the Petitioners' said Power of Conservatorship destroyed'.[9]

A considerable Parliamentary battle resulted, during which the London Trinity House were asked by the Lords[10] to make a report on the Aire, Calder and Ouse. This they did, but then Parliament was prorogued, and the Bill had to be re-presented in January 1699. The Trinity House report favoured the Bill; it held that given certain precautions the navigation of the Ouse would not be harmed, and considered that the many likely advantages outweighed the clear disadvantage the measure would be to Selby in diverting much of its transhipment trade.

This time there were less difficulties, and the royal assent was given in May. The Act named nine Leeds undertakers, all corporation members, including William Milner and the then mayor, and nine others, gentlemen of Wakefield,* empowering them 'at their proper Costs and Charges' to make the rivers 'navigable, portable and passable', including cuts, locks and horse towing paths, to demolish mills and weirs on payment of compensation, and to charge per ton of cloth or other goods between Weeland or Leeds and Wakefield, 10s (50p) between 1 May and 1 October, and 16s (80p) during the winter, and so proportionately for distance. Property owners were protected by the appointment of commissioners, the tidal flow of the Ouse by preventing the undertakers from interfering with Knottingley mill dam or the Aire below it except by building locks.

The ownership of navigation property was now vested in trustees on behalf of the subscribers: these trustees, with elected shareholders, then formed Leeds and Wakefield committees, which worked separately, each temporarily paying their own expenses and sharing those below Castleford. Five days after the Act, John Hadley was engaged as engineer at a fee of £420, the work to be finished in two years from Michaelmas 1699. Locks were quickly built upwards from Knottingley. A single boat reached Wakefield in December 1699, though Bottom Boat became the practical waterhead until the Calder line was finished about the summer of 1702. The first craft reached Leeds on 17 November 1700. Hadley's work was done, and with the building of Beal and Haddlesey locks and weirs by George Atkinson and James Mitchell, the original navigation was completed in 1704. About 1709 the Leeds line reached the form it was to have for the next half century when the Crier Cut near Woodlesford, about 1½ miles long, was made.†

Twelve masonry locks with timber flooring were probably built on the Aire between Haddlesey and Leeds, and four on the

* Wakefield was unincorporated.
† The Crier Cut may not all have been made at one time.

Calder.* They were probably 58–60 ft long × 14 ft 6 in to 15 ft wide, with 3 ft 6 in depth over the sills. The river depth was likely to be less than that over the lock sills, for in 1700 the Leeds committee had a boat built for them at Selby, to be 44 ft × 13 ft and draw 2½ ft, which would 'carry 15 or 16 Tun weight att seaventeen Inches water'.[11] It was to have a crew of four.

The works below Knottingley almost at once involved the undertakers in complaints from landowners that they caused the river channel to silt and their lands to be flooded. The people of Knottingley, who now had to pay tolls for the stretch of river below their wharves, joined in, as did Pontefract corporation who claimed an ancient river toll they seem never to have tried to collect, and others with a grievance. After commissioners' meetings and lawsuits, the undertakers in 1714 settled with the landowners on the basis of increasing the number of weir sluices, and so the scour obtainable. They also reaffirmed a promise of 1699 that the inhabitants of Knottingley would not have to pay from Weeland more than one-third of the toll to Wakefield. Pontefract kept its claim.[12]

Money was raised separately by the Wakefield and Leeds groups of undertakers, from themselves and outside subscribers: to begin with, £4,100 at Wakefield and £5,000 at Leeds. No new shareholders were admitted after December 1699. Early in 1702 the Wakefield subscribers began to trade in coal in a small way from Bottom Boat, then dropped out as regular trade began. After a complicated series of capital and interest movements, in 1721 the total nominal capital was stabilized at £26,700, and there it remained until 1774. Regular dividends began from 1718–19, with 7 per cent.[13]

The first toll list, dating from 1703–7, divided the navigation into three sections, Weeland–Knottingley, Knottingley–Castleford, and Castleford to either Leeds or Wakefield, with collection points at Knottingley, Castleford and the two termini. Beal was added later. Against the authorized tolls of 10s (50p) (summer) and 16s (80p) (winter), the highest was 8s (40p), made up of 2s (10p) on each of the two lower sections and 4s (20p) on either of the upper, on cloth, spirits, merchandise and similar goods.

* Haddlesey, Beal, Knottingley, Castleford, Methley (added after 1700), Fleet, Woodlesford, Greywood, Thwaite, Knostrop (New Mill), Hunslet Mill, Leeds; Penbank, Lake, Kirkthorpe, Wakefield. The number was reduced to eleven with the elimination by 1709 of Greywood lock upon the lengthening of Crier Cut and the making of a deepened Woodlesford lock. I do not know when Crier Cut flood-lock was added.

Timber was charged 2s 6d (12½p), 10d each section, and coal, corn, beer and most English agricultural produce is 6d (7½p), or 6d (2½p) each section.

In November 1704 the undertakers first leased the navigation at £800, and thereafter at slowly increasing figures until 1715, when they resolved not to let it at less than £1,800 p.a. However, they could not, and the undertakers had to take it into their own hands, contracting with the previous lessees, Thomas Clark and Joseph Shaw, to carry all goods on the navigation except coal, corn and seed at 4s 6d (22½p) a ton, and with another to rent the wharf and warehouse at Weeland. In that year tolls were revised, whole-length charges being raised, for instance on coal to 3s (15p) from Leeds, 2s 6d (12½p) from Wakefield, cloth 6s (30p) in summer, 12s (60p) in winter, and 9s 6d (47½p) for spirits and groceries.

The undertakers were now willing to take less, and at the end of 1716 the rivers were again leased, to Clark, Shaw, John Burton and George Dover (the last two being undertakers) for seven years at £1,600 p.a., the lessees to pay all outgoings, do repairs, and buy the three craft the undertakers owned. One disadvantage of leasing was, of course, that the undertakers had no means of knowing the takings. In 1720 they minuted that they would make an allowance of £100 for the effect of stoppages due to lock repairs, etc., on condition that the lessees showed the books that revealed the navigation's profits. It does not appear that they did.

Another lease was executed at the end of 1722 to four undertakers, two of whom were new, at a rent rising from £1,600 to £2,000 p.a. At this time moves were being made to make the river Don navigable (see Chapter III), and these the Aire & Calder opposed, having no wish to encourage a second coal trade to and from Hull. The lease was again renewed to the same undertakers in 1729 at £2,600 p.a., and this time 'The Farmers' books touching the product of the farm, and the outgoings, to be inspected'.[14] The freight and toll receipts of the lessees for the five years 1724–8 averaged £6,016 p.a.,[15] as the undertakers discovered when they did get access to the books.*

In September 1705 a central committee of ten was appointed; it included four trustees, two of each from the Leeds and Wakefield groups, and three other representatives of each. This combined committee was 'to Let, manage and order the whole Navigation upon both Rivers and shall Imploy such Persons under them for

* But the lessees did not charge tolls on their own boats.

collecting Tolls and profitts and in maintaining all Locks, wears and other things'.[16] The Leeds and Wakefield committees still continued, however, and dealt with their own finances. As the undertakers moved into the ranks of the landed gentry, so they drifted away from involvement in their navigation property, and control passed to those of their body who were also trustees. It is worth remembering how very few shareholders there were. The maximum attendance at any meeting up to 1758 was 17; the usual was under ten.

The early trade of the navigation was mainly based on carrying woollen goods made at Leeds, Wakefield, Halifax and Bradford. Small river craft, most of them probably owned by the lessees, took them to Rawcliffe, where wharf and storage accommodation was provided. Goods were transhipped there for Hull, or taken along the coast to northern or southern ports, or 'shipped for Holland, Bremen, Hamburgh and the Baltick'.[17] Wool and corn came inwards, much of it from Lincolnshire and East Anglia. In the early 1720s Defoe described the river carrying 'coals down from Wakefield (especially) and also from Leeds, at both which they have a very great quantity. . . . These they carry quite down into the Humber, and then up the Ouse to York, and up the Trent, and other rivers, where there are abundance of large towns'.[18] This trade, he pointed out, was exempted from the duty on coal carried by sea which had to be paid by cargoes from Newcastle.

In 1728 Brandling had two coal-loading staiths at Hunslet (Leeds) and Fenton one at Rothwell. There were also two near Methley and one below Lake Lock on the Wakefield line. The building of tramroads accompanied this development: for instance, by 1745 there was a waggonway from Outwood collieries to near Bottom Boat on the Calder, and in 1755 a line was made from Middleton colliery to the river. At Wakefield, coal brought down the Calder valley was stacked on the narrow Stennard island to await loading.

In 1736 the undertakers tried to acquire land at Airmyn, lower down the Aire than Rawcliffe and so more accessible to incoming craft, especially on neap tides. They did so in 1744, and the lessees, who had previously been developing Rawcliffe, then advertised their intention of building warehouses, wharves and cranes there.[19] By 1774, when the company itself and not lessees were working the waterway, most of their staff were at Airmyn. For the next ten years or so, the lessees developed Airmyn, while others used Rawcliffe, where additional staiths and woolsheds were ordered to be built by the undertakers in 1751. Then Airmyn seems to have drawn ahead because of its deeper water and easier access, and to have become generally used. By 1750, staiths, a crane, woolsheds and other buildings had been built there, the undertakers then reimbursing the lessees and so taking ownership. At Leeds, a warehouse and crane had been provided by 1716.

Any eighteenth-century river navigation was likely to clash with millowners whose interests were to keep the water level up, who saw an increase in the number of boats passing their weirs as a menace to their trade, and who had to be compensated for every hour their wheels were idle by reason of boats passing. Companies therefore tried to get control of mills, and so of their water. In 1700 the Aire & Calder undertakers had leased Sir John Bland's Castleford mill, which governed the water back to Penbank on the Calder and Methley on the Aire. Where they had no control, conflict followed, as for instance in 1731, when the committee decided to move the Court of King's Bench for an information against Arthur Ingram, owner of Knottingley and Brotherton mills and his tenant, 'for Stanging and ffastening the Wheels of his Mills and drawing his Clows of the same Mills, and thereby drawing of the Water in the River Air above his Mills to the intent to damage the Navigation of the said River'.[20] This quarrel was settled later in the decade, when an alteration was made to Knottingley weir, but the war went on intermittently until 1776, when the company bought both mills.

In 1736 the lease was again renewed to the same group at £3,200 p.a., with a clause allowing the farmers to renegotiate it should the Don be made navigable to Rotherham. They did not do so, however, when this happened in 1740, so their trade cannot have been much affected.

In 1741 the putting forward of the first Bill for the Calder & Hebble (see Chapter II) caused the undertakers to have a survey made of the river from Wakefield up to Thornes; they were perhaps wondering whether they should try to exclude the new concern from Wakefield to avoid losing their wharfage profits. But it failed. There was also much Parliamentary bustle over various turnpike roads which appeared to be competitors rather than feeders to the Aire & Calder or the proposed Calder & Hebble, including one from Wakefield to Weeland, the preamble of which stated its purpose to be mainly to benefit the woollen manufac-

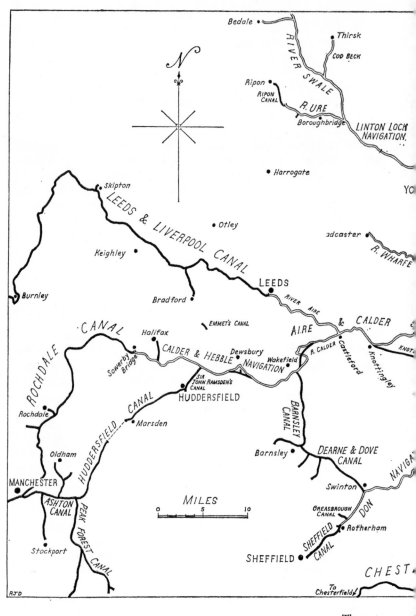

1. The waterways o

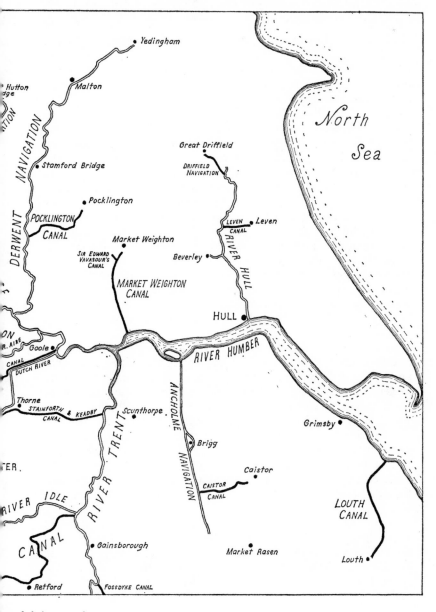

and their connexions

ture and to carry coal to the lower Aire for shipment to 'York, Hull, Malton, Boroughbridge, Lincoln, and divers other Places'. It was perhaps more to control the charges and tolls on the Aire & Calder.[21] A number were authorized, but in practice they were not well enough maintained or sufficiently convenient to give the rivers serious competition.

In 1744 another lease, at £3,600, was granted, this time to Joseph Atkinson and two associates, and it was at the same time decided that £200 p.a. should be held back from dividends until it amounted to £600, as a reserve fund in the hands of the trustees. In 1744, hearing that Wakefield was seeking a Bill to compel the lessees to pay rates, they sent representatives to London to try to get clauses inserted in it to amend their own Act, notably by empowering them to search all trading craft, move boats after a certain time, restrain mill occupiers from interfering with the navigation, make further locks and weirs, and repeal the present restriction on making cuts below Knottingley. These proposals effectively wrecked the Bill, as presumably they were intended to.[22] Meanwhile trading development went on. In 1751 an old Leeds warehouse was pulled down and a new one built. For the five years 1744–8 the freight and toll receipts of the lessees averaged £9,279 p.a.

In 1750[23] Joseph Atkinson* and Thomas Wilson leased the navigation, now at £4,400 p.a., to include the Airmyn wharves and others at Rawcliffe. There must have been complaints to the undertakers of damage while the lessees were transhipping goods, for it was made a condition of the 1750 lease that the lessees pay £50 p.a. to an official to be appointed by the undertakers, who would inspect the condition of goods transhipped at Rawcliffe. In 1758 Sir Henry Ibbetson, Bt., and Peter Birt took it on at £6,000 p.a., which represented a dividend of over 20 per cent to the undertakers, plus £2,000 cash on taking over the lease, to be used for new works or other improvements. Later, Birt became sole lessee.

A regular coasting service started from Airmyn to London in 1758, charging the same as from Hull to London.[24] In the 1760s the trade done on the rivers steadily increased. During this time John Gott, Birt's engineer, who had been appointed in 1760, spent some £4,000 on capital improvements and £9,000 on maintenance, chiefly by rebuilding old weirs to restore their

---

* In 1751 Atkinson, who had been concerned with the Don since 1722, also became one of that river's three lessees.

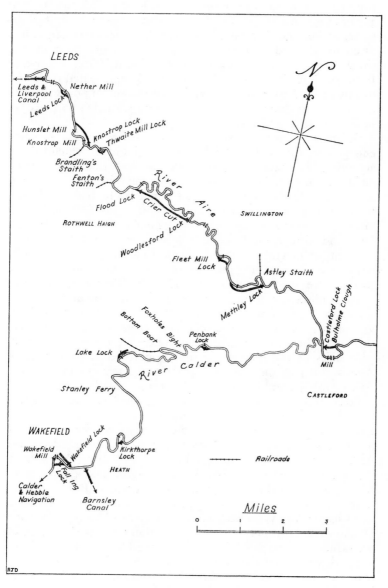

LEEDS

Leeds &
Liverpool
Canal

Nether Mill

Leeds Lock

Hunslet Mill

Knostrop Mill

Knostrop Lock

Thwaite Mill Lock

Brandling's
Staith

Fenton's
Staith

Flood Lock

River Aire

Crier Cut

ROTHWELL HAIGH

SWILLINGTON

Woodlesford Lock

Fleet Mill
Lock

Astley Staith

Methley Lock

Castleford Lock

Bulholme Clough

Foxholes Bight

Bottom Boat

Penbank
Lock

Lake Lock

River Calder

Mill

CASTLEFORD

Stanley Ferry

WAKEFIELD

Wakefield Lock

Wakefield
Mill

Kirkthorpe
Lock

Fall Ing Lock

HEATH

Calder
& Hebble
Navigation

Barnsley
Canal

- - - - - Railroads

Miles

0   1   2   3

RJD

2. The Aire & Calder Navigation in 1805

original height and so get more depth. This enabled craft to draw 3 ft or more instead of 2 ft 6 in, and carry 40 to 50 tons, but all the same, flashes and dam boards to give the weirs extra height had often to be used to keep craft moving and get them off the shoals. Boats normally took 3 to 4 days upwards from Airmyn to Leeds or Wakefield, 2 to 3 days down. The high-rated trade was mainly in the import of merchandise and wool, and the export of cloth, though three-quarters of the tonnage carried was in coal, lime, limestone and manure.

Before concerning himself with the Aire & Calder, Birt had engaged in the coal trade; he now had greatly extended his activities, his boats having most of the cloth trade. In 1773 he had between 50 and 60 craft on the river out of some 300 using it, and a share in a dozen or more. From 1767 he had also begun to trade in timber and iron, and later in stone. Finally, he had interests in some of the vessels working between Airmyn and Hull, and Airmyn and London.[25] John Gott in 1774 thought that the number of craft on the navigation had increased by half in ten years.[26] This trading pressure on a navigation most of whose works were seventy years old, and Peter Birt's long career as lessee combined with major carrier and trader, naturally created grievances against what was considered his oppression and engrossment, especially of the coal trade; these seemed worse than they were because a remedy now offered for the seeming inadequacies of the river navigations, one forecast in a letter of August 1764 to the *York Courant*[27] suggesting a canal to join Aire to Ribble, and so Leeds to Preston and the Irish Sea.

From July 1766 what was to become the Leeds & Liverpool Canal[28] was being promoted to run from the Aire & Calder at Leeds bridge up Airedale and into Lancashire. Simultaneously north of York projects were being planned that emerged as three Acts of 1767 to make navigable the Ouse above York from Widdington Ings to beyond Boroughbridge and extend it to Ripon, and also the Swale and Bedale Beck to Bedale and to near Northallerton, and the Cod Beck from the Swale to Thirsk (see Chapter V). As far back as 1741, an Act had been passed for a Halifax–Selby turnpike. In 1751, a petition for a new Act said of the earlier one 'the good Purposes intended by the said Act (have been) defeated and the said road between Selby and Leeds remains in a most ruinous condition'.[29] From 1767, therefore, it was inevitable that a canal line from Leeds to Selby would be canvassed, one that would bypass the Aire and its difficulties by shortening the route to the Ouse, one that would also open the promising trade likely to offer on the upper Ouse once the works authorized by the Acts of 1767 had been done. In 1769 the *Leeds Mercury* said of the turnpike proposal: 'The confessed original design ... was to make Selby the shipping port for Leeds',[30] and now a Leeds–Selby canal was being promoted, Thomas Yeoman having made a preliminary estimate of £65,350 for it. Once the Leeds & Liverpool's Act had been passed in May 1770 and construction above Leeds had begun, those who were trying to assess the future naturally took a critical look at the capacity of the river navigation to cope with the trade that promised, hard put as it was to carry what already offered. It was indeed the case that the undertakers, because they had been able to lease their property at steadily increasing rents, had on the whole been satisfied to see it kept in repair but to make few major improvements. The Aire & Calder in 1770, with its four Calder locks and eleven on the Aire from Leeds to Haddlesey, was not very different from the navigation of 1720:

'the original projectors . . ., not having had any notion of the extensive trade that was likely to be carried on by means thereof . . . formed their plan upon too diminutive a scale, and particularly with respect to depth . . . of water'.[31]

Many lock sills only gave 2 ft 6 in depth at normal summer water. To this limitation of construction had to be added shoaling below the locks, due, John Smeaton considered, to 'endeavouring to save locks in point of number, and to save length of cutting', and also the lack of water in the tideway below Haddlesey lock, the lowest. In ordinary dry seasons 'there will not be two feet of water up to Haddlesey lock at high water neap tides'. Finally, about a mile below the Aire & Calder's limits at Weeland there was another shoal 'over which, though the neap tides sensibly flow, yet they do not make, in the whole, above two feet depth of water'. Therefore in dry seasons when little water was coming off the Pennines, flashes had to be provided but, because of millers' requirements and of the need to keep pounds up, perhaps only two a week, 'wherefore, vessels will be frequently from Stock Reach to Leeds or Wakefield, a week or more in making good their passage, that otherwise would be performed in fifteen hours'. The result, Smeaton considered, was underemployment of boats and men, delays and expense.[32]

The pressure of increasing trade, some of it consequent upon the west Yorkshire clothmaking boom of 1769–71, upon inade-

quate transport facilities focused in discontent with the undertakers and attacks upon their lessee, Peter Birt. In addition,
prospects of efficient canals replacing inefficient navigations were
added to hopes of new markets north of York. The undertakers
put a match to this explosive mixture when in February 1771
they agreed to lease their tolls again to Peter Birt from 12 November 1772 for £8,500 p.a., this time for 21 years.

A shower of memorials from traders and carriers descended on
them. They quickly promised

'to set apart a round share of the increased rent, for the making
the navigation more speedy, more certain, and, of consequence, less liable to those abuses, to which long delays on
shallows etc. naturally lead the boatmen',[33]

and called in John Smeaton (who had already proposed minor
changes at Birt's request) to survey the navigation and recommend general improvements. He set himself 'to procure the
essential of a navigation, the means of keeping vessels always
afloat' and recommended improvements that would provide 3 ft
6 in to 4 ft of water, to take craft carrying 30 to 45 tons. These
included dredging, rebuilding some mill locks, new cuts,
especially a by-pass canal from just above Haddlesey lock to run
on the south side of the river to Gowdall above Snaith with two
locks[34] or a similar one on the north side from Chapel Haddlesey
to Newland beyond Rawcliffe[35] to avoid low water and shoals.
There was to be a second by-pass with one lock from Brotherton
on the north side of the river below Knottingley: this because 'the
Water is in general so shallow, that it becomes necessary, not only
to raise the Water higher by temporary Boards placed on Beal
Dam below, but to let down Flashes from the Mill Dam to carry
the Vessels over the Shallows; and, for want of sufficient Water
for the Purpose, the Vessels are often detained there in their
passage many Days together'.[36] He proposed other cuts at Leeds
(¼ mile, with a lock to replace the old one), Knostrop (⅞ mile, with
two new locks to replace three old ones at mills), Woodlesford
(1½ miles, with two new locks to replace two old ones), Methley
(⅜ mile, with floodgates and a lock to replace the old Methley
lock) and floodgates and a lock on the ¼ mile cut to Castleford.
Finally, he recommended powers to the undertakers to remove
obstructions and build a towing path right to the Ouse.

Smeaton's report was published in January 1772, soon after a
very hostile meeting at York on 30 December 1771. The undertakers, perhaps underestimating the seriousness of the opposition,

had petitioned for leave to introduce a Bill to improve their navigation on the lines of Smeaton's proposals, including the cut below Haddlesey. It was strongly opposed by those who alleged that:

'the present navigation, on the Rivers Air and Calder, is very insufficient to do the necessary Business of the Country in a proper Manner; and the powers exercised on the same are very grievous and oppressive, and tend to the establishing an exclusive Monopoly in the Hands of the Undertakers . . . and their Lessees, not only of the Carriage and Freight of all Goods conveyed along the said Rivers, but also of the Sale and Merchandize thereof',

but also by supporters of a new and dangerous project. The Calder & Hebble Navigation had been finished to Sowerby Bridge in 1770 (see Chapter II), and before that, in 1766, a scheme had been put forward for a canal from it to Manchester. A petition now proposed

'one or more navigable . . . Canals, from . . . Wakefield and from . . . Leeds, into the River Don, the River Ouze, or the River Air, below Weeland . . . in such Manner as to be intirely unconnected with the present Navigation . . . or with the Undertakers'.[37]

Realizing now the strength of opposition that was developing both to themselves and Peter Birt, and the dangerous forms it was taking, the undertakers withdrew from Parliament. Two schemes developed, subscriptions for which were opened simultaneously as the most effectual way of obtaining redress of grievances against the Aire & Calder.[38] One, following the petition, was surveyed by John Smith: the Went Canal from Wakefield by way of the Went Valley to the Dutch River at Went Mouth, to enable the Calder & Hebble and Wakefield trade to by-pass the Aire & Calder. It was to be 24 miles long, with 19 locks 56 ft by 15 ft 6 in, and a 2,128 yd broad tunnel, to cost £36,414, a proposition good enough to beat the Aire & Calder with, but certainly not to build.[39] After a few months, doubts of its usefulness, the lukewarm attitude of landowners, the reluctance of subscribers to support the scheme (only £14,000 was raised), and lack of confidence in the engineer after his troubles on the Swale, caused it to be dropped at the end of 1772 without getting to Parliament. The Leeds & Selby, pressed by those with grievances against the Aire & Calder and supported by some of those behind the Leeds & Liverpool, employed John Longbotham to survey for a canal direct from Leeds to the tideway. The Leeds & Liverpool company themselves remained quietly neutral, though Longbotham was their engineer.

Longbotham confirmed Selby as the termination. His line ran from the Leeds & Liverpool at Holbeck, Leeds, to the north of the river past Hunslet and then across it by a long aqueduct near Methley. This was to have four river and six land arches, 11 ft to the crown above normal river level. Thence it would run by Fairburn, where there would be a 400-yd long tunnel under the Great North Road, Hillam, Hambleton and Thorpe Willoughby to the Ouse at Selby. The canal was to be 23⅛ miles long with ten locks arranged in two staircases of three each and two staircase pairs, was to take 50 to 60 ton craft, and shorten the Leeds–Hull route by 9 miles, and Leeds–York by 34 miles. His estimate was £59,468. A subscription was opened in September, and by the end of October the necessary £60,000 had been offered.

A petition for the canal Bill reached Parliament in December 1772, a week after the Aire & Calder again petitioned for leave to bring in their own. This was to embody Smeaton's previous proposals for improving the navigation above Haddlesey, but a new one for the lower section. After they had withdrawn from Parliament earlier, they had gone back to Smeaton and asked him to do a detailed survey and estimate of his proposed by-pass cut to the north of the Aire. Being too busy, he got his young assistant, William Jessop, then aged 27, to do it for him. Jessop proposed a canal 7¼ miles long, nearly double Smeaton's, from above Haddlesey lock to near Newland above Airmyn and about three miles from the Aire's confluence with the Ouse.[40] This Smeaton approved, after increasing the estimate. In Parliament, Thomas Yeoman broadly supported Longbotham; the Aire & Calder had Smeaton. Criticism of the canal scheme concentrated upon its doubtful water supply, obstruction likely from the aqueduct, unknown geological dangers in the tunnel (no barge tunnel of that length had yet been built in England), danger from the canal passing over coal workings, and Longbotham's probable underestimate of the cost, which Smeaton put at about £100,000. Contrariwise, the Aire & Calder came fairly well out of the evidence, which more clearly showed the need for navigation improvement than for a by-pass canal. The session ended without the House having accepted the report of the committee that had closely attended to both proposals.

The Aire & Calder seem to have spent the breathing space

more profitably than the canal party. They did it, first, by stealing their opponents' clothes, deciding that the Selby route had too many advantages over an improvement of the lower Aire not to be adopted. Jessop therefore surveyed the whole route, accepting Smeaton's proposals between Leeds and Castleford, and preparing under Smeaton's direction new proposals below Castleford for a cut from above Ferrybridge to above Beal, and then, from a little above Haddlesey lock, a canal $5\frac{1}{4}$ miles long to the Ouse at Selby, with floodgates at the Haddlesey end and a lock at Selby. The result would be an improved, though no shorter, route to Hull, but a considerable reduction in the length of that for coal to York. Second, they directed attention from Birt to the always unpopular millers: finding 'the principal Inconveniences complained of to be occasioned by certain Mills belonging to private persons . . . one* of which, the most capable of distressing the said Navigation, has been purchased'.[41] But, reckoning that, right or wrong, something had also to be done about Birt, the undertakers bought him out from 12 May 1774 by giving him a one-tenth share of their navigation and its property, an agreement confirmed in their subsequent Act. James Hebdin, their future law clerk, writing to a committeeman on 14 February 1774, said:

'every Body seems very glad that you have purchased Mr. Birt's Interest but then they say if he is to have a Share in the Navigⁿ he will be as great a Tyrant as ever, however I hope it will answer your purpose to prevent the Canal'.

Birt became a committeeman and sat until 1790, but he was not assiduous at meetings, and did not attend at all after 1782. Meanwhile the Leeds & Selby promoters had met at Leeds to reopen subscription books and again seek a Bill 'to exterminate every Idea of a Monopoly or any Intention of it'.[42]

The spring of 1774 saw Parliamentary battle joined, with rival Bills for the Aire & Calder, now well organized, and the Leeds & Selby Canal, now supported by the Leeds & Liverpool company. Though heavily supported by petitions the latter was decisively lost on 3 March by 105 votes to 33, helped perhaps by the sharp recession that had followed the earlier boom, and so a current scarcity of money; the former passed three months later,[43] authorizing the main Aire cuts,† the Selby Canal, and the keeping

---

* Knottingley and Brotherton were bought at this time, and Castleford (already leased) agreed for.

† In Parliament the Knostrop cut was shortened by one lock so as not to by-pass Thwaite mill, as was that proposed from Ferrybridge to Beal, which was reduced to a new weir and short cut at Knottingley.

C

navigable of the Aire from Weeland to its confluence with the Ouse, though this section remained toll-free. The Act also provided the company with a revised administrative framework, power to make bye-laws, and a new toll-structure. Cloth bales from Leeds or Wakefield to Selby or Weeland were now to be 7s (35p) a ton maximum, and coal ½d a ton/mile. Apart from the navigation tolls, five mills were authorized to make a charge, usually 1s (5p) per loaded boat only, as compensation for loss of water. Peculiarly, the concern remained unincorporated, a state of affairs that lasted until 1948. The former practice of vesting all property in four trustees, two each from Leeds and Wakefield, was continued. Three others were to be elected by the Leeds undertakers, three more by those of Wakefield, to join them and make up a management committee of ten. Power to borrow was given, without naming any limit.

With William Jessop as engineer, John Gott as resident and James and his brother John Pinkerton as contractors, cutting on the Selby line began early in 1775. It was Jessop's first big part-time job, for which he was to get £250 p.a. He carefully set out his own duties for the committee's approval, and added that he intended to make the business the principal object of his attention 'for the Advantage of the Proprietors and to my own Credit'.[44] The Selby Canal was opened on 29 April 1778, when 'a large Concourse of People assembled, and the same was conducted in very great Order with firing of Cannon, Music, and ringing of Bells, to the great Satisfaction of the Gentlemen and others at Selby and that neighbourhood'.[45] Though successful and heavily used for nearly fifty years, experience revealed some things about it that could have been better done. In 1791 it was reported 'that great Damage has arose to the Canal . . . and the Ground near thereto by the Cloughs being out of repair, and want of Bye Washes and Drains for taking the Water therefrom',[46] and with hindsight, Elias Wright, the navigation's engineer, looking back in 1797, complained that with 3 ft 6 in of craft depth it had been made too shallow, so compelling extra height dam boards to be maintained on Haddlesey weir. He also complained of the two miles of canal which had banks of loose sand, which in rain washed, and in dry weather blew, into the canal, necessitating constant dredging.

By 1785 four of the Aire cuts had been finished: Castleford was opened about the spring of 1775, and those of Hunslet and Knostrop were completed by 1779, the year Methley was begun.

Woodlesford was not made, the purchase of Fleet mills having rendered it unnecessary. A new cut at Thwaite, 206 yards long, had been authorized in 1778 to avoid possible subsidence on the existing cut due to mining. The following year, the undertakers were told that coal probably lay beneath the land they owned there, and they agreed to sink a mine at the joint expense of themselves and James and John Smyth of Holbeck, who owned neighbouring pits. It was worked out in 1794. Jessop himself was not regularly employed after 1779, though he was consulted about the remaining works. A set of replacement locks had by now been built on the whole line. Those on the Calder and below Castleford were later to be duplicated at a width of 18 ft, the new locks being built alongside or near the replacements of the 1780s. The Aire & Calder also used some flood-locks, but not flood-gates at the cut heads as on the Calder & Hebble.

In early 1775 the undertakers had a debt of about £45,000, and authorized the raising of £60,000 more for their improvements. In fact, Priestley said they had spent over £70,000, of which some £20,000 was attributable to the Selby Canal, though he may have exaggerated in order to make a case for the Aire & Calder's 1820 Bill. Their money had been well spent: in July 1775 the general assembly decided that in future £9,000 p.a. should be paid as dividends; this was increased to an annual rate of £12,000 in 1777, £16,000 for 1784, £17,000 for 1785, £18,000 for 1786, £20,000 for 1787, £24,000 for 1788 and £32,000 for 1791.

In 1775 the undertakers made an important purchase at Wakefield, of land and warehouses at Fall Ing for £600, and in 1776 of more land there for £1,450. In 1783 a new warehouse was built, but, sadly, it collapsed early in 1784, 'having been undermined by the flood, when a large quantity of wool, bale goods, and other articles fell into the river. The damage is very considerable'.[47]

About the time the Selby Canal opened, 2,200 loaded boats a year were noted as passing Thwaite mill, 1,550 Knostrop and Hunslet. Brandling's staiths, to which coal was brought from the Middleton colliery, accounted for 650 of Thwaite's figure. As on the Don and elsewhere, it was the early practice on the Aire & Calder to calculate the tonnages of coal loaded by the number of waggons, whether these were emptied into the boat, or, as later sometimes happened, were carried in it. Needless to say, difficulties arose when waggon sizes were increased, sometimes without the company knowing. In 1774 they were reported to vary from 38 to 46 cwt.

By 1774 the company possessed a number of the most important mills: Castleford and Allerton, Brotherton and Knottingley, for instance, with shares in Knostrop and Hunslet; Fleet mills were added in 1777, and about the same time some at Wakefield were leased to improve control of the Wakefield cut. These mills were let on conditions that safeguarded navigation interests.

Unlike the Calder & Hebble, the Aire & Calder had no objection to Sunday trading. In 1779 they minuted:

'The Hailers of Vessels being much oppressed by being prosecuted for Hailing on Sundays not only by suffering the Punishment but afterwards sent to the House of Correction for Costs, Resolved that the Clerk do Assist the Hailers of such Vessels against such Oppressive Prosecution and proceed therein as he shall be advised'.[48]

Towing on the navigation was done by separate groups of hauliers, with whom masters of craft agreed for their services. Charges for towing in 1785 were: upwards, Selby to Wakefield, 13s 6d (67½p) with one horse, £1 3s (£1·15) with two; Wakefield to Sowerby Bridge, 12s 6d (62½p) and 16s 6d (82½p); Selby to Leeds 15s 9d (79p) and £1 3s (£1·15). Downwards, always with one horse, Sowerby Bridge to Wakefield, 11s (55p), Wakefield to Selby 11s 10d (59p), Leeds to Selby 12s 9d (64p).

Until the opening of the Selby Canal re-routed most traffic, Airmyn was a transhipment point where the contract vessels* working there from Hull and an occasional trader from London would transfer their goods to river craft. In January 1776 the undertakers, anxious to improve the service, told seven owners of vessels that were reported by William Martin, the Aire & Calder manager, to be old and in bad condition that unless they provided better vessels they would no longer be employed as contractors. In 1775 a woolshed was ordered to be built there, and there was also a yard for the sale of coal and a place to inspect and weigh incoming cargoes. A staff of six worked there in 1776. Airmyn was also the main base for the undertakers' own carrying fleet. A letter from the company's agent there of 30 July 1775 says: 'we have loaded 19 Boats this week & have a many goods &c on hand'. During the four days 26 to 29 July, eight vessels had arrived there from Hull and one from London. It must have been a busy place. In 1775 a horse was bought for the staff there to come upriver to expedite boats as far as the junction, where the

* A contract vessel was one independently owned, but worked under contract to the Aire & Calder company.

expediting was taken over by a man at Castleford, who had to keep an eye on those doing the towing, see the undertakers' boats had enough horses, check the waybills of the bye-traders, and generally keep an eye on the traffic above Castleford. Another officer inspected undertakers' craft working on the Calder & Hebble. Warehousing seems then to have been free, but in 1785 the company began to charge for wharfage and warehousing, so accepting liability for theft or damage. Previously they had denied liability.

The Selby Canal open, most of the trade on the river passed that way instead of by Airmyn, and early in 1779 the coalyard and other offices were closed. Soon afterwards, the clerk was told to buy ten or twelve acres of land on the river banks at Selby for building warehouses and wharves 'in Order to Establish a large and extensive Trade there';[49] in the event, they leased eight acres.

Late in 1779 the company seem to have wondered whether after all Airmyn should be a main base: certainly the old river course was busy enough for a towing path to be built from Weeland to Stock Reach, and for Stock Reach itself to be dredged. But they did not turn away from Selby: in 1781 they removed such remaining premises as they had to the north side of the river, and relinquished the south to Peter Birt. Soon afterwards the Airmyn boat repair yard was given up. The river continued to be used, however, to some extent: boats were generally sailed up as far as Weeland, then sailed or horse-towed on to Haddlesey. In November John Gott was told to proceed immediately to erect and finish the Selby staiths, plans of which he had produced, and in February 1782 to put up two more. In February, also, he was instructed to prepare plans and estimates for such warehouses, cranes and lay-bys as he thought necessary there. In July he was told to build 'the Counting House, Warehouse, Crane, Rigging House, Tarring House, Sailmaker's Shop and a Place for depositing old Ropes at Selby',[50] in accordance with his plans and estimates. In 1785 a warehouse and staith were built for letting to Walker and Reed, in 1787 Gott was told to 'erect two Cranes at Selby, one to the River and one to the Canal, with three Gantries',[51] and in 1788 an assistant lock-keeper had to be appointed because of the great increase of trade. The Selby Canal had triumphantly justified itself.

The opening of the Selby Canal greatly increased Selby's importance.[52] Already the limit of convenient navigation on the Ouse for most seagoing ships, it now became a key transhipment

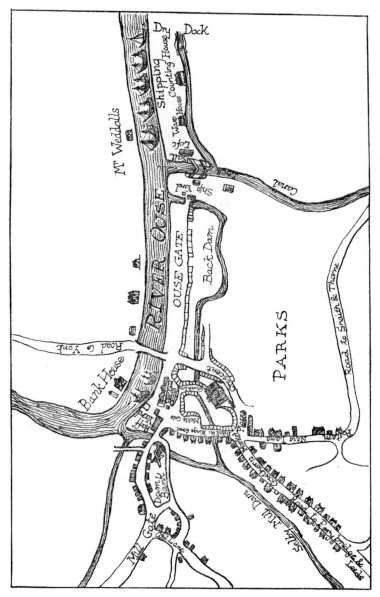

3. Selby in 1800: redrawn from James Mountain's *The History of Selby*, 1800

port for most goods except coal. The canal could only take craft of 60 tons or so. Smaller keels and sloops using it did go down river to Hull, Humber estuary ports or the Trent, or up to York and beyond, but most traffic for the Humber and the coast was transhipped to the bigger Humber keels, sloops (similar to keels, but differently rigged), schooners and brigs, some of them 200 tons or so. In 1800 it was estimated that 369,780 tons of goods were handled there.[53] This business stimulated Selby's own commerce, much of it, like shipbuilding, rope and sailmaking, connected with the river trade, so that the population grew from 2,861 in 1801 to 4,097 in 1821.

One consequence of the ending of Birt's lease was that the company took over his carrying business, putting William Martin, formerly chief agent of the Don company, as manager from the beginning of 1775. He was an able man, who much improved relations with customers which had been impaired in Birt's time and by the quarrels over the canal Bill. In 1774, when the lease ended, they took over Birt's Haigh Moor coal boats, which then had a monopoly. They cut the business back to modest levels, at which they continued it, buying from some colliery owners on their own line and also the Calder & Hebble, among them Charles Brandling of Hunslet, the Fentons and Peter Birt, and selling it to coal merchants at places like York and Ripon where they wanted to develop their trade. They also bought from smaller producers, among them William Jessop after he had ceased to be their engineer—with Pinkerton he ran a colliery near Mirfield on the Calder & Hebble. Later, supplies were supplemented by some of the output of their own Thwaite pit. This trading averaged sales of £7,301 in 1776–8, fell away to run at about £3,000 p.a. to 1790, then declined to an average of £1,633 for 1791–5, and continued on a small scale for half a century more.

Twice a year William Martin or another official went from Wakefield to York and other centres to collect money due from the coal trading. In 1776 he had ridden to York, but after that the company could afford a post-chaise. He entertained customers at his York inn, went round tipping their coal porters, and sent in a bill like this of September 1779:

	£	s	d
Chaise &c to Castleford		9	6
do &c from do to York	1	5	1
Mr. Hall's Porters 2s 6d, Son 5s		7	6
Mr. Carrack's Porters		2	6

	£	s	d
Mr. Atha's do		2	6
Messrs Gibson's do		2	6
Expenses at Howletts		1	7
Mr. Cooper's Porters		2	6
Expenses at York at Falcon	7	18	11
Chaise to Harrogate	1	0	3
Turnpike 1s 6d, Boy 2s, Ostler 1s		4	6
Chaise from Harrogate to Leeds, Boy &c		16	3
do from Leeds to Wakefield		8	3
Boy 1s 6d, Ostler 6d, Turnpike 6d		2	6
Expences at Leeds		5	0

$$£13 \quad 9 \quad 4\,(£13\cdot46\tfrac{1}{2})$$

Entertainment was mostly from the bottle. We have not got his bill on this occasion, but in September 1777, when he stayed at the Minster in Micklegate, his bill was £2 for food, £6 10s 5d for drink, 10s 6d for keep of his servant and horse, and 9s 6d for tips and being spruced by the barber before meeting customers, £7 10s 5d (£7·52) in all.

In 1783 William Martin reported that the company's sloops working between Selby and Hull were 'in such bad Repair that the Trade . . . is likely to be much injured, if not entirely lost',[54] and that new ones would cost some £6,000. A consortium of the company themselves, shareholders and merchants put up the money, and nine 70-tonners were built; these ran in connection with the Aire & Calder's services from Leeds, Halifax and Sowerby Bridge. The company had subscribed £900, and by the end of 1791 had had £845 in dividends, a very respectable return.

A growing part of the Aire & Calder's trade was via the Calder & Hebble to Sowerby Bridge and then by road transport over the Pennines to Manchester. In 1784 William Martin held a meeting in Manchester of 'Merchants and others Trading on this Navigation from Hull to Manchester', to tell them the water routes available and the charges made between Sowerby Bridge and Selby, and also of the Aire & Calder's 'Intention of Building new Vesssels to Navigate from Selby to Hull'.[55] It was a good piece of salesmanship. In 1794 the company started an experimental carrying service on the Leeds & Liverpool and Bradford Canals to Bradford.

In 1787 a bridge over the Ouse at Long Drax below Selby was promoted and a meeting was called at Selby on 11 January. The

Aire & Calder sent representatives to oppose it as injurious to the navigation,[56] and the Calder & Hebble later subscribed £100 to oppose a possible Bill. It was not built, but soon afterwards Jessop built his well-known Selby bridge, in spite of the Duke of Bolton's revival of an older proposal for a 19½ mile canal from Blacktoft on the Humber to Water Fulford below York to take 400-ton ships[57] and by-pass the proposed bridge.

Increased business resulted in a growing network of staff: in 1787 a part-time man at Manchester to investigate damage claims, an office at Sowerby Bridge, whence the company's boats worked, and an arrangement with Sir John Ramsden's agent at Huddersfield to act as part-time freight collector. Increased business also brought increased efforts to defraud the undertakers. In 1791 a gauging station had been ordered to be set up at Castleford where goods could if necessary be weighed, and in 1792 Bertram of the Aire & Calder's staff was appointed to take charge of the business, and have suspected vessels weighed. At the same time he was to see the undertakers' own craft had a proper number of crew, and used 'due Diligence in the proceeding on their several Voyages'.[58] The station was set up late in 1793, and by 1794 was having a useful effect. A novel form of publicizing frauds appeared in 1795, when the company agreed 'that the Penalty arising on the Conviction of John Senior for giving a false Account of his Loading be distributed . . . for the benefit of the Poor at Castleford'.[59]

By early 1792 the 'Trade of the West Riding . . . having lately increased so much and is now so much increasing that it is Adviseable for the Undertakers to use all possible means to improve this Navigation so as to Accommodate the Trade of the Company in every possible degree'. William Jessop was asked whether he would survey the navigation and recommend improvements.[60] Meanwhile a warehouse was to be built at Wakefield.

Seemingly Jessop was then too busy, but the undertakers in London made some suggestions, perhaps after seeing him; to improve Selby lock to make it usable at all times; to double Castleford lock, make a cut at Cross Channel and improvements at Beal. In August it was decided to build 'a Dock* and other conveniences' at Selby, and Jessop was asked to look over William Martin's plans and give his opinion and estimate.[61] Martin also proposed granaries at Leeds and Wakefield, as there was 'great want' of them, and was told to prepare plans. Jessop

* A graving dock.

came in November, and reported in January 1793 to a meeting which ordered the repairs he suggested to be 'set about immediately'. Land for the Selby dock took time to find—it was obtained in August 1793. The dock then seems to have been privately built by John Foster, who made a cut some 300 yds long to join it to the canal. This ran southwards parallel to the Ouse. A rather longer cut, 580 yds, and dry-dock had been approved by the undertakers in 1784, but not then built.

At this time the Aire & Calder claimed 'nearly the Whole of the Consumption of Coal in the City of York, the Towns of Malton, Howden, Selby, Snaith, and Boroughbridge, and places on the Ouse and Derwent: much of that of Hull, Hedon, Louth, Market Weighton, Brigg, Lincoln, Gainsborough and other places on the Humber and Trent;' and 'at Times, when it can be had, there are considerable Quantities sent Coast-wise to Boston, Lynn and Wisbich &c. by the Ships and Vessels which bring Wool and Corn to Selby'.[62] But this supply was insufficient, and was therefore a motive for promoting a new canal, the Barnsley (see Chapter VIII).

In July 1792, the Aire & Calder undertakers authorized spending up to £100 for a plan and estimate of a canal from near Barnsley to their navigation near Wakefield, and thereby triggered off a contest between themselves, the Calder & Hebble and the Don Navigation to promote canals from their separate lines to Barnsley. Agreement between the Aire & Calder and the Don was reached at a joint meeting of representatives on 20 October. This approved the Barnsley Canal scheme as accepted by the public meeting at Barnsley on 15 October, and also a line from it to the Don at Swinton, the future Dearne & Dove. Hence rivalry by the two big concerns, each backing one of the new projects, was lessened. Both parties agreed not to oppose a future extension by either the Barnsley or the Dearne & Dove towards Manchester.[63] It may have been against this idea, later developed as a link with the proposed Huddersfield Canal, that the Aire & Calder, Calder & Hebble and Sir John Ramsden were later to be protected by a toll clause in the Huddersfield Canal's Act of 1794.[64] The Calder & Hebble's scheme failed (see p. 172), the Dearne & Dove and the Barnsley Canals were built. The latter was authorized in mid-1793, and we must remember this preoccupation of the Aire & Calder in the year from July 1792. They seem to have been much less interested in the Rochdale and Huddersfield Canal schemes that concerned the Calder & Hebble, and perhaps not to have realized the importance the former especially would have for them. Both were authorized in 1794. The Aire & Calder had come a long way since the Act of 1774. Here are averaged figures since 1777:[65]

Years	Coal	Stone & Lime	Corn	Miscel- laneous	Total	Dividends
	£	£	£	£	£	£
1777–78 (2 yrs.)	7,710	2,048	4,178	8,921	22,857	11,625
1779–81	7,661	1,680	4,290	9,051	22,682	12,750
1782–84	7,368	1,622	4,346	10,390	23,726	15,333
1785–87	10,199	2,953	5,142	13,751	32,045	18,333
1788–90	11,150	4,287	6,192	16,212	37,841	26,000
1791–93	10,742	4,858	7,488	20,288	43,376	32,000

Tolls (spanning Coal, Stone & Lime, Corn, Miscellaneous columns)

Until 1785 the old navigation might still have carried the trade that offered. But the Selby Canal was essential to the tremendous leap forward that followed the ending of the American War in 1783. This showed itself especially in the 'Miscellaneous' category of toll receipts, covering, e.g. cloth bales, wool and groceries. Coupled with the hope of major coal carrying from the Barnsley Canal and merchandise from the new Pennine waterways, the future looked good. (*To continue the history of the Aire & Calder Navigation, turn to Chapter VI.*)

CHAPTER II

Upwards from Wakefield

✦✦✦✦✦✦✦✦✦✦✦✦✦✦✦✦✦✦✦✦✦✦✦✦✦✦✦✦✦✦✦✦✦✦✦◆✦✦✦✦✦✦✦✦✦✦✦✦✦✦✦✦✦✦✦✦✦✦✦✦✦✦✦✦✦✦✦✦✦✦✦

Calder & Hebble Navigation

In 1735 Yorkshire's first turnpike Act had authorized the turnpiking of the road from Rochdale by Blackstone Edge to Halifax
and Elland. It needed it, for it had been described as in many
parts almost impassable for wheel-carriages, and in others 'so
strait that two pack-horses cannot pass each other without
danger and difficulty.[1] By 1740 some work had been done, but
toll receipts were low. Clearly the road should be extended, for
Lancashire as well as Halifax traffic, and in 1740 proposals were
made, and Bills promoted, to turnpike the roads from Halifax by
Bradford and Leeds to Selby, from Halifax to Wakefield, from
Elland to Leeds and from Wakefield to Weeland. These road
schemes, and others discussed at the time, seem to have been
aimed partly at getting the Aire & Calder tolls reduced, partly
also to make sure that any promoters of a navigation of the
Calder from Wakefield up to Elland and Halifax would start in a
proper frame of mind. Dr Unwin[2] quotes a letter of William
Marsden of December 1740:

'wee have petitions for Turnpikes without end going forward. . . . The exorbitant Lock dues upon the river to Wakefield and Leeds, and ye petition for carrying it up to Ealand and
Hallifax seems to have put em all upon mettle prodigiously. . .
Mr. Milnes and the tradesmen of Wakefield are . . . solicitous for
em to distress, and reduce ye navigators and ye Lock dues upon
ye river up to Wakefield'.

In 1740, indeed, Halifax, Ripponden and Elland had petitioned
for the navigation of the Calder to be extended upwards from its
junction with the Aire & Calder at Wakefield to the Hebble, and
then up the latter to Salterhebble bridge 'and so far up a River*

* They called it the Halifax Brook.

to the town of Halifax',[3] arguing that road transport was very costly, and that such a navigation would help trade with London and other places by reducing road costs from Wakefield to Halifax from 15s (75p) to 9s (45p).[4] John Eyes of Liverpool made a survey and he jointly with Thomas Steers[5] 'a projection of the then Intended Navigation'[6] in 1740 and 1741. It was ambitious, providing for 21 locks on the Calder and 3 on the Hebble and three long cuts at Horbury (2 miles), Cooper bridge–Kirklees ($1\frac{1}{8}$ miles) and Kirklees–Brighouse ($1\frac{1}{4}$ miles) within a total of nearly 10 miles of cuts.[7] A Bill was introduced, but opposition to the application came to Parliament from landowners who feared that their lands would be flooded, and from owners of fulling and other mills, especially Cavendish Nevile and Sir Lionel Pilkington. It was argued that navigation would 'so much interrupt their Working in dry Seasons, as wou'd not only injure the particular Cloths in the Stocks, but so far obstruct the Fulling of it in general, as to prevent the Demands of Trade being supplied in due Time'.[8] Opposition came also from the rival promoters of turnpike Bills, and in combination these defeated the Calder & Hebble Bill in committee. In their turn, navigation supporters attacked the road Bills, but succeeded only in amending, not stopping, them. In 1744 and again in 1751 Bills seem to have been intended, but nothing reached Parliament.

Halifax was at this time a busy, crowded town of some 8,000 people: Dr Pococke said of it in 1751: 'They have a great manufacture in serges and cloths and a very plentifull market, and are all people of business'.[9] On 2 September 1756, a meeting of the Union Club at the Talbot there decided to seek an Act to make navigable the Calder from Wakefield 'to Elland, and so on to Halifax'. One purpose in mind was to improve the transport of raw wool to the Halifax manufacturing area, which some years earlier was said to employ 60,000 people in the trade.[10] This came from Lincolnshire, Nottinghamshire and East Anglia by water to Leeds and Wakefield, and then by land, 16 miles from Wakefield, 17 miles from Leeds. Another purpose was to make corn cheaper: that was 'brought partly upon Wheel Carriages, partly upon Horses, but the greatest part on Horses'.[11] A committee was appointed and John Smeaton was invited to do a survey. He replied that for the time being he was too busy with the Eddystone lighthouse, but after another invitation sent in June 1757, he agreed to come in the autumn, and meanwhile asked for a scale plan of the river.

They sent him Eyes' and Steers' plans, told him that expense had been less a hindrance in 1740 and 1741 than landowners' and millowners' objections, and explained, when he asked why it had not then been proposed to continue the navigation up the Hebble to Halifax, that the reasons had probably been 'the great Difference of Level, the Scarcity of Water, the Rockiness of the Channel, and the great No of Fulling and other Mills situate upon this Brook'.[12] Meanwhile a subscription was advertised in August and September, a copy of which was sent to Lancashire.

Smeaton, basing himself on Eyes's work, concluded a navigation could be built with very little damage to millowners compared to the general advantage. Ending his work on the Eddystone for the season, he did his survey in October and November 1757. A meeting was held at the Talbot on 23 November, to which Smeaton produced a scheme to dredge shoals, build short cuts and 26 locks to overcome the 178 ft rise from Wakefield to the mouth of the Halifax brook and then up it for half a mile to Salterhebble bridge,[13] with a reservoir at Salterhebble, so providing a navigation 23½ miles long (including 5¾ miles of cuts) to take craft carrying 20–25 tons drawing up to 3 ft 6 in, of the type then working between Wakefield and Rawcliffe. Such a navigation, he considered, would not hurt the thirteen mills concerned. His estimate of cost was up to £30,000, and of time seven years. Though he had never built a navigation before, Smeaton was confident of his ability. He had seen locks in Flanders and Holland, and told the Parliamentary committee that 'he proposed to make the Locks better than most of the Locks he had seen on any River in England; and that he never saw worse Locks at Exeter',[14] and that he saw no reason for locks to leak excessively.

The survey, and the committee's tactful proposals for tolls, including the free carriage of building materials for mills, were accepted, and a letter was sent 'to the Gentlemen in Lancashire who are wel-wishers to the propos'd Navigation',[15] asking them to appoint a local committee and solicit subscriptions. In December a land and mill owners' meeting approved the scheme. Then, much to the embarrassment of the promoters, the Lancashire committee that had been set up at Rochdale with Manchester and Bury support (Rochdale got its wool from the same source as Halifax) proposed that powers should also be sought to extend the navigation to Sowerby Bridge, 'which lies in the great Turnpike Road that forms the Communication between the Eastern and Western Part of this Island'.[16] The Halifax committee thought this might well imperil the Bill by giving an impression to Leeds and Wakefield businessmen that 'the Trade of the West Riding is likely to be remov'd Westward',[17] and by antagonizing land and millowners who had already agreed to the original plan. However, the Rochdale committee, though their subscription was only a small proportion of the whole, employed John Eyes to do a survey, and refused either to give way or make theirs a separate scheme within the same Bill. They were proved right, for in 1758 the Bill was successfully amended in Parliament and the Act[18] passed in June to make the Calder navigable from Wakefield through to Sowerby Bridge, and the Hebble brook to Salterhebble bridge, at a cost of £2,075 to the promoters, in spite of the efforts of a strong turnpike lobby. The extension from Brooksmouth to Sowerby Bridge was estimated at £3,400. It had perhaps originally been intended to establish a company,[19] but if so, this plan was also changed in Parliament, the proposed undertakers being replaced by a body of commissioners qualified by a landed estate of the annual value of £100, or personalty of £3,000, and nine of whom could act,* perhaps on the analogy of the Thames Commissioners. They were given power to raise money on the security of the tolls and to pay 5 per cent interest out of capital until sufficient revenue was earned. Tolls were set at 1s 1½d (5½p) a ton for coal, lime, limestone, stone and slate carried the whole distance from Wakefield to Sowerby Bridge, and 8s (40p) for merchandise, but with most of the mills on the line having the right to free carriage of gravel, timber, sand and other materials. There was a prohibition on coal carried downstream, presumably inserted by the influence of coalowners on the Aire & Calder, and a limitation of craft tonnages to 24 tons that was ignored from the start. Millers had to be paid 1s 3d (6p) an hour for stopping their wheels to let vessels pass.

The commissioners first met on 7 July 1758; they appointed John Smeaton as part-time superintendent (i.e. engineer) at £250 p.a., and agreed to borrow £36,000 at 5 per cent, the works not to start until this sum had been raised. Although this was to be loan capital, the sums subscribed were to be called in instalments as they were needed. At this point John Kemmett of Tewkesbury wrote offering his and his partners' services in making the Calder navigable without affecting the mills, by using cranes to tranship

---

* Though daily administration was done by a committee, annual meetings were sometimes attended by large numbers of commissioners. There were some 180 present at that on 20 June 1765.

containers from one boat to another at each mill weir, a technique he also offered the Don company and which was tried on the Stroudwater.[20] They were not accepted.

Work does not seem to have begun on the first, Wakefield–Dewsbury, section until after 25 November 1759, when Smeaton's pay began. He had Joseph Nickalls from the Eddystone as assistant, and Joshua Wilson as master mason. They also appointed Thomas Simpson clerk. He was a Halifax man, and thereafter the company remained based upon that town, with its growing textile industry. At first Simpson worked from the Talbot; in January 1761 he moved to a room in his own house, for which the company paid him £3·15 p.a. The treasurer was then Richard Townley of Belfield, who in 1766 was to promote the forerunner of the Rochdale Canal.[21]

Nickalls arrived in the spring of 1760, and the work of collecting materials and opening quarries began. Smeaton followed on 25 May. Some cutting appears to have been done by a contractor, some by direct labour. The engineers seem to have driven the men too hard, for in 1761 the commissioners minuted 'that the Men at Work upon the Calder who are under the Direction of Mr. Smeaton or Mr. Nickalls shall not work more than 12 Hours p Day unless in Cases of Emergency'.[22] Perhaps Nickalls was to blame, for in November his conduct was described as 'culpable', and he was dismissed. He was replaced by two surveyors, one for carpentry and smith's work, one for masonry and digging, John Gwyn and Matthias Scott. By November 1762 some part of the lower river was navigable, for Gwyn was told to receive such tolls as did not belong to the Aire & Calder lessee, Peter Birt, himself a (non-active) commissioner, and note the lading of boats passing up and down.

It seems that 90 per cent of the original £36,000 subscribed in July 1758 had been spent by September 1763, when a further sum of about £20,000 was borrowed. By November 1764, however, with the navigation open for some 16 miles to Brighouse, there was a crisis. One group of commissioners seemingly wanted work to stop at Brooksmouth,* and earnings to be applied to servicing the debt, another to raise more money and complete the navigation. The second group prevailed by 56 votes to 28. A third subscription was agreed upon at a meeting significantly held at Rochdale, a new committee appointed especially to oversee construction and the clerk told to write telling James Brindley that

* Where the Hebble joined the Calder.

Page 49 (*above*) Sir John Ramsden's Canal near Huddersfield in 1795;
(*below*) Ledgard Bridge dry-dock, Mirfield, before 1914

Page 50   (above left) On Frodingham Beck: *Skelfleet* using steam and sail, *Faxfleet* sloop, *Prosperity* keel. *Skelfleet* and *Faxfleet* were Market Weighton Canal boats; (above right) a keelman and his wife on the Hull River 'he is fixed upon as a proper person to undertake the Works for perfecting the Calder Navigation, and that he be desired to attend as soon as possible to survey the Works, and prepare the plans and Estimates thereof'.[23]

Brindley came to a meeting on 31 January 1765, at which the commissioners, among the most energetic being several connected with the Aire & Calder, ordered the navigation to be extended 'with all convenient expedition' to Sowerby Bridge according to his plan, and also from Brooksmouth to Salterhebble bridge. Brindley was thereupon appointed 'Surveyor, Manager and Undertaker' for carrying out the works, at 1½ guineas per day employed and expenses, and Smeaton was discharged. So were Gwyn and Scott. Smeaton took his discharge well, saying that he would claim no salary after 15 November 1764, and 'shall never envy any Man the praise of doing better than myself while I am conscious of having done as well as those that have trod the same (or perhaps less difficult) Steps before me'.[24]

In late March the company advertised for a contractor for the 2½-mile Brooksmouth–Sowerby Bridge length,[25] about the time the navigation was opened to Brighouse. Above, Brindley had proposed a cut to cross the Calder on an aqueduct and run on the south side to Sowerby Bridge. On 20 June 1765 he was told to continue to Brooksmouth, and then re-survey his cut on the north side. He came back with a plan to continue to Brooksmouth on the north (with the cut up the Hebble), then cross the Calder and continue to a basin opposite the Ryburn at Sowerby. It seems likely that the navigation was opened to Brooksmouth about the end of 1765. Wharves and warehouses were now ordered to be built at Wakefield, Salterhebble and Sowerby Bridge. Profits from these were anticipated, which would 'not only benefit the Public, but tend to strengthen the Calder Security'.[26]

At a committee meeting in June 1766, the clerk, Thomas Simpson, was appointed superintendent, and told to give the committee reports on the state of the works, the implication being that Brindley had left. Certainly we find him two months later surveying for a possible Rochdale Canal from Sowerby Bridge to Manchester, with men like John Royds, a Calder & Hebble treasurer, among the promoters.[27] This project was partly a natural prolongation of the Calder & Hebble's authorized extension to Sowerby Bridge, and partly also an immediate, though temporary, retort to the first suggestion of what was to become the Leeds & Liverpool. He was also now to be concerned not

D

4. A Calder & Hebble subscription certificate, 1760

only with cutting the Bridgewater Canal extension to Runcorn, now beginning in earnest,[28] but with the Trent & Mersey[29] and Staffordshire & Worcestershire Canals,[29] the Acts for which had been passed in May. By December the third subscription had been spent, and to everybody's consternation still more money had to be raised. The navigation was completed to Salterhebble,[30] probably during 1767, including a staircase pair of locks at Salterhebble and a single lock and small aqueduct at Brooksmouth. Then, on the nights of 7 and 8 October 1767, 'violent and uncommon' floods damaged the works. Repairs were made. Another flood followed in February 1768, and again locks, bridges, and cuts were damaged.*

The commissioners promptly called 5 per cent on the subscribers to make good the damage and complete the navigation, and advertised for an engineer. Smeaton generously came back to survey the river, and reported that the flood had been 'higher than any flood in man's memory, or of which there is any tradition'.[32] The damage was mostly by breached banks, less to weirs and locks. He recommended repairing the damage, raising and strengthening certain banks, and building floodgates at the entrance of some of the cuts, at a cost of some £3,000. The commissioners repaired the damage, 'and several new additional Works were made at a very great Expence, and the said Navigation again restored'.[33] Then, a few days after the work had been done, another flood did so much damage that the navigation had to be closed. Some £64,000 had been spent, of which £56,900 had been borrowed and the rest taken from toll receipts.

Given the undertaking's precarious position, fresh capital could not be borrowed, and the commissioners decided to seek an Act 'for more encouraging Terms', and to raise enough money to pay off their debts and get the Act they wanted. Meanwhile lock cuts were to be dammed, and gates padlocked on the upper sections of the navigation to prevent further damage.

Smeaton having supported them in Parliament, in 1769 the 81 holders of loan stock were incorporated[34] as the Company of Proprietors of the Calder & Hebble Navigation,† with power

---

* About this time John Longbotham surveyed, apparently on private account, a canal 2⅝ miles long with some 20 locks from the navigation at Brookfoot just above Brighouse up the Red Beck valley to Godley bridge about a mile from Halifax[31], a precursor of the later Halifax branch.

† The name Calder & Hebble dates from this Act. Previously the concern had been known as the Calder, or to distinguish it from the Aire & Calder, the Upper Calder, Navigation.

to extend the navigation to near Sowerby Bridge, convert the existing debt and accrued interest into £100 shares, admit new subscribers, raise what money they needed in shares, and borrow up to £20,000 also. Tolls were considerably raised, for coal, lime, limestone, slate and stone carried the whole distance to a maximum of 4s 2d (21p), for merchandise 9s (45p). The Act also laid down (for the first time in a navigation Act) a dividend limitation, stating that if in any year more than 10 per cent were to be paid in dividends, then in the following year rates should be reduced by 2s 6d (12½p) in the £ upon the surplus over the amount needed to pay the 10 per cent. Sixty years later it was said this limitation of dividends arose from those who were 'Shocked with the enormous gains, as they are pleased to term them, of Wakefield and Leeds adventurers on the Aire & Calder.³⁵ Millers were required to stop their mills when the water fell to 18 in below the tops of their mill weirs, though the hourly payment to them for stopping their mills was raised from 1s 3d (6p) to 2s (10p). The restriction on coal being carried downstream was got rid of, to the benefit of local collieries.

The new company first met on 18 May 1769 at Halifax under the chairmanship of Richard Townley; they thanked Sir George Savile for his help with the Act, reappointed Thomas Simpson as clerk, and nominated Luke Holt and Robert Carr* as surveyors or resident engineers. Work was energetically pushed on, starting with floodgate building, £5,612 being called on existing shares, and £7,500 raised from new ones upon which 5 per cent was paid from September 1770. In August 1769 a newspaper announced the reopening of the Wakefield–Salterhebble section,³⁶ and the whole line, 24 miles long, was finally opened to Sowerby Bridge on 26 September 1770 with John Jackson's *Sally*,³⁷ on a line that now ran north of the Calder all the way. In December Smeaton surveyed it,³⁸ and 'finds the River now put into as good a State of Security as could possibly be expected in the Time and is indeed in the General in a very defensible Condition'. Even before the opening, a meeting at the Coach & Six, Birstall, on 15 January 1770, had discussed a branch canal from Birstall to the Calder & Hebble at Dewsbury, which was then surveyed by John Longbotham, who was also employed about the same time to survey a branch from the navigation by Cleckheaton and the Spen valley to Bradford.³⁹ In addition to locks, the navigation now had a

---

* West Riding bridge surveyor and architect, father of the better known architect John Carr.

number of separate floodgates to control the entrances to cuts and so protect their banks. John Longbotham, in evidence on the Leeds & Selby Canal Bill, said that the cost had been £75,000. The ruling length of the locks was 61½ ft,[40] to allow use by craft some 57 ft 6 in × 14 ft. A towing path had been built; towing for some years at any rate was by men as well as horses.

In 1771, Smeaton was asked how best the water supply to the summit Sowerby Bridge pound could be improved, and advised the building of 'a Tunnel made in the way of an Adit or Sough, such as those made for draining Collieries'[41] to bring it from Hollins Mill through the high grounds. It was begun in June 1772, and finished in March 1774. Luke Holt now left the company's service, and Carr continued alone until he was succeeded in 1779 by William Brassey.

A coal toll of 1½d per ton/mile, less than the 2½p authorized, was decided upon in July 1773, perhaps because the building about that time of a waggonway to the navigation at Horbury bridge from the coal pits at Flockton owned by Richard Milnes and his sons suggested that Flockton coal would compete in West Yorkshire markets. This and its successors were used until 1893, when the Lane End and Emroyd collieries it served were closed. Other lines built over the years were from Storr's Hill colliery to a little above Horbury bridge; one from the White Lee colliery above Heckmondwike to just above Dewsbury, until the mine was worked out in the 1820s; from Sir George Armytage's coal mines to Kirklees; and from the Earl of Cardigan's at New Park to Wakefield.[42] Though some mining had gone on since medieval times, colliery development took place at Flockton, Horbury, Crigglestone and elsewhere above Wakefield once the Calder & Hebble was there to carry the coal which was also brought by plateway and road waggon for shipment from Wakefield's wharves. But the produce could only with difficulty compete with that mined below Wakefield or (from the 1820s) towards Barnsley, and so some of it went upwards, to Halifax, Huddersfield and, once it had been opened, the lower part of the Rochdale Canal.

Completion of their navigation brought the company into close relations with the Aire & Calder. The latter's lessee, Peter Birt, in 1771 was both slow in paying tolls for his boats, and rude into the bargain. His lease ended in 1774, when these craft were transferred to the Aire & Calder company. They were busy: there was a request for more to be sent in 1775, when it was noted that the

river 'is not so well supply'd with Undertakers Boats as usual'.[43]
The previous year the company had sent a representative to watch
the Aire & Calder's 1774 Bill, to solicit and promote 'proper
regulations of Public Utility with which the Interest of this
Company is closely united'.[44] But the concern was still an un-
sophisticated one, which in 1773 could order 'That no pigs or
Fowls be kept at any of the Warehouses or Wharfs belonging to
the proprietors'.[45]

Curiously enough, not only the preparations for, and the passing of, the Act of 1774 for Sir John Ramsden's Canal, from
Huddersfield to join the Calder & Hebble at Cooper Bridge,
passed unnoticed in that company's books, but Ramsden's Canal
is thereafter hardly mentioned at all for some fifty years after it
was built. They do not seem to have been interested.

Our company was becoming established. In December 1775
they decided to get rid of 'the great inconveniences complained
of'[46] on the river between Shepley bridge and Mirfield by a cut;
William Jessop was engaged to build and John Pinkerton to cut
it. Another sign of incipient prosperity was an order of 1776 'That
the boarding of the Dams be put into Execution if Mr. Jessop
thinks it Proper'[47]; that is, raising the height of navigation dams
by adding boards, so increasing water depth and allowing craft
to carry more cargo. Coal-loading staiths were now built, and
new warehouses put up at Wakefield and Dewsbury. In June
1778 the company were prosperous enough to add 1 per cent to
the 5 per cent interest they had been paying on their capital since
24 September 1770, so making a 6 per cent dividend.

In 1779 Smeaton again examined the navigation. He recommended some changes, among them the replacement of Brindley's
staircase pair of locks at Salterhebble and the single at Brooksmouth by three new single locks. His proposals were commended
to the committee by the annual meeting, which also decided to
raise another £4,091 from shareholders, and further sums in
subsequent years. Because of the dividend limitation clause of
their Act, the company preferred to finance all the improvements that were steadily made throughout the 1780s, 1790s and
early part of the new century by increasing their share capital
than by borrowing on fixed interest, as an unrestricted company
would probably have done. These additional subscriptions, being
offered to shareholders only in proportion to existing holdings,
were similar to modern rights issues. Jessop reported on Smeaton's
proposals, a situation that must have amused the older man who

had indeed taught Jessop his business. He approved them, and was then told in 1780 to proceed with work at Kirklees and a new cut at Brighouse. In 1782 and early 1783 Samuel Hartley, working to Jessop, replaced the Salterhebble and Brooksmouth locks with three new ones. Then, in 1785, Battye Ford cut was extended, also to Jessop's plan. Jessop was also in business himself on the navigation. He and John Pinkerton for many years had a dry-dock at Mirfield made out of the old cut they had replaced in 1776, and also in 1786 began to send down coal for lime-burning

MASONRY and DIGGING,

ON THE

Calder and Hebble Navigation.

M A S O N S

W HO would undertake the Build-ing of a LOCK, and Two Pair of FLOOD-GATES on the RIVER CALDER, not far from *Brighouse*, may deliver in Pro-pofals for the fame on *Wednefday* the 26th of *April*, at the Houfe of Mr. CLEGG, in *Brighouse*, to Mr. JESSOP, Engineer, who will be there on that and the two preceding Days, and will explain the Circumftances and Situation of the Work.

A L S O, about three Quarters of a Mile in length of Cutting, will, at the fame Time, be contracted. for, of which a proper Explanation will be given upon the Place.

A P R I L 17th, 1780.

[Halifax: E. Jacob, Printer.]

5. Jessop at work in 1780

from a colliery they owned near Whitley Wood, for which he was given a special toll.

In 1779 Thomas Walpole had been engaged as agent or superintendent at £130 p.a., a house, and keep for a horse. Two years later he was told to contract with road carriers on suitable terms, to carry between Sowerby Bridge and Burnley. Two years later again Simpson the clerk died, and was replaced by William Norris at £25 p.a.—a family that was long to be associated with the Calder & Hebble.

The Calder & Hebble company were not carriers on their own account, but their table of charges included both tolls and freight. They accepted goods for despatch, freight paid, and themselves found carriers, the wharfinger using the first suitable craft (many of them the Aire & Calder company's) unless the consignor had stated a preference. This system, also used on the Don, could be so managed that a regular service resulted. In 1779 the navigation company were advertising in Manchester that

'one or more Vessels will set out regularly from the Warehouses at Sowerby-bridge, and Salter-Hebble, for Wakefield, Selly (Selby), and Hull, every Tuesday and Friday at four o'clock in the afternoon; and goods sent by the carriers from Manchester on Mondays and Thursdays about noon, will reach Sowerby-bridge the next day soon enough to be sent by the said Vessels without loss of time'.[48]

Goods, the advertisement said, should be consigned to the care of Thomas Walpole the company's agent.

In the 1780s the main traffics of the company's warehouses were wool, corn and other grains, beans and casked goods. Important downwards traffics to the Aire & Calder were cloth from the Halifax district and quarried stone, much of it shipped coastwise to London as paving stone. By 1783 warehouses were getting so crowded that the company decided to start charging for space. Two years later an assistant had to be put on at Fall Ing lock, 'the Business . . . being much encreas'd',[49] and by 1788 new warehouses had been built at Sowerby Bridge and Fall Ing.

In 1788 boats were leaving Huddersfield for Wakefield three times a week, connecting at Huddersfield with land carriage from Manchester, and at Wakefield with boats to Hull.[50] It was probably the starting of this service, unwelcome to the Calder & Hebble because Manchester trade was only passing over part of their navigation, that persuaded them a month or so later to start subsidizing their agent to run a road transport business between

Sowerby Bridge and Manchester. This was continued for some years.

An advertisement of April 1786, offering five shares for sale, described the company as 'a flourishing Undertaking, having long yielded far more than legal Interest, exclusive of the Money invested in the Funds from the Redundancy of the annual Income thereof'.[51] Late in the decade the company were indeed growing so prosperous, and had so much in reserve, that they could contemplate paying a regular dividend of over 10 per cent. In 1787, therefore, they took counsel's opinion whether the Act meant they could divide 10 per cent profits as well as the 5 per cent legal interest, and whether they could add to their capital upon which dividends were paid money later raised for capital purposes—as they had been doing. Seemingly the answer to the first question was 'no', to the second 'yes'. When their dividend went over the permitted 10 per cent maximum, therefore, toll reductions had to be made, the first at the beginning of 1791. Here are averaged figures:

Years*	Dividend per cent
1771–77	5‡
1778–79†	8
1780–82	8·16
1783–85	7·66
1786–88	11·66
1789–91	12·66
1792–94	13

These figures must greatly have encouraged the promoters of the Rochdale Canal[52] from Sowerby Bridge to Manchester, among whom were several Calder & Hebble committeemen and shareholders. They sent a deputation in March 1792 to get our company's formal consent to a junction; this was given, but the Bill was lost. They were back again in the autumn before introducing their second Bill, and were followed a fortnight later by another deputation, from the committees of the Manchester, Bolton & Bury Canal and of its proposed extension by the Bury & Sladen Canal and a long tunnel to the Calder.[53] The Calder &

---

* The company's financial year began in mid-June. These figures are for calendar years, adding together the two half-yearly dividends declared in June and December.

† Two years.

‡ Statutory interest.

Hebble agreed to both in identical terms, saying that the engineers could arrange the junction once the Acts had been passed.

Both Bills failed, and in October 1793 the persevering Rochdale deputation made a third appearance. Again the Calder & Hebble agreed, but this time with stipulations. At that time the Rochdale promoters did not know whether the Duke of Bridgewater would withdraw his objections to a broad canal, and the most important of their stipulations was designed to support them against him. They insisted that, were a waterway smaller than the Calder & Hebble to be built, all craft off the Rochdale should stop at Sowerby Bridge or Salterhebble, below which only boats owned by the Rochdale company should pass, and then only in pairs through the locks. The company were envisaging short narrow boats of the type later used on the Huddersfield Canal,[54] which if allowed to pass singly would waste a great deal of water. Simultaneously the narrow Huddersfield was being promoted from Ramsden's at Huddersfield to the Ashton-under-Lyne Canal near Manchester. This was much less attractive to the Calder & Hebble, as craft passing by it to Wakefield would only move over a part of their line. Therefore, while not opposing the Huddersfield in Parliament so long as the Rochdale succeeded too, they actively supported the latter, now to be a broad canal, the Duke having withdrawn his objection, and sent representatives to London to help it through Parliament.

It passed, enacting among other provisions that the Calder & Hebble company were to build whatever warehouses and wharves at Sowerby Bridge the Rochdale company wanted, the latter to pay ½d per ton per day for goods deposited. Should the Calder & Hebble company not do so, the Rochdale or landowners could. Our company were so pleased that they voted £105 each to their two representatives and their engineer Thomas Bradley (who had succeeded Brassey early in 1792) for their work in London. As regards the Huddersfield, they had joined Sir John Ramsden and the Aire & Calder in agreeing with the promoters while the Bill was in Parliament that should any other canal be made later from the east—that is, from the Barnsley or the Dearne & Dove Canals—to join the Huddersfield Canal, all the benefits it brought should accrue to those three alone. However, early in 1795 they petitioned in favour of a turnpike road from Ripponden (above Sowerby Bridge) via Marsden to Manchester, much of it along the Huddersfield's proposed route.

Bradley was to become a very competent engineer. After his

appointment, William Jessop, who had been employed as consultant on all the improvements made since 1776, ceased to be used, Bradley himself undertaking both planning and execution.

Meanwhile, in February 1793 the committee had decided to oppose the proposed Barnsley Canal (see Chapter VIII) from the Aire & Calder at Heath to Barnsley and on to Barnby (for Silkstone) and Haigh Bridge, and instead to support a Barnsley-based alternative (see p. 172) from Horbury on their navigation to Haigh Bridge, and thence by way of Barnsley to the Don, since this would 'be of the greatest Utility to the Calder and Hebble Navigation',[55] by communicating with their line instead of the Aire & Calder. A Bill was promoted, the Calder & Hebble subscribing £10,000, but in Parliament a compromise was reached whereby the Barnsley Canal Act went through without the Haigh Bridge branch, and with clauses authorizing a 6-mile line from that canal at Barugh to Horbury, to be built by the Calder & Hebble. Its likely cost had been estimated by the Barnsley's engineers, William Jessop, Elias Wright and John Gott, at £72,115, but no more was heard of such a very doubtful economic proposition. (*To continue the history of the Calder & Hebble Navigation, turn to Chapter IX.*)

Sir John Ramsden's Canal

A canal or river navigation to link Huddersfield with the Calder & Hebble must have been in mind in 1758, for a section of that year's Calder & Hebble Act stipulated that the commissioners it established should have no power to interfere with any future navigation 'from the Mouth of the River Coln, to the Town of Huddersfield'. A similar clause was repeated in the 1769 Act. Before then, indeed, Robert Whitworth had in 1766 surveyed from the Calder & Hebble at Cooper Bridge to King's Mill, Huddersfield.

Sir John Ramsden was under age when Luke Holt, helped by Joseph Atkinson, a former lessee of the Aire & Calder, made another such survey in 1773, and his trustees therefore promoted a Bill early next year to build a canal. The Ramsdens had a strong motive to develop Huddersfield, for in 1774 they owned every house in the town except one, and a third of the land upon which the canal was to be built. Luke Holt[56] had formerly been a master carpenter, who with John Topham had from 1763 worked for the Calder & Hebble as a contractor on their locks from Cooper

Bridge upwards. When after their flood damage a new company was formed in 1769, he and Robert Carr were appointed surveyors or resident engineers to rebuild and complete the navigation, but in June 1772 he was dismissed and Carr went on alone, perhaps because Holt was now to work for the Ramsden interest.

Joseph Atkinson gave evidence for the Bill. He told the Commons committee that Huddersfield, 'the only Market for Narrow Woollen Cloths' in the West Riding (it wasn't quite true) would benefit were the canal to be built and carry cheaply coal, lime, corn and general merchandise. Lime, he said, from Cooper Bridge to Huddersfield then cost 4s (20p) a ton by road transport and could be taken for 1s (5p) by canal.[57] The line was estimated to cost £8,000 and take twelve months to build. Following the Calder & Hebble's 1769 Act, but more severe, the Act compelled toll cuts of one-eighth for each £1 rise in the clear profits above 6 per cent p.a., commissioners appointed by it being given powers to examine the canal accounts. The upper 1½ miles were to be cut deeper than the rest, to form a reservoir that would prevent interference with the working of the mills.[58]

The Act[59] was passed on 9 March 1774. Sir John was empowered to take 8d a ton on coal, lime and stone and 1s 6d (7½p) a ton on all other goods. Though authorized to enter the Colne just below King's mill,[60] the canal in fact ended at Aspley, where wharves and warehouses were built. Originally the water supply was from the Colne, by way of the Shaw Foot Mill tail-goit, but after the opening of the Huddersfield Canal, most of the water came from its lockage water. Later tramroads were built to the canal from the Colne Bridge and Upper Staith collieries, and perhaps also from that at Fieldhouse.

The canal, with nine broad locks, was opened in the last quarter of 1776, when Aire & Calder boats started to trade up it,[61] the cost being some £11,975, though this figure seems to include some maintenance work also.[62] A local historian was to say later that it was 'the principal means of raising the town of Huddersfield to be one of the principal marts for woollen goods in the West Riding'.[63] In 1788 a new thrice-weekly carrying service from the town to Wakefield was advertised, connecting there with another to Hull, with a promise of a daily service should enough business offer.[64] (*To continue the history of Sir John Ramsden's Canal, turn to p. 206.*)

Emmet's Canal

In 1782 John Emmet senior and three partners began to build an iron furnace, followed by a foundry, near Birkenshaw, four miles south-east of Bradford. In order to bring coal and iron-stone to the works, they built a one-mile-long level small canal from a place called Blue Hills. The works closed in 1815, but much of the canal can still be traced.[65]

CHAPTER III

The Don Navigation

++++++++++++++++++++++++++++++++++++++◆++++++++++++++++++++++++++++++++++++++

THE Don,* running past Tinsley near Sheffield, Rotherham and Doncaster, had two outlets before Vermuyden's work, one to the Trent at Adlingfleet just above Trent Falls, the other to the Aire above Rawcliffe. The river had always been navigable in favourable conditions to Doncaster. In 1343 a commission was made to men to inquire into obstructions from 'bridges, weirs and other things' to 'the passing of ships from the town of Donecastre to the water of Trent'.[1] In the fourteenth and again in the fifteenth century, stone was carried by water from Doncaster up the Ouse to York for York minster.[2]

On 24 May 1626 Cornelius Vermuyden signed an agreement with Charles I to drain Hatfield Chase, and in the same year the scheme was begun. Among other works, the waters of the Don were concentrated into a single channel and washland running into the Aire. This served its drainage purpose, but caused severe flooding around Fishlake, Sykehouse and Snaith. In 1628 there was rioting, followed by a judgement in 1633 to compel the undertakers to cut a new channel from Newbridge to Goole on the Ouse. This Dutch River cost nearly £30,000.[3] Its greater fall attracted the flow, and the old Trent and Aire outlets gradually silted up. Perhaps also it lessened the depth in the Don's upper reaches. Originally sluices had been built at the Goole end of the Dutch River to keep out the tides, but about 1688 a flood carried these away, and they were not replaced. The tide could now enter, with two consequences: it reduced the tidal flow that went up the Ouse towards York, and it widened the Dutch River.[4] By using it, 'large Barges and Vessels† both Summer and

---

* The river is now spelled 'Don', the navigation often 'Dun', following the older spelling used in the Acts. To save confusion, I have used 'Don' throughout, except in quotations.
† Those of 10 to 30 tons were meant.

Winter'[5] could reach Fishlake, and usually Wilsick House (Thorpe in Balne) above Stainforth; small craft could reach Doncaster during three-quarters of the year and large ones at floodtides.[6] Above Doncaster, there was then no water carriage. Sheffield and Rotherham, and maybe Doncaster also, sent goods by land to Bawtry and then by water down the Idle to the Trent.[7]

In November 1691 Doncaster corporation gave £5 towards making the Don more navigable.[8] A Bill for this purpose was introduced in 1698 by Sir Godfrey Copley of Sprotbrough,[9] who was also closely concerned with the promotion of the Aire & Calder.[10] Though backed by West Riding interests and Leeds corporation, the Bill was not supported by Sheffield or by Doncaster corporation, who feared their mills would be affected, and was successfully opposed by Idle and Trent interests. Another Bill was initiated in 1704 by Doncaster corporation[11] and backed by Sheffield and Barnsley, but by now the riparian landowners, frightened that the building of locks and weirs would cause their lands to be flooded, were organized enough to defeat it.

When the project was revived in 1721, it was initiated by Sheffield (both town authorities and the Cutlers' Company) and

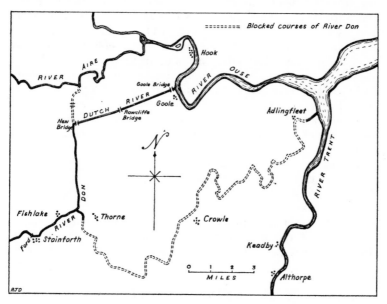

6. Vermuyden changes the course of the Don

by Rotherham.[12] They hoped the transport of export goods would be cheapened by a navigation which would also carry locally-produced lead, coal and millstones, as well as trade from Cheshire, Lancashire and the Midlands brought by the Trent and the Idle, and by land carriage to the Don. Upstream, they sought trade from London, Hull, York and the east coast. Farsighted men also saw a link being built to the recently authorized Mersey & Irwell Navigation at Manchester.[13] A Bill was introduced at the turn of the year 1721, and early in 1722 Doncaster corporation started to negotiate with Sheffield on tolls and costs, though a group which feared that trade would by-pass Doncaster to enrich Sheffield combined with lower-river landowners to oppose the idea. The Aire & Calder proprietors despatched one of their number to oppose it,[14] however, and it got no further.

In September 1722 a meeting of representatives of the Cutlers' Company, Doncaster corporation and landowners commissioned William Palmer, Joseph Atkinson and Joshua Mitchel[15] to survey the Don. There were then about nine mill weirs on the river, and a number of fords, especially below Doncaster. In November Palmer produced a survey[16] showing how the whole river could be made navigable up to Sheffield itself, including alternative plans for dealing with the part below Doncaster; to build locks and weirs, or make a 4-mile cut from Doncaster to Barnby Dun to avoid the worst stretch. The landowners preferred the second. The Cutlers' and Doncaster corporation, supported now by the Aire & Calder, then agreed[17] upon a navigation for 30-ton craft, to have 3½ ft river depth, and petitioned for a Bill prepared after 'Copying ye Manchester Act of Parliament'* with the intention of building locks, but were defeated when the landowners organized the House of Commons Committee to refuse leave to bring in the petition.

The Cutlers now worked to reduce the hostility of the landowners, and those with water-power interests; these in turn were trying to detach Doncaster from Sheffield, by letting the idea get about that if Doncaster went ahead on its own, Sheffield's Bill might fail and Doncaster could then become the riverhead. This so that the landowners on the lower river might have greater influence. Although Doncaster agreed to a petition in December 1724,[18] they did not follow it up with a Bill, and Sheffield was first in the following session, with a Bill of February 1726 to make the Don navigable from Holmstile, ¾ mile

* That for the Mersey & Irwell.

Page 67 (*above*) On the Ouse near Selby. An early postcard; (*below*) Leeming
lock on Bedale Beck

Page 68　The Ripon Canal: (*above*) the first lock, near Ripon, seen from the second lock. The derelict barge is moored near the entrance to a dry-dock; (*below*) the basin at Ripon, before 1900

below Doncaster, to Tinsley above Rotherham and 3 miles from Sheffield. In spite of opposition from landowners and Aire & Calder and Idle interests, it passed,[19] helped by the dropping of any effort to make the river navigable above Tinsley, which could have interfered too greatly with water-powered industry, and by a carefully organized set of petitions from towns all over Yorkshire and as far away as Middlewich, Stockport, Derby and King's Lynn. But there were some bad moments: William Palmer caught a fever and was for a time dangerously ill while the Bill was in the Commons; there was opposition from Bawtry, Gainsborough and higher up the Trent, and John Smith the Sheffield cutler, piloting the Bill through, was glad to catch the Derby coach on his way to Rebecca, to whom he was united 'in all the Tyes of Conjugall Affection', happy that 'We had a Quicker Dispatch yesterday in the house than has been known this 7 years (the Lords in a Comitee went thro our bill then made a report & read it a 3rd time & past it without any amendmt'.[20] Not surprisingly, £10 was 'Paid for the Entertainmᵗ' at ye Return of Mr. Steer and Mr. Smith from London . . . when the Navigation Act was gained',[21] and an item appeared in the Cutlers' accounts: '1726. 30 Aug. Paid Wm Moore for glasses which he said was broak at the Navigation Feast, 3s 9d'.[22] By the Act, the Company of Cutlers were appointed undertakers, to make the river navigable for 20-ton craft, and levy tolls of 6d (2½p) a ton on lime, 2s 6d (12½p) on lead, 3s (15p) on iron and some other goods, and 3s 6d (17½p) on the remainder, charges notably lower than had been authorized in 1699 for the Aire & Calder. They were also to make a good road from Tinsley to Sheffield and keep it repaired, for which they could levy 1d a ton on waterborne goods. Unlike most river Acts, however, this one included a number of restrictions, the price of its passing. The most important of these barred them from building any new weir—that is, locks had to be made at existing mill and other weirs—or from altering the height of any of them.

The Act passed, Doncaster corporation followed with a Bill to improve the river downwards from Holmstile to Wilsick House, Sheffield, at this time agreeing to transfer the small portion of their authorized navigation between Holmstile and the corn mill dam in Doncaster to Doncaster corporation.[23] Joseph Atkinson appeared as engineer, there was no opposition, and the Bill passed in 1727.[24] It appointed the corporation as undertakers, empowered them to levy 8d a ton on limestone (with certain

E

provisions for free carriage) and English timber, and 10d on everything else. It was specific, like its predecessor, about what could be done. Below Fishlake, the undertakers were enabled to convert three fixed bridges* to drawbridges and to charge for opening each one. The Commissioners of Sewers for the Level of Hatfield Chace were then the river authority from Wilsick House down to Newbridge, while the Corporation of York claimed the conservatorship of the Dutch River.

Both Acts gave power to borrow, neither specified how much or in what way. Doncaster decided to create 50 shares and then make calls on them, 10 to belong to the corporation as a body, 40 to members as private individuals. This did not, of course, constitute the shareholders a company. Sheffield, on the other hand, divided expenditure between the Cutlers' Company and the town. Each raised money by borrowing at interest, the Company also by annuities, until in 1730 the Sheffield interest in the river was also converted into 100 shares. Many outstanding loans were now exchanged for shares, 6 of which were assigned to the Cutlers' Company, 10 to the town of Sheffield and held by trustees, and 84 for others. These shares were issued at £95, which probably covered what had already been spent, and were subject to further calls. A management committee of seven were appointed and empowered to make such calls.

Maybe Sheffield's adoption of the share principle was a conscious preliminary to the amalgamation of the two sets of undertakers. This was agreed in October 1730, and came into operation in August 1731. It established that the amount expended per share of each group should be equalized, after which the shares should rank *pari passu*.[25] On amalgamation, all shares were vested in trustees for their owners, because under the Bubble Act of 1720 the amalgamated concern could not act as a joint stock company with transferable shares without a royal charter or an Act. The shareholders decided to regularize their position as soon as possible by a new Act. By now Sheffield had built 'five Chargeable Locks, and several long Cuts', and had extended the navigation about 11 miles for 20-ton boats; Doncaster had built 'one Chargeable Lock, and several other Works below Holmstile',† [26] the two bodies having spent £12,000. However, they also included in their Bill new powers, notably to improve the river and take

---

* Middle (or New), Rawcliffe and Goole bridges.
† Doncaster's lock was probably at Doncaster, Sheffield's five those at Kilnhurst, Swinton, Mexborough, Conisbrough and Sprotbrough.

tolls, from Wilsick House down to the Ouse, and to remove two of the three bridges over the Dutch River. The landowners rallied against this, and the Bill was lost in 1731.

The shareholders therefore had to make a start without it, calling a general meeting at Sheffield in August 1731, and appointing a chairman, treasurer, and committee. The last in turn appointed John Smith engineer and Thomas Radford accountant, and made a call on the Doncaster shareholders that brought their shares to £95, equal to the current level of the Sheffield ones. Earlier, in May, a collector of 'ye Ship Keel and Boat Freights' had been appointed to Sheffield, and told: 'Keep your Books true and exact and let us have no complaints from the Lead Merchants; be quick in answering letters'[27] A first dividend of £1 16s 4d (£1·81½) or about 2 per cent was paid in June 1732, and one of 5 per cent in 1733, though calls were still being made and work going on.

In 1733 the shareholders tried again with a Bill, this time solely to set up a single corporate body, explaining to Parliament that they had so far spent £17,250 upon 8 locks and several cuts above Holmstile and 2 below, and on other navigation works. This time they were unopposed. The resultant Act[28] established the Company of the Proprietors of the Navigation of the River Dun, gave power to make an additional cut from Bromley Sands above Rotherham High Dam to Ickles Dam, and authorized the Cutlers' Company to continue construction from the current head of navigation at Aldwarke 2 miles below Rotherham should the Don company fail to do so. Eleven locks had now been built, to which that at Barnby Dun below Long Sandall was soon added. The new company first met at Sheffield on 9 August 1733, and appointed a committee of nine whose chairman was George Bradshaw, recorder of Doncaster. This authorized new tolls of 1s 8d (8½p) for English timber from Aldwarke to Barnby Dun, 2s 4d (11½p) for coal, lead and lead ore, and 4s (20p) for most other goods, the lower lead figure presumably reflecting competition from the Idle and Trent route.

Below Wilsick House, there was a Bill of 1736, seemingly promoted by a group that included Don interests and also a merchants' group at York, to improve the river down to Sykehouse Ferry by dredging shallows, as well as the Ouse above York. This failed to get beyond first reading,[29] but may have encouraged the Don company in 1737 to seek their own powers to do the same thing, as well as to remove Rawcliffe bridge and make the other

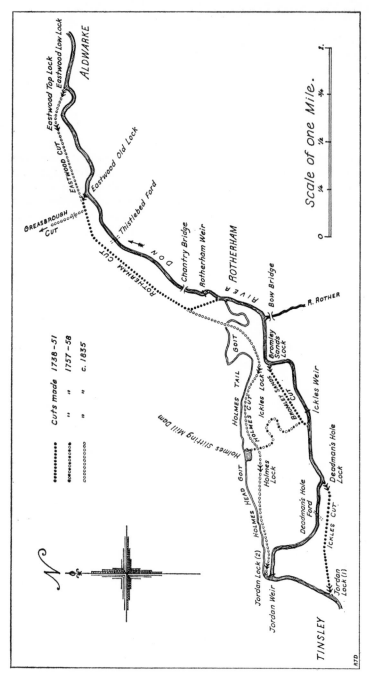

7. The upper Don

two bridges over the Dutch River more convenient for craft to pass. But their Bill also failed.

The company, prevented from improving the river below Wilsick House, turned to the upper river, and after some years of litigation with Lord Effingham, who owned mills at Rotherham, opened the navigation to that place by 1740, by building East-wood Lock and the long Rotherham Cut, so giving local coal access to the markets of the east. With three more locks and two considerable cuts, the line was extended to Tinsley in 1751, though the Tinsley–Sheffield road was not built until about 1755. The Aire & Calder evidently feared that the extension to Rother-ham would seriously affect their trade, for in 1737 their lessees were given the option of giving up their lease should the Don be made navigable to Rotherham before it had expired.

Meanwhile, the Don company had once more tried to get powers to extend downwards and, this time, in 1740, they succeeded. Giving evidence before the Parliamentary committee, their spokesman said that £26,550* had been spent between Rotherham and Wilsick House, so that 'Four Men can do as much work in the River Dun as Six in the River Eyre and Calder'.[30] Below Wilsick down to Fishlake Ferry, they claimed that 20-ton craft often got stuck for days in water sometimes less than a foot deep, though at spring tides 40-ton vessels could sail from Fishlake to Hull. They said that £3,750, spent mostly on a lock and a 2-mile cut, would complete the work. In spite of opposition, the Act[31] passed, enabling the company to improve the river to Fishlake Ferry, but again specifying in detail how the work should be done. An additional toll was granted of 2d a ton on coal, lime, stone and timber, and 4d on other goods, though much local traffic not going to, or coming from, beyond Goole was exempted. A petition on the Bill tells us that 'great Quanti-ties of Coals' are carried down the Don for use at Gainsborough and its neighbourhood: and another that great quantities of corn and coal went to Hull. Finally, a petition from Manchester shows that the Don was used for imported goods going west over the Pennines, and other goods returning.[32]

The channel was now deepened from Wilsick House to Bram-with, and a long cut made thence to Stainforth, with a lock at Bramwith and another at Stainforth, the lowest on the river.

* Calls of £165 (the £115 mentioned in the 1733 Act, plus subsequent calls) had been made on each £150 share, raising £24,750. The balance had come from receipts.

Thorne now became the effective end of the navigation and the transhipment point for goods for Hull, a wharf and warehouse having been built there by 1737. In this year also the company decided to trade in coal, stocking it at Thorne wharf presumably to be loaded into keels coming up the Dutch River from the Humber or the Trent. But the business seems only to have lasted for a year. The lower part of the old river was still sometimes used: in 1749 the company ordered

'that a Flood gate be fixed up immediately in the South End of Bramwith Wash to help the Light Boats up the Channell of the old River, without the Trouble and hindrance of passing through the Cutt'.[33]

The navigation was now some 33 miles long from Tinsley to Fishlake, with twelve locks from Doncaster upwards and five below. A horse towing path had probably been built downwards from Doncaster when the river was first made navigable. Above, men may have hauled the boats when they were not being sailed, for in 1762 the shareholders' meeting had gates and bridges for horse towing made on the towing path.

Up to 1750 £40,500 of capital had been raised, and some income also spent on construction; perhaps we can put the total cost at about £45,000. The 150 shares then had a par value of £270. Meanwhile the company, having spent some time looking for a lessee, and having resolved 'that the River be lett to no person concern'd in the River of Air and Caldare, upon any Terms whatsoever',[34] let the tolls to Henry Broadhead, Francis Cripps and Richard Ellison* for seven years from Lady Day 1738 at £1,200 p.a., and for a further seven at £1,500 p.a., plus interest on new money spent on the navigation, 5 per cent in the first period and 6¼ per cent in the second. The lessees were to maintain all works except the Dutch River bridges. In 1751 a new lease was given, this time to Joseph Broadbent, Joseph Atkinson and Thomas Smith,† out of several applicants, at £3,500 p.a. plus 6¼ per cent on any new capital expenditures they should ask for.

When the lease expired, the company were undecided whether to lease again or to manage the river themselves. After advertising

---

* Broadhead was the first chairman of the company after the 1733 Act and held more shares than any other private person; Cripps was a Doncaster resident; Ellison had given evidence for the Doncaster Bill of 1727, and been a committeeman from 1731 to 1737.

† Broadbent had been a committeemen from 1742 to 1750, Atkinson had helped to do the original 1722 survey, had given evidence on the Doncaster Bill of 1727, and was at that time a lessee of the Aire & Calder.

either for lessees or for managers, in 1759 they took on John Hill of Thorne and William Martin of Tinsley, who had formerly been agents to the lessees, as manager and assistant manager at an inclusive combined salary of £590 p.a., responsibility to include running the navigation and the freighting business, recruiting staff, and keeping the accounts. At the same time they fixed the coal toll along the whole navigation from Tinsley at 3s (15p).

For the ten years from Lady Day 1759 the tolls averaged £7,006 p.a., £3,733 of which came from the coal trade, £366 from lead, £179 from stone and lime, and the balance of £2,728 from other goods, about £1,500 of which was said to be from Sheffield manufacturers. For the same period, an average of £5,024 p.a. was paid out in dividends. Calls continued to be made, however, until the end of 1763, by which time the capital value of each of the 150 shares was probably £349. Here are averaged dividend figures to 1793:

Years	Total annual dividend payment	Payment per share			
	£	£	s	d	
1759–63*	4,647	30	17	9	(£30·89)
1764–68	5,100	34	0	0	(£34)
1769–73	6,907	46	0	11	(£46·04½)
1774–78	7,905	52	14	0	(£52·70)
1779–83	6,835	45	11	4	(£45·56½)
1784–88	7,008	46	14	5	(£46·72)
1789–93	8,896	59	6	2	(£59·31)

Trade was now responding quickly: on 4 May 1765 Josiah Wedgwood wrote to Samuel Garbett that toll receipts on the Don had increased by £2,000 in the previous four years.[35]

Figures that we have for 1764 to 1767† are illuminating.

	1764	1765	1766	1767	1768
	£	£	£	£	£
Coal, charcoal, cinders	4,028	3,851	4,495	4,287	5,255
Lead	793	816	1,160	1,056	1,473
Corn	517	640	532	569	500
Stone, lime	196	192	219	215	211
Timber, bark	134	72	59	60	48
Sundries	5,825	6,195	6,187	6,501	7,351
Total	11,493	11,766	12,652	12,688	14,838

* Excluding the first quarter of 1759.
† Years beginning 25 March.

As we see, the sundries traffic is far the most important: under this heading will be both manufactures, such as Sheffield goods, and also groceries and all kinds of merchandise. Coal is growing steadily, as is lead.

The company did not then possess their own craft, but like the Calder & Hebble, accepted goods freight paid and then found carriers. These could be contract boats* or bye-keels working mainly to and from Hull, though by 1789 there was also a regular service from Thorne to London.[36] In 1782 it appears the company were also carrying through to Hull in their own vessels, but such craft must have been few. In 1771 a regular bye-traders' service was announced from Rotherham to York.[37] Independent craft also worked, of course. In 1764 a four-year-old 60-ton keel drawing 6 ft and working between Thorne and Hull was advertised for sale.[38] For these years the following sums were paid out as freight: 1764, £3,059; 1765, £3,309; 1766, £3,320; 1768, £4,023.

While the navigation was leased, there was trouble with riparian landowners over the towing path. In 1749 the company had to support a man who had forced towing path gates that had been locked against him, and in the following year agreed to defend anyone 'who shall hale with Men or Horses according to the Powers given by the Statutes'.[39]

An amusing situation arose in 1754. The Act of 1733 enacted that of the committee of nine, three should be elected from existing shareholders below Holmstile (Doncaster) and six from those in the upper river, so long as any were alive, and after that, from any other shareholders. In that year only five original upper river men were still eligible, and a woman, Mrs Elizabeth Drake, was elected as the sixth. She was too bashful to appear, however, and two years later counsel's opinion was taken upon the construction of the Act. Seemingly nothing could be done, and she continued to be elected up to 1759, though she never attended, and in 1760 was reported 'very infirm' (she died in 1765, aged 82). Thereafter the shareholders' meeting ignored the strict wording of the law, which they had been unable to amend 'by Reason of several Discouragements they had . . . met with'[40] by appointing four committeemen not proprietors at the time of the 1733 Act.

The navigation back in their own hands, the company took steps to reorganize their business. Martin, accompanied by some keelmen, presumably to answer practical carrying questions, went

---

* A contract boat was one working for the company under a regular contract; a bye-craft one running independently.

'to Manchester and other places in that Neighbourhood, in order to keep up Correspondence with the Traders in those parts',[41] and also put advertisements in papers there. At the same time a shipper at Hull was appointed forwarding agent. It does not seem likely that much Manchester trade resulted, especially after the Calder & Hebble opened. Certainly a cargo of yarn brought from Hull to Rotherham and then taken by land to Manchester in 1769 was exceptional enough to be minuted.

In 1760 began the company's long quarrel with Samuel Walker & Co,* who had ironworks at Masborough between Tinsley and Rotherham, and a forge at Rotherham mill. Walker's had started by wanting lower rates on their vessels than others paid. Then in 1757–8 they had made a navigable cut from their works to the navigation to avoid using the little Holmes Goit, with floodgates where it entered the company's Bromley Sands cut.[43] Soon afterwards, it seems, the Don company were given by Lord Effingham a lease 'of his power of erecting a Work (not being an Iron Forge, blast Furnace or Slitting Mill)' on the Holmes Goit,[44] and proposed to make a weir across the goit to provide it with water. Walker's seem to have seen this as a threat to their water power, and then to have blocked their own cut and started to use Holmes Goit again, sometimes also drawing down the water at Rotherham to hinder passing craft. This effort to prevent them damming Holmes Goit caused the Don company to minute that a new cut out of the lower part of Holmes Goit, where their weir was to be made, to the Ickles cut, would be as good as the blocked cut, and also useful to their new works.[45] They then took to the law against Walker's, and also promoted a Bill, only to find Lord Effingham supporting Walker's; so it had to be dropped. They then sought the advice of James Brindley, 'a judicious Engineer'[46] and other 'Skillful Workmen' on how to alter their own navigation. At the same time they asked Brindley to estimate for altering the three fixed bridges on the Dutch River to swing bridges, so that craft need no longer lower their masts. He made a model, and John Needham, now acting as John Smith's deputy, built them.

---

* The firm of Samuel Walker & Co started in a small way at Grenoside near Sheffield about 1741, and began business at Masborough near Rotherham in 1746, the site being chosen to provide water power, river transport, and access to raw materials. The works grew, keels were built, and in 1757 the firm bought the Holmes estate from Lord Effingham, and later expanded to other sites, including Rotherham mill in 1792. Walker & Co closed in the early 1820s, not long after they had completed the castings for Rennie's Southwark bridge in London, which was opened in 1819.[42]

In August 1763, having won their lawsuit against Walker's, the shareholders bravely resolved 'that such a Work as the fall of the Water will best serve, shall be immediately built, and the Committee are desirous to hasten the doing of this with Courage and Resolution'.[47] Walker's continued to divert water, and refused to reach agreement on water supply unless their demands on charges were first met. They also complicated matters with further works at Thrybergh, and the enlargement of what they already had, so using still more water. Now a landowner, Finch, who had built an oil mill at Ickles near Rotherham, and took too much water, joined the battle. Skirmishing went on. In August 1770, for instance, water taken for their new rolling mill at Thrybergh stopped boats, Samuel Walker announcing that 'they were aggrieved by the Company, and till those Grievances were removed they shou'd take every Opportunity to impede the Navigation, and he hoped his Children wou'd do so after him'.[48] In September he delayed 70 or 80 craft by running his Thrybergh rolling mill even on Sundays, and in October stopped another 30 vessels.

This quarrel brought about a conference which, having lasted until 2 a.m., decided to differ. The company did, however, produce a revised toll list, which gave traffic in unmanufactured iron, timber and stone to Rotherham an advantage over that to Tinsley. In January 1771 a temporary agreement was reached, whereby the company was to give Walker's free navigation from Rotherham to the Holmes for their own goods, including coal, and to pay them £90 p.a. for supplying water; in 1773 Walker's were also repaid dues paid before November 1770 over agreed minima.

The coal trade was growing, and in 1763 a toll was fixed from a Denaby colliery to Doncaster. The company started to contract with carters to carry goods over their road from Tinsley wharf to Sheffield at 2d per cwt upwards and 1½d down. Increasing trade led to new warehouses at Rotherham and Swinton being ordered in 1765.

In 1766 John Thompson of Sheffield was appointed engineer under John Smith's supervision: the following year it was agreed to allow Smith, now elderly, 3s 6d (17½p) for every day he worked.

In 1768 we may see the navigation like this. Downwards from Tinsley a cut with two locks, Tinsley and Deadman's Hole, then a section of the Don (the Ickles dam); out of this led the Bromley Sands cut and lock to the Don above Rotherham. Thence the Rotherham cut ran to the north of the river to Eastwood, where it locked down to the river. Beyond there was a short cut and a lock at Aldwarke. Thence the navigation followed the river to the Long Cut, the entrance of which was protected by a flood gate (the later lock is still called Kilnhurst Flood Lock). There were three locks in the cut, Kilnhurst Forge, Swinton and Mexborough, and a wharf at Swinton. Below the Long Cut, there were locks and cuts at Denaby, Conisbrough, Sprotbrough, Doncaster, Redcliffe (later Milethorn), Long Sandall and Barnby Dun. Finally, there was a long cut from Bramwith, where there was a lock, to Stainforth lock, from which craft entered the tidal Don. Below, there was the sometimes shallow and always hazardous navigation of the Dutch River with its three bridges.[49]

The Tinsley and Bromley Sands lock and cut system by-passed a great curve to the north, where was Jordan weir. Above this the Holmes Goit fed Walker's works and then continued to rejoin the Don below its confluence with the Rother. From this goit the winding canal made by Walker's ran to Bromley Sands cut: it had two sets of flood gates to prevent work being stopped by the back water at flood times.[50]

On 10 August 1769 a delegation was ordered to go from the company to see Lord Rockingham 'to sollicit his Concurrence to the making the River Rother navigable from Chesterfield into the River Dun at Rotherham',[51] after which the committee were to call a meeting of shareholders and local residents to consider promoting a Bill. This was presumably a kite flown to see whether there would be support for a navigation from Chesterfield to the Don as an alternative to the Chesterfield Canal, plans and estimates for which Brindley was to produce at a meeting at Worksop on 24 August of the same year.[52]

In 1772 a possible canal line was surveyed from Conisbrough to near Barnsley and Haigh, with a branch to Cawthorne, for coal and iron traffic:[53] it was 18¼ miles long, plust 1⅜ miles for the branch, with 23 locks in all.[54] Discussions lasted until the autumn of 1773 when a Bill was announced, but it then petered out.[55] In this year also some Halifax and Wakefield merchants promoted a canal from the Calder at Wakefield to the Don by way of the Went valley at a cost of £36,000 (see p. 31). It was perhaps intended rather to bring pressure on the Aire & Calder than to be taken seriously.

In 1772 the company were providing a navigable depth of 3 ft 9 in., and were trying to stop overloading and consequent delays. Like other river companies, the Don shareholders found that if they wished to control depths, they had to control the more important mills. In 1773 they took a 60-year lease of Doncaster mills, in 1775 agreed to lease Aldwarke mill, which would then be demolished and a new big one built, in 1776 that at Sprotbrough, and in 1780 took over the big mills at Rotherham, which cost them £6,000, and caused them for the first time to borrow money.

In the 1760s and 1770s coal was becoming a steadily more important trade. The toll, now 2s 7½d (13p), was charged on a customary ton of 81 cu. ft. This was much more than an ordinary ton, for the Sankey Brook Navigation in Lancashire, working on a customary ton of 63 cu. ft, found that it represented about 27 cwt. To save trouble, the Don charged on tramroad waggon loads, until in 1776 the company found some coal owners had been quietly enlarging waggon capacity. They then increased their charges correspondingly, and threatened toll increases if standard waggons were not used.* Later, in 1782, a drawback of one-third was given on coal taken to sea and sold 'in any Port where Duties are paid upon the same to the Government';[57] these were duties at that time levied on coal carried coastwise. Available coal meant that lime could be burned for land improvement at kilns at many places including Tinsley, Sprotbrough and Warmsworth.

In 1783 the company went back to trading in coal, telling their agents to buy and load it on their own vessels 'for supplying the Town and Neighbourhood of Thorne therewith for ready Money, and at such a reasonable Rate as they can be afforded for, without Loss to the Company'.[58]

Trade was now improving. By 1787 the company were reporting 'a great Increase of Business at Tinsley',[59] and in 1790 they granted the collieries at Attercliffe and Darnall exemption from the Tinsley–Sheffield road toll. It was perhaps the first sign of that impetus which, when the canal mania began in 1792, was to lead to the company's involvement in the schemes which later became the Sheffield, Dearne & Dove and Stainforth & Keadby Canals. (*To continue the history of the Don Navigation, turn to p. 208.*)

Greasbrough (Park Gate) Canal

By 1762 a waggonway had been built from the Don near Eastwood lock to collieries leased by the Fentons south of Wentworth Park and near Bassingthorpe. Then in 1769 the Marquess of

*In the 1830s, coal waggons were actually carried on the boats.[56]

Rockingham commissioned John Varley, one of Brindley's assistants, to survey and estimate for a canal from the Don to Cinder bridge (Greasbrough Ings) on the road from Greasbrough to Rawmarsh, then the turnpike from Wakefield to Rotherham, or to the nearby Sough bridge towards Greasbrough, to serve his collieries in the area. Varley proposed a canal 1½ miles long with three locks, each having an 8–9 ft fall.

His proposals seem to have been laid aside. In 1775, however, John Smeaton was employed to re-survey the line. He did so, altering Varley's three locks to five of 5 ft fall, and estimating the cost at £5,952, including some £1,000 worth of Lord Rockingham's own land.[60] Smeaton's strong feelings that much lock-building was inadequate comes out in his sentence: 'True it is, that Locks have been and may be built at very different Expences, but Experience teaches me, that even in a Country where Stone is plentifull, they cannot be made good sound Work of, even without any Finery, for less than what I have rated them at'. This was £500 each.

This report also was laid aside, until in 1778 Lord Rockingham employed William Fairbank once more to survey a line.[61] This came out similarly, and William Jessop was then employed to build it. He began in 1779, after he had altered Smeaton's plan to allow for four broad locks and a reservoir, and probably completed it in 1780. The main canal ended at Cinder bridge, where limekilns were built, but a short branch was built to Sough bridge. From these terminals tramroads ran to the mines the Fentons leased from the Marquess.

Oddly in a coal-carrying canal it inspired verse:

'. . . the Bason wide
Bears many a vessel in its pomp of pride;
Where solid ground once bore the goodly row,
The Sailor's wife now turns the vessel's prow'.[62]

(To continue the history of the Greasbrough Canal, turn to p. 225.)

Thorne and Hatfield Moors Peat Canals

Peat from Thorne Moor and Hatfield Chase may originally have been carried to the old mouths of the Don that ran to the Trent and the Aire. When they were closed after the building of the Dutch River in the 1630s, a canal seems to have been cut from Hatfield Chase to the Trent, possibly that shown as 'The Cutt by Thorn into Trent' on a plan of 1752, part of which is still called

'Boating Dyke' on the O.S. map. By the mid-eighteenth century the Thorne moors were being worked adjacent to canals which ran for short distances generally westwards and out of the Moor, to join another Boating Dyke, which ran down to Thorne and the Don. In about 1790 between 30 and 40 boats were using this drain to carry turf for transhipment to the Don. These waterways are shown on Thomas Jefferys' map of Yorkshire, surveyed in 1767–70. This map shows a pound lock between Thorne town end and the Don, and there may also have been another on the system.[63] (*To continue the history of the Thorne and Hatfield Moors Peat Canals, turn to p. 226.*)

CHAPTER IV

To Driffield and Weighton

+++++++++++++++++++++++++++++++++++◆+++++++++++++++++++++++++++++++++++

THE Hull river is narrow and winding, navigated now, as it always
has been, as much on the tides as by sail or power.[1] The Arch-
bishops of York claimed privileges on the river; in 1213 their
right to navigate was confined to a 24-ft wide channel, and in
1321 the archbishop was, much to Hull's annoyance, claiming 4d
a bushel on all goods carried between Emmotland, near North
Frodingham, the usual limit of navigation, and the Humber.[2]
Subsequently it became, as it remains, a free navigation (except
for the bottom mile, controlled by Hull Corporation), along with
its tributary the Arram Beck. In the Middle Ages seagoing ships
went regularly at least to Grovehill, Beverley's ancient port,
whence the Beverley Beck was made navigable to the city. In the
seventeenth century it was navigated fairly regularly to the
Wansford area;[3] in the mid-eighteenth the Driffield Navigation
was made from it, and later the Leven Canal.

Before the Old Howe, running north and then east from
Frodingham bridge, and its former extension towards Barmston,
the Earl's Dyke or Watermill beck, was about 1800 incorporated
in the Beverley & Barmston drain, small flat-bottomed boats were
used on it, to carry farm products (and, it is said, some smuggled
goods also) to Frodingham market.[4]

The Hull river was central to the local drainage system. In
medieval times efforts were made to drain the southern salt-
marshes bordering the Humber and the Hull. Further inland, the
monks of the abbey of Meaux in the twelfth and thirteenth cen-
turies cut boating channels through the carrs or fens to join their
various properties to the river. In time these channels became
part of the drainage system. In later times, at the end of the
eighteenth century, the drainage was greatly improved when
Chapman and Jessop built catchwater drains on both sides of the
river.[5]

Not only was the Hull River a navigation and central to a drainage system: its outfall to the Humber, the Old Haven, was until 1778, when Hull's first dock was opened, the town's only harbour. Here were continuing causes of conflict.

Beverley Beck

Beverley Beck[6] or creek runs from the town of Beverley for ¾ mile to Grovehill where it joins the Hull River. In 1296 the Archbishop of York negotiated with local owners for the removal of fish-weirs that were obstructing the Hull so that boats could approach Beverley. Grovehill then became Beverley's wharf. The archbishop transferred the agreement he had made to the burgesses, and probably not long afterwards the Beck was made properly navigable. It certainly was by 1344.

Beverley corporation dredged and kept it in repair out of specially-raised funds. The corporation regarded themselves as having a monopoly, letting the navigation to tenants who agreed to provide two boats, one decked, in which all goods were to be carried. Tolls were substituted in 1704, but some time later the corporation were still maintaining a right to farm out two market boats.[7]

Funds available were not always enough for maintenance, and in 1727 the corporation, after having considered various schemes for widening and deepening the Beck, obtained an Act[8] to cleanse, deepen and widen it, repair wharves and also roads leading to it. A complicated schedule of 43 classes of goods granted tolls high by later standards—4d per chaldron on coal, for instance—and enabled the corporation to borrow money on assignment of them. These could be levied on goods loaded or unloaded on the Beck and also on the Hull River within the liberties (later the municipal boundaries), of Beverley, and were additional to those of 1704.

Between 1727 and 1731, when work ended, the corporation spent £1,395 on improvement work. After crediting toll and other receipts, £1,000 was left as a permanent debt. For the year from 1 June 1730, the main traffics were coal, bricks, turfs, wool, wheat, oats, barley and malt.[9] From 1731 to 1742 the corporation made an average profit of £23 p.a. on the Beck after expenses and interest. It was clear that revenue would not be enough to maintain the navigation and pay off the debt: indeed, the Beck was tending to silt, the banks needed piling, and up to £400 was needed to put it right.[10] In 1745 a second Act[11] increased and altered the

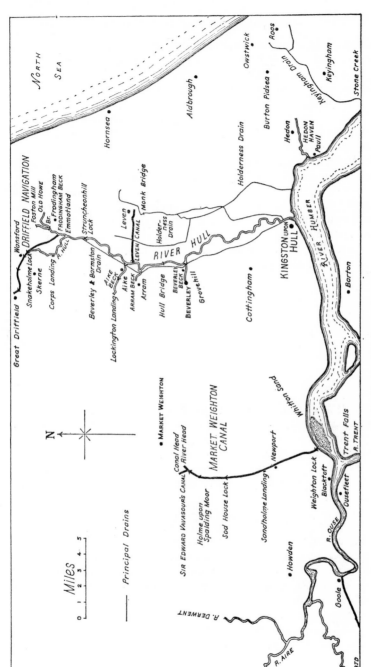

8. The East Riding waterways

authorized tolls, many of which were not related to the value of goods carried. This laid it down that the whole revenue collected was to be spent on repaying capital borrowed, and in maintaining the navigation and the roads leading to it.

At this time the Beck entrance was tidal. In the eighteenth century a level in the upper part seems to have been obtained by using a plank-type stop gate. A minute of 1752 empowers the surveyor to take up the old barricade and fix it near the head of the Beck.[12] Beverley Fair was a trading attraction, London goods being sent to it by way of the Humber and Hull River[13]

Up to 1747 the Beck tolls had been taken by the corporation. From 1 May 1748, however, they were let, and continued to be so until well into the nineteenth century, the corporation maintaining the waterway—which chiefly meant a lot of dredging—and the roads leading to it. Here are averaged figures, gross receipts up to 1 May 1748, after that receipts from the Beck rent:

Years	£	Years	£
1732 only	79	1763–67	110
1733–37	109	1768–72	129·50
1738–42	111	1773–77	140
1743–47	174	1778–82	150
1748–52	102	1783–87	180
1753–57	110	1788–92	182·50
1758–62	110		

Notable here is the jump in rent from the last quarter of 1770, almost certainly following the opening of the Driffield Navigation with increased up-river trade, and the further rise in 1780, probably the result of greater coal and other imports as a result of improved access to the Aire & Calder through the newly-opened Selby Canal. (*To continue the history of Beverley Beck, turn to Chapter XIII.*)

Driffield Navigation

About 1765 the merchants of Great Driffield, a small town on the upper part of the river Hull, and Kilham 4 miles beyond it, then a market town for grain and wool, with support from the Malton district where perhaps there was restiveness over the Rockingham monopoly of the Derwent,[14] called in John Smeaton to advise them on making the upper river navigable for keels to Driffield. He proposed a short cut from the river above Wansford to Driffield Beck, 1¼ miles long with one lock, to cost £2,586.[15]

John Grundy from Lincolnshire, then consulted, enlarged this modest plan. His report of 18 December 1766[16] suggested instead that a canal should be cut from Fisholme on Frodingham Beck a little above its junction with the Hull river at Emmotland to Driffield with a basin there 'to moor and wind the Keels in', at a cost of £7,000, with a branch also up the beck to Frodingham bridge. The river was already navigable to Fisholme, though 'capable of being greatly improved'.[17]

His plan was accepted, and an Act[18] passed in May 1767. It appointed a long list of commissioners, seven of whom would be a quorum, and gave them power to make a navigation through Brigham and by Wansford to Great Driffield. It also gave them some control over the river's navigability down to Aike Beck mouth, a little above the later junction of the Leven Canal. Money could be raised on the security of the tolls granted.

On 17 June the first meeting was held at the Blue Bell, Driffield. The commission arranged to borrow money at 5 per cent, on which calls were to be made as necessary. They appointed Richard Porter, a local man, as resident engineer. His father was at one time landlord of the Blue Bell, and Richard was to become a corn merchant and be a mortgagee of the navigation for £510. But after six weeks he was replaced by Samuel Allam of Spalding, recommended by Grundy (himself a Spalding man) to work under him. By October 1767 two small contractors had been appointed, and work began. However, they seem to have taken the job too cheaply, and given up, for in May 1768 they were replaced by James Pinkerton in partnership with James Dyson; these in successive contracts took on the whole work, including building the basin at Driffield and the culvert under the road at its head that brings water to it.

There was partial navigation probably from 12 December 1768 when Allam was authorized to receive tolls, and on 25 April 1769 a newspaper reported the line completed to Wansford.[19] The canal was opened on 25 May 1770, the day tolls were first authorized over the whole line from Fisholme, and a proper toll-collector appointed. Driffield was told that it now had communication without transhipment with, for instance, Ripon, Leeds, Doncaster and Gainsborough 'at an easy Expence'.[20] Tolls were set well below the maxima: 2s (10p) a chaldron of 48 bushels for coal, raised to 2s 6d (12½p) in 1776, against 3s 6d (17½p) authorized, and 3s (15p) for merchandise against 4s (20p). The canal was 5 miles long: this length, added to the ¾ mile from

Fisholme to Emmotland, compared with 8⅞ miles by the river from Driffield to Emmotland. There were four timber-floored locks. The works had probably cost about £13,000. Because this was more than the estimate, the clerk had been told in May 1769 to 'wait upon the several Gentlemen or Freeholders and others who have any Estate or Estates in Driffield or in the Neighbourhood thereof to Soleicit them to Enter into the Subscription for making and compleating the Navigation'.[21] Pinkerton's bill was not paid off for a long time—meanwhile he got interest on it.

The navigation did not for many years earn enough to pay 5 per cent on the original expenditure and another £2,000 raised in 1776. Lower interest was paid as it was earned, beginning with 1½ per cent in 1774, the balances being set aside to be paid later. By 1790 the amount paid had reached 4 per cent. Here are early figures:

Y.e. 1 *April*	*per cent*	Y.e. 1 *April*	*per cent*
1774	1½	1783	2
1775	1½	1784	4
1776	nil	1785	3
1777	1½	1786	2
1778	nil	1787	2½
1779	2½	1788	2½
1780	2½	1789	3
1781	1	1790	4
1782	2		

With the additional money raised in 1776, it was intended to dredge the river down to Aike Beck mouth, and also to build an additional lock at Thornham Bottoms, between the lowest lock at Snakeholme and Brigham. However, the commissioners seem to have decided it would be cheaper to convert Snakeholme from a single lock to a staircase pair, and then done so.

In September 1777 proposals were put to the commissioners to extend their powers, by making Hull bridge, below the then end of their navigation at Aike Beck mouth, 'more commodious for the passage of Vessels',[22] making locks or cloughs down to Aike Beck, making a proper navigation for the 1⅜ miles from Fisholme up to Frodingham bridge (with power to charge one-third of the tolls to Driffield) and in vague terms to improve that up the by-passed section of the Hull river to Corps Landing. However, they were turned down, partly because of opposition from Beverley corporation who thought a swing bridge instead of the present stone Hull bridge would cut their chief communication with

Holderness, whereupon some dredging was probably done to enable keels to reach Frodingham bridge.

In 1783 the commissioners for the first time exercised their powers by ordering the river from Emmotland down to Aike Beck mouth to be 'scour'd, deepen'd and widen'd and be made completely navigable',[23] and over the next few years a good deal of money was spent on dredging. No permanent buildings seem to have been put up at Driffield basin until in September 1784 the commissioners decided to build a warehouse and granary. It was finished the following year. Trade was improving, and in 1787 Richard and William Dunn, cornfactors, agreed to lease land at the basin to build another warehouse. The following year lock-keepers were appointed for the first time.

An interesting development took place in 1789, when Bainton, Boyes & Co, having just started a carpet factory at Wansford, agreed with the commissioners for a lump sum payment of tolls to cover both manufactured goods and Brandling's coal from the Aire & Calder that they were using. This temporary arrangement was replaced in 1790 by specially-negotiated rates. After thirty years or so, the factory became a corn mill. (*To continue the history of the Driffield Navigation, turn to Chapter XIII.*)

Market Weighton Canal

The Market Weighton Canal grew out of the threefold need of the Vale of York in the middle of the eighteenth century for drainage improvements to some 20,000 acres, enclosure in the interest of agricultural productivity, and better transport.[24] It was first discussed in October 1765[25] and revived in August 1767 as a line to Wholsea,* with branches to Weighton and Pocklington.[26] Not until the Driffield Navigation had been opened, however, was it again raised in April 1771, now as a proposed navigable drain from these two towns.[27] By December, Pocklington was no longer an objective, and the scheme finally emerged as a proposal to cut a channel from Market Weighton through Wallingfen to the Humber at what was then called Fossdike Clough, which should be both a main drain and a navigation, the bottom 5 miles of which would be a canalization and straightening of the Foulness river.

The Act[28] of 21 May 1772 set up two authorities: five commissioners who were to make the channel and works upwards

* Where Sod House lock was later to be built.

from the Humber, and borrow the money, and trustees to whom they were to be handed when finished. These were substantial subscribers or rateable landowners. Two sets of accounts were then to be kept for drainage and navigation, drainage revenue being raised by rates on the drained land, navigation by tolls, and costs apportioned. Each contributor of capital was than to be allotted a proportionate share in the revenue, on which dividends could be paid. Tolls were stated as 4s (20p) a ton on merchandise, 2s (10p) a chaldron of 32 bushels on coal, 1s 6d (7½p) a chaldron on lime, 1s (5p), a ton on stone, and 6d (2½p) on manure.

The Act made it clear that drainage was the primary consideration. No navigation works were to prejudice it, and a most important clause was inserted in the Act, that no lock should pen water higher 'than within Three Feet of the natural Surface of any of the Lands . . . above such Lock or Staunch, and such Lock or Staunch shall be opened or pulled up whenever the Water shall run above Four Inches over the Top of such Lock or Staunch'.

John Smith, the engineer, put his plans and estimates to the first meeting of the commissioners on 12 June at the Black Swan, Market Weighton, when £6,500 was promised. His proposed line ran to Market Weighton with a sea-lock and four other locks with rises up to 16 ft, the canal reducing in size as it rose. It was accepted. After his debacle on the Swale, Smith's reputation was not good, and some thought it would be safer to have Smeaton or Grundy as consultant to keep an eye on him. But the meeting decided this would be too expensive (Grundy had stated his terms), and went ahead with Smith as consultant, and Samuel Allam as resident—he had just done a similar job on the Driffield Navigation. Priestley's statement[29] that Whitworth was the engineer is a mistake, perhaps caused by the appointment in May 1776 of John Whitworth as lock-keeper at Weighton (Humber) lock. James and John Pinkerton were then taken on as contractors to cut from Weighton lock upwards to Sod House lock, the second on the line, with separate contractors for the sea-dam that was to protect the sea-lock works, and for its construction.

By August, however, 'some Principal Proprietors of Lands'[30] had sent for Grundy to check Smith's plans and estimates. Grundy disliked Smith's high-rise locks, and suggested eight above that at the entrance, each of 8 ft rise, and one more of 6 ft to the basin at Market Weighton.[31] However, as nearly 46 ft of the rise was between Weighton Common and the town, Grundy asked whether, if this section were to prove too expensive, 'will it not be more advisable to stop in the . . . Common, which is not more than 1½ Mile short of the Town, and pretty near the Holme Road?' Finally he wrote hearteningly:

'it appears to me that it is not only very practicable to accomplish a very perfect Drainage of the aforesaid low Grounds and Carrs, but also to make a four Feet Navigation perfectly compatible therewith, to be carried along the Mother Drain of such Drainage'.

He was promptly taken on as consultant, and Smith paid off. In November 1772 a newspaper advertisement for labourers said: 'The Works are clear of Water, and near good Lodgings, and are now going on with great Spirit'.[32]

In spite of Grundy's opinion, the commissioners then intended to complete the line to Market Weighton, and in August 1773 Allam showed his survey of it to Grundy. Construction, however, went on slowly, linked as it was to drainage. On 6 May 1776 the entrance lock and section of canal to a point probably near Sandholme Landing above Newport was opened, and a short further section of the Foulness river in 1777. There for the moment cutting of the main line stopped among complaints of the Pinkertons' slowness, William Jessop being called in to measure the work done and settle their account. It had taken almost all the £8,675·50 originally subscribed, and in 1778 John Holt, who had probably succeeded Allam as surveyor, was asked to estimate for finishing the canal to Market Weighton 'upon the smallest Scale which he shall judge to be effectual'.[33] The original subscription had been contributed by 21 people, of whom seven had found over £5,000 between them, the largest sum, £1,269, by the Duke of Devonshire.

Then in 1780, after the first of many arguments whether the water depth should be maintained for navigation, or reduced to help drainage, was settled on the basis of craft drawing 4 ft maximum, work began again with James Pinkerton back as contractor, but little was achieved. The arguments remained: for instance, in 1788 the trustees ordered that when drainage required the water to be low, a lighter should be lent to free vessels compelled to transfer part of their cargo.

In early 1781 three men proposed to finish the canal to Weighton Common along Holt's lines for some £2,500. An agreement was made in May and £2,900 raised. On 15 February 1782 a first settling up occurred. Those who had participated in the original subscription then had a dividend; they and the new ones got another in May 1783, paid on a capital of £11,575·50. It amounted to rather under 5 per cent. On 3 November 1784, after a third subscription, a final capital of £12,004 was designated, on which dividends were paid thenceforward.

The extension was probably completed about mid-1782, when the last call on the second subscription was made. Tolls, £76 in 1777, £192 in 1779, £332 in 1781, reached £522 in 1783. The canal was now 9⅝ miles long, with three locks additional to that at the entrance. The Weighton lock and lower pound took craft 66 ft by 14 ft 10 in, the rest 57 ft by 14 ft 2 in. A visitor, riding from Beverley to Market Weighton, saw 'The new made canal, which . . . made the smaller land and householders imagine their possessions would double in value'.[34]

The canal's upper end was not, as at Driffield, in a town, or, as at Pocklington, on a main road. Instead, it was some 2 miles from Market Weighton and over ½ mile from the turnpike road, and had to be sought down a by-road. The basin, therefore, never had the same importance as the others. Originally, very little was done there, for in 1784 the trustees asked the committee to 'widen the Canal at the Head of the Works so that two Vessels may conveniently lie abreast and pass each other'.[35] In 1789 a meeting of the trustees was called 'to give Orders that may prevent further obstruction in the roads from Market Weighton to the Canal',[36] a phrase that suggests difficulties of access: about 1790 the head was widened to allow a vessel to lie across the canal and timber staithing provided, and in 1795 a crane was installed. It is noticeable that Baines in 1823[37] lists a number of road carriers working from Market Weighton, three to Hull, but no water carrier.

In 1790 the toll system was changed, a single charge being now made for goods to any part of the 6-mile lower pound between Weighton and Sod House locks, and a lock charge thereafter. Coal and merchandise paid 1s (5p) for the lower pound, and then 1d a lock; manure 3d and ¼d. Then, in 1791, the first* of a series of fairly regular but modest dividends appeared, 5 per cent.[38] (*To continue the history of the Market Weighton Canal, turn to Chapter XIII.*)

---

* Except for 6s (30p) in 1787.

CHAPTER V

From Ouse to Tyne

THE Yorkshire Ouse begins at Ouse Gill Beck about 2 miles above Linton Lock, and flows down past York to its confluence with the Trent to form the Humber. At some time its tributaries the Foss, Wharfe, Derwent (with its canal branch the Pockling-ton), Aire and Don were all navigable, while two canals were made to it, the Selby and the Knottingley & Goole. Above York itself the river was considered to be navigable at most times to Widdington Ings, about 8 miles above the city near Newton upon Ouse. At Ouse Gill Beck the stream becomes the Ure, which passes Boroughbridge and Ripon on its way to Wensleydale. At Swale Nab the Swale runs north to Richmond, and from it the Bedale Beck runs to Bedale, the Cod Beck to Thirsk. The Ure was made navigable for $5\frac{1}{4}$ miles past Boroughbridge to Ox Close, and then continued by a canal to Ripon. Schemes to make navig-able the Swale, Bedale Beck and Cod Beck all, however, failed.

Farther north, no inland navigations of significance were built but there were many schemes in the period: to extend the Derwent navigation above Malton to Yedingham, for a canal to bring coal from the County Durham coalfields to Stockton, to make the Wear navigable to Durham, and to extend the navigable Tyne.

The Yorkshire Ouse

The Ouse[1] has always been navigable, though never an easy navigation, and until 1757 craft could work up to York on a succession of tides. Throughout the medieval and into the modern period, however, the increasing size of sea-going ships caused York to yield as a seaport to Hull and Selby, keeping only the trade of small sea craft and an inland barge and transhipment business. In 1462 Edward IV, by charter, established the corpora-tion of York as conservators of the whole Ouse and Humber, the

Wharfe (to Tadcaster bridge), Derwent (to Sutton bridge), Aire (to Knottingley mills) and Don (to Doncaster mills), a position the corporation still holds upon the Ouse for the section from Widdington Ings above the city to the railway bridge above Goole.

York, as a trading city and a cloth town, watched with disquiet the growth of industry in the West Riding, whether on the Aire, the Calder or the Don. She tended to blame the condition of the river for her growing inability to compete with them successfully, and strongly to oppose any improvement to the channel of the Aire or Don which might, she thought, reduce the amount of water coming up the tidal Ouse. Therefore the corporation saw that dredging was done, and from the early seventeenth century had in mind either building locks and cuts, or even a by-pass canal like the ambitious scheme of 1616 for a tidal canal from Fulford below York to Blacktoft on the Humber.

In 1621 a York Bill for river improvement got as far as second reading, but failed on the opposition generated by the proposal to finance the works by a county assessment. The city hoped to try again, and meanwhile helped to resist proposed Aire & Calder Bills in 1621 and 1625. After a Dutch engineer had surveyed the river, the corporation got their enactment in 1657,[2] but whether for lack of money or other reasons, almost nothing was done.

About 1688 the sluices Vermuyden had built in the Dutch River, the artificial new mouth he had given the Don, collapsed and were not replaced. Thenceforward York was convinced that water flowing up the Dutch River was depriving the Ouse. In 1697, when the Aire & Calder scheme was revived, therefore, York and all the communities along the Ouse, frightened that both water and trade would now be diverted to the Aire, bitterly opposed it. In 1699 York called in an engineer, Thomas Surbey, to survey the river and make recommendations. He did a thorough job, which ended in recommending a 100 ft × 20 ft lock at Naburn. Incidentally, he did not think the Dutch River deprived the Ouse of water, saying it made 'no sensable hindrance to ye Influx in Ouze'.[3]

On the day Surbey had arrived in York, the Aire & Calder got its Act. Two months later the corporation called in Hadley, at work for that company, and got him to re-survey the river. He having reached Surbey's conclusion, and agreed to build the lock, the corporation decided to raise money and promote a Bill. However, this failed on second reading in 1700.

The early seventeenth century had seen great changes in the Ouse below York, as new trades were added to the older ones of sea-coal and merchandise upwards to the city, cloth, corn, cheese and lead (from the Ure) downwards. The Aire & Calder Act of 1699 removed the city's claimed conservatorship from Knottingley to Weeland; it was followed by the Derwent Act of 1702 and Don Acts of 1727 and 1740 which also reduced York's claims. Thus great new trades began to use the lower Ouse.

In 1727, after a new survey from York to Trent Falls by William Palmer, York promoted a new Bill. This time it was passed. The Act[4] established a body of trustees from members or officials of the corporation—a form of council committee, which in 1835 it indeed became—and authorized them to levy tolls above Wharfe mouth. These had, however, to be amended by a new Act of 1732.[5] After the first of these Acts had been passed, Palmer was taken on as engineer and manager and began to build jetties to restrict the river's effective width and so increase its scour, and to undertake dredging. But the river showed little signs of yielding to treatment. Therefore the idea of a lock was revived, and this was supported by John Smith, called in from his work as engineer of the Don. The yield of tolls, some £500 p.a., was not enough to finance it, so the city raised money in £50 shares, and Naburn weir and lock were opened in 1757, the latter 90 ft × 21 ft 6 in. It raised the river some 4 ft 6 in back to York, and so gave a good increase of depth. On the other hand, the lock reduced the flow below it, a large shoal forming at Acaster Selby. In times of low water flashes from Naburn had to be given to vessels trying to pass it until the late 1820s. Duckham reckons that in the thirty years to 1757, about £18,000 or £20,000 had been spent on the river.[6] *

The rise of Selby after the opening of the Selby Canal in 1778 caused some jealousy in York, and the planned Selby bridge some perturbation. An editorial of February 1790 in the *York Courant* accused Selby of endeavouring 'to monopolise nearly the whole Coasting Trade of the County. It is said they are favouring the Plan of a commodius Street from the intended Bridge to the Canal, with Warehouses along the Bank of the River ... The People of Hull and York will surely do well to be upon their Guard'.[8]

* The result was a better navigation, but not good enough for seagoing craft. William Jessop, reporting in 1790, said of them: 'I am informed there are not above three in a Week to York and all other Places (above Selby) ... and this Number includes the Hull Sloops, and the small Vessels from Gainsborough and Rotherham'.[7]

Other important developments on the Ouse are dealt with elsewhere: the extension of the navigation above York past Linton Lock to Boroughbridge and Ripon opened in 1772, which gave the Ouse trustees some increase in tolls and traffic, the efforts to make navigable the Swale, and its tributary Bedale and Cod becks; and below, the opening of the Aire & Calder's Selby Canal in 1778, which put a largely increased trade on the lower Ouse. Finally, in 1793 an Act was passed to make navigable the river Foss, branching from the Ouse in York itself.

The trustees' annual toll receipts kept remarkably steady throughout the period. The fall after the 1730s probably reflects the pull of trade away from York towards the Aire & Calder as that navigation's trade increased. The opening of Naburn lock in 1757 improves takings, as to some extent does the extension of the navigation to Ripon. But then receipts decline, the improved communication with Leeds and Wakefield offered by the opening of the Selby Canal in 1778 being offset by the pull of trade away from York. Here are averaged figures:

Year	Tolls £	Year	Tolls £
1728–30*	591	1755–57	447
1731–33	643	1758–60	597
1734–36	756	1761–63	533
1737–39	716	1764–66	551
1740–42	403	1767–69	
1743–45	424	1770–72	623
1746–48†	456	1773–75	
1749–51	455	1776–78	487
1752–54	434	1779–81	431
		1782–84	502
		1785–87	437
		1788–90	
		1791–93‡	483

* 1729 and 1730 only
† 1746 and 1747 only
‡ 1792 and 1793 only

(*To continue the history of the Ouse Navigation, turn to Chapter XIV.*)

Derwent Navigation

The Derwent[9] runs upwards from its junction with the Ouse at Barmby-on-the-Marsh, about half way between Selby and Goole, to Malton and on to its source near Scarborough. The lower part

was already navigable after a fashion. A Trinity House report of
1698 says that at its mouth:
'ye depth thereat at Low water is 3 foot & it flowes abt 9, ye
breadth of ye said River Darwent being abt 70 foot. We were
Informed that there were 2 Keeles of 20 and 30 Tuns besides
some few open Boates of 5 and 6 Tuns which were imploy'd in
fetching & carrying to ye next Towne some 10 or 20 Miles up
ye River ye Comodityes of ye Country, Corne especially'.[10]
This probably meant that craft could get to Sutton and Stamford
Bridge when there was enough water.

George Sorocold, the engineer, had in 1693 agreed with Leeds
corporation to build them a water works, and this was being
done in 1694 and 1695. While at Leeds he seems to have become
concerned with making the Derwent navigable, producing the
plans on which unsuccessful Bills were promoted in 1695 and
1698.[11] However, the passing of the Aire & Calder's Act in 1699
probably encouraged similar action for the Derwent, perhaps with
coal imports especially in mind. George Sorocold again surveyed
it and a Bill was introduced in 1700. It failed, but another[12] passed
in 1701, empowering five undertakers* to make the river navigable from the Ouse right up to 'Scarborough Mills', provide a
horse towing path, and levy tolls, 8s (40p) a ton from the Ouse to
Malton, another 8s for the remainder, or proportionately by distance and weight.

In April 1704 the navigation was transferred from the original
undertakers to Sir William St Quentin, Sir William Hustler and
Walter Strickland, £250 then being paid to William Palmes of
Malton, 'who had been at the Expense and Chges of passing the
sd Act of Parliament', by the Hon Thomas Wentworth.[13] They
authorized Edward Watson, Charles Leigh and William Aslabie
to make the river navigable, but again nothing seems to have
happened until 1715, when the undertakers made an agreement
with four others. Then it seems that control fell to William Palmes,
who sold it with the Malton estate to Thomas Wentworth. In
1720 he agreed with Joshua Mitchel who two years later was to
work with William Palmer of York to survey the Don, and Mark
Andrew of Knottingley, seemingly to build it, and only then did
serious work begin, the commissioners meeting for the first time
on 10 June.[14] Some local landowners now began to protest, on
the one hand against having to pay tolls on the lower part of the

* Richard Darlay, Chris: Pertchay, Nath: Harrison, Ralph Cheatham and James
Hebden.

river which had previously been free, and on the other against a lock at Sutton, which they thought might cause flooding. They petitioned Parliament in January 1723, but witout success. At this time Wentworth said he had spent £4,000 on making the navigation.

Between 1723 and 1724 Wentworth leased the tolls to Andrew and Mitchel; by this time the river was probably navigable as far as Malton, 38 miles from Barmby, with a towing path for bow-hauling by men and five locks big enough to take Yorkshire keels, 55 ft × 14 ft. The lowest of these was at Sutton, 15½ miles from Barmby, to which point spring tides affected the water level.* Neaps, however, only ran to Cottingwith, 11½ miles from the Ouse, later to be the junction with the Pocklington Canal. The navigation's ownership descended from Thomas Wentworth, in 1744 Earl of Malton, to his son and grandson, the first and second Marquesses of Rockingham, and then in 1782 to the second Marquess's nephew, Earl Fitzwilliam, who lived until 1833. In 1744 the navigation was leased to James Fenton, probably for £440 p.a.,[15] and it remained in the hands of the Fentons until 1805. They were coal masters, corn merchants and much else, but their main interest in the Derwent was the coal trade. In 1756 the towing path from Stamford Bridge to Malton was converted for horse towing.[16]

Trade seems to have been modest. Probably most of it was to and from Hull, some of it coal from the Aire & Calder. In 1776, for instance, a Malton craft damaged Kirkthorpe lock weir on the Calder. In 1752 the annual rent seems to have been £500 plus maintenance cost, from 1755 to 1776, £684. In 1777 the rent increased to £1,300, and we may guess that this rise reflected expectations of greatly increased trade from the Aire & Calder by way of the Selby Canal, to be opened in April 1778.

In 1772 a number of landlords interested in improving the Derwent mainly above Yedingham in order to drain their lands better held a number of meetings and employed Isaac Milbourn and Thomas Tofield as engineers. Though primarily concerned with drainage, they did very tentatively consider also seeking new powers to complete the original navigation line from Malton to Scarborough.[17]

---

* Others were at Stamford Bridge, Buttercrambe, Howsham and Kirkham Abbey. That at Stamford Bridge, with its rock channel approach, seems later to have been converted to an occasional staircase pair, by providing a second pair of gates below the original lock for use when water levels were low.

'Resolved that a clause be inserted in the Bill to be presented to Parliament for making a Navigation as well as a Drainage, and that the Corporation of Scarbro' shall defray the Expences of such Clause & that in Case any Opposition to such Navigation Clause sho^d be made in Parliament to hinder the Drainage, then the Corporation promise to consent that the same shall be drop'd.[18]

In September a newspaper announced a Bill which would include power to make a navigable canal from Malton to Scarborough Mere if the Corporation of Scarborough asked for it, and would pay.[19] After that, the navigation scheme was quickly dropped, followed in 1775 by the whole drainage plan.

An interesting statement of the river's trade in 1793 records 35 craft regularly trading to Malton, 15 of them belonged to the Fentons of Malton. These averaged 16 trips a year, often running a triangular journey outwards from Malton to Halifax carrying 50,000 quarters of corn and probably wool also, then moving to the Leeds area for coal, bringing 28 chaldrons each time,* or to Skipton on the Leeds & Liverpool, presumably for stone from the Springs branch.[20] In addition, several other craft used the lower stretches of the river. Finally, two sloops worked between Hull and Malton, making perhaps 48 to 50 voyages a year, and probably carrying merchandise.[21] Financially, the results were:

	£
Tolls on coal carried by the 35 craft	1,960
Corn ditto	1,250
Vessels working below Malton	600
Two sloops	350
	4,160

'The Rent paid by Messrs Fentons is £1,300 and they repair the Locks, Dams Etc which may be supposed to amount to £350 or £400 more, which with the Exp of collecting the Dues Etc, say 2,000

Annual profit £2,160

In 1793 Fenton, the lessee, had an agent at Barmby, to collect tolls. There was a warehouse there, and another, with a stable and coalyard also, at Stamford Bridge. John Jackson, Fenton's agent, lived here, selling coal and accepting freight on Fenton's account, and keeping three vessels busy in the lime trade. There were

* 28 chaldrons were charged for, but craft actually carried 32 to 45 according to the river's depth.

flour mills at Sutton and Stamford Bridge, which brought corn and flour traffic to the navigation. In 1792, the Aire & Calder company claimed that 'nearly the whole of the coal consumed at Malton came from their navigation'.[22]

In the early 1790s, schemes to extend the river navigation upwards and into its tributaries, or to link the river by canal to Scarborough or Whitby, began to enliven the scene. (*To continue the history of the Derwent Navigation, turn to Chapter XIV.*)

Wharfe River

In 1698 the London Trinity House, in the course of a report on the Ouse,[23] had this to say of the Wharfe:

'ye mouth whereof is about 70 foot wide. It is there abot 2 foot deep at Low water & Flowes abot 6. We were imform'd that some few small vessells or Boates did upon Spring Tides, tho not without difficulty, get up to Tadcaster, being som 7 or 8 miles'.

Tadcaster's petition opposing the Aire & Calder's 1698 Bill said cloth and other commodities were brought from Leeds by land carriage, and then sent on by water to Hull. Given that Trinity House were accurate, it cannot have been a large trade, for most of it went by Selby.

An Act of 1751 gave powers to turnpike the Leeds–Tadcaster road. Two years later, Robert Fretwell advertised his service of 'a Number of good close-deck'd keels' between Hull and Tadcaster, connecting with covered waggons thence to Leeds: the total freight was the same as via Rawcliffe, the speed greater.[24] In 1758 a witness upon the Calder & Hebble's Bill said he and others sent goods from Leeds to Tadcaster by land: 'the Navigation on the Rivers Air and Calder, is a Monopoly; and that by sending their Goods Ten Miles by Land, they can send them to Hull down a River that has no Works on it'.[25] It looks as if the pressure on the Aire & Calder, due to elderly locks and works and to what traders considered too high charges and so profits, was forcing some trade towards Tadcaster. In 1756 two of the piers of Tadcaster bridge, which belonged to the West Riding, had to be piled, as they were being damaged by boats.[26] Then in 1762 an advertisement appeared[27] which indicates the Robert Fretwell, who had owned the 'Navigation, Mills, Grounds, Wharfs and Warehouses', had died or given up, and they were therefore to let. It seems likely that the business was not sold, but remained in the hands of trustees, presumably for the heir, for in September 1762 the newspaper announced that William Bowling of Leeds and George Holden of Hull had been appointed to conduct the navigation's business by Sir William Wentworth, Edwin Lascelles and the trustees of the Tadcaster Navigation[28] In 1763 Edmund Knipe of Tadcaster was added to the previous two. It seems then to have been rumoured that Peter Birt of the Aire & Calder was connected with them, for a denial was issued.[29] In 1764 Knipe was replaced by John Adamson from Wakefield, who took over at Tadcaster, working with Holden at Hull and Bowling at Leeds. He was described as having:

'Wharfs, Granaries, and Warehouses, now put into good Repair, and proper Persons to attend, in order to take in Goods &c at Tadcaster, Leeds, and Hull; also very good Sloops, Lighters, and experienced Masters &c likewise good Waggons and other convenient Carriages . . . which it is hoped will induce Gentlemen, Merchants, Tradesmen, and others to send their Goods that Way . . .'[30]

In 1773 the newspaper offered on rental Lord Egremont's wind and water corn mill at Tadcaster, fishing in the Wharfe, and 'the Cloughs for making Flushes, whereby the Navigation of the said River is in great Measure commanded'.[31]

In 1774 there was talk of a canal, probably for tub-boats, projected by Sir Thomas Gascoigne and surveyed by George Dixon, from Garforth, between Tadcaster and Castleford, to the Wharfe below Tadcaster, by way of the Cock Beck valley.[32]

In 1779 Peter Birt of their committee was asked by the Aire & Calder to talk to the proprietors of the Tadcaster Navigation about buying out their interest,[33] presumably to prevent competition with the newly-opened Selby Canal. (*To continue the navigation history of the Wharfe, turn to Chapter XIV*.)

Linton Lock, the Swale and Bedale Beck

The Ouse was usually navigable to Widdington Ings near Newton upon Ouse, and onwards to near Linton. When conditions were favourable, however, craft could get up the Ure to Boroughbridge, and up the Swale to Topcliffe and sometimes beyond. When the Aire & Calder's Bill of 1698 was in Parliament, Boroughbridge, petitioning against it, said that 'Abundance of Goods and Corn are brought thither, by Water, for supplying the adjacent Towns, and several Places Northwards',[34] while North-

G

allerton said that 'great Quantities of Lead, Butter, and other Commodities are daily carried from thence to Borough-Briggs; and thence, by Water upon the River Ouze'.[35] In the early eighteenth century coal was reaching Ripon from the Aire & Calder by way of the Ouse, for in 1726, when the Don Navigation Bill was in Parliament, the Aire & Calder had sent representatives 'to York and Ripon with petitions against the River Dunn'.[36]

In this year William Palmer surveyed the Ouse above York while working for the corporation: his survey later proved useful to Smeaton. Then ten years later a curious alliance took place between Don interests and a group of York merchants, with the object of making the upper Ouse and Swale navigable from York to Richmond, and also of improving the lower Don between Wilsick House and Sykehouse, so facilitating trade between Ouse towns and Doncaster, Rotherham and Sheffield. The merchants petitioned in 1736, alleging that 'great Quantities of Goods are carried by Land from Sheffield to Borough Bridge, the Carriage whereof costs 50s per Ton', while Richard Ellison for the Don did a survey, now modifying the original idea by proposing to limit the Swale navigation to Morton bridge on the Bedale–Northallerton road. But York corporation supported other York merchants who opposed the idea, and it was dropped.[37] However, in 1742, by which time a Don Act to improve the river to Fishlake Ferry had been passed (see p. 73), Ellison was reported to be again proposing a Bill for the Swale: the corporation asked members of Parliament 'to have a watchfull Eye in that respect to give all the Opposition in their power to the Bill'.[38]

The first discussions of what were later to become the Leeds & Liverpool and the Rochdale Canals in the summer of 1766 may perhaps have encouraged those who in September announced meetings to consider opening a 'Communication from' Hull by York to Ripon by river and canal, and then to seek subscriptions towards a Bill.[39] This led the 'Proprietors of Estates and others . . . interested in the Navigation of the River Swale' to meet at Thirsk in December to consider whether any lock built below Swale Nab would interfere with navigation of the Swale, and whether an Act to make it 'more navigable' would not be useful.[40] Smeaton, using the earlier surveys by Palmer and Ellison, then resurveyed the Ouse and Ure, proposing a lock at Linton, the point to which water was penned by Naburn lock below York, and a navigation to Ripon by three Ure locks and two staircase pairs on a cut thence from Ox Close.[41] In turn, a group at Thirsk were encouraged to make the Cod Beck navigable from the town down to the Swale, for 'one of the chief inconveniences of Thirsk, and the whole Vale of Mowbray is the scarcity and high price of coal, which is brought from the county of Durham in small carts containing from 18 to 22 bushels and varies in price according to the season'.[42]

Petitions for the Ouse above Widdington Ings, the Ure and Ripon Canal, the Swale and Bedale Beck, and the Cod Beck were considered together by Parliament early in 1767.[43] Smeaton gave evidence. His estimate for the Ouse, Ure and Ripon Canal was £13,844, though £15,000 had been subscribed. John Grundy appeared for the Swale and Bedale Beck, estimating them at £19,844 against a subscription of £24,950, and was supported by Robert Wilson who, however, wanted a 4-mile canal from Morton bridge to Bedale, considering that 'without a Canal it is impractical to make this Navigation'. Evidence for the Cod Beck was given by Richard Firth, who estimated it at £6,100 without the land, of which £6,000 had been subscribed. John Smith, the inexperienced son of the retired engineer of the Don, supported him. Later, on the Bill itself, John Grundy, who had by now been called in, raised the estimate to £8,710.

Three Acts were therefore passed in 1767, for the Swale to Morton bridge, now with a branch to Bedale up the Bedale Beck; the Cod Beck; and the Ure and Ripon Canal: the Ouse trustees at York minuted hopefully that there was a prospect of 'great Alterations and more Business upon the River'.[44]

The first Act[45] proposed to extend the navigation from Widdington Ings for 9¾ miles to Swale Nab, with one lock at Linton, and then the Swale for 28 miles of winding course past Helperby, Topcliffe, Skipton-on-Swale and Maunby to Morton bridge, some 4 miles from Northallerton. Robert Wilson must have changed his mind, for now the Bedale Beck was to be made navigable from its junction with the Swale about 1½ miles below Morton bridge for 2 miles to Bedale, though with considerable cuts.

The Act named two sets of commissioners, one for the Ouse section, the other for the Swale and Bedale Beck together, with power to raise money by borrowing or annuities. Interest was to be paid during construction, and afterwards lenders were to receive a share of the tolls. Linton lock was to take craft at least 60 ft long × 15 ft 4 in. and drawing 4 ft, for which tolls could be charged of 4d on coal and stone, and 9d on merchandise. On the

Swale, locks were planned at Myton, a little above Helperby,* Topcliffe Mill, Wiske mouth, and Gatenby[46] with two on the Bedale Beck at Leeming and below Bedale itself, where a basin would be built. Authorized tolls were 1s 10½d (9½p) from Swale Nab to Bedale, and presumably also to Morton bridge, for coal and stone, 3s 9d (19p) for merchandise.

The Linton Lock commissioners took charge of their section; those for the Swale and Bedale Beck, of theirs. They all had one engineer, John Smith the younger, but each had its own resident, and competed with the others, and with the Ure, for scarce skilled labour.

Linton lock itself was estimated at £4,000. Work began early in 1768, and the timber and masonry lock was opened on 24 August 1769, the day tolls were first taken,[47] though the weir took longer. By early 1770 about £8,400 seems to have been spent, and another £2,000 that year. The work was announced to be completed in an advertisement of 13 August 1771,[48] when surplus materials were offered for sale: John Smith, also working on the entrance lock of the Market Weighton Canal, was told to try to 'buy the Crane now lying at Linton Lock'.[49] The commissioners now let the tolls and, the Ure and Ripon Canal having also been completed soon afterwards, the Linton Lock Navigation settled down as a useful part of a through route, even though it never had any substantial traffic from the Swale or its tributaries.

While Linton Lock was being built, work was at the same time going on upon the Swale, with John Jackson as resident engineer. John Smith decided to build his first lock at Topcliffe, apparently so that stone could be boated down to it from Holme, where there was land access to Rainton quarry whence it came. Jackson had to cope with labour troubles due to a sudden scarcity of skilled men. Modern managers would recognize his problem when he wrote:

'As by advancing the Wages on Mond last from 15d to 18d a Day wee had got the last Week 12 able Men, and more I expected this week, that the work might go on with expedition. Instead of that, they confederate, and seeing that the works cannot go on without them, come all to me this Morning in a Body, saying, unless we will advance their wages to 20d a Day, they will not come and work, but go somewhere else where they could get it'.[50]

He managed, however, but sometimes by borrowing the men

* Later altered to Leckby higher up, near the Cod Beck junction.

BY Virtue of an Act, *for making navigable the River Ouse from below Widdington Ings, near Linton, to the Junction of the Rivers Swale and Ure, and for making navigable the said River Swale from the said Junction to Morton Bridge, and also the Brook running from Bedale, into the said River Swale, in the County of York*, We, seven of the Commissioners, appointed to put in Execution so much of the said Act as relates to the Navigation from below *Widdington Ings* to the Junction of the *Swale* and *Ure*, do assign unto *William Law Esquire* ——————— his Executors, Administrators, or Assigns, in Consideration of the Sum of *Sixty Pounds* ————————————————— from this *Sixteenth* ——————— Day of *March* ——— in the Year of our Lord One Thousand Seven Hundred and *Sixty Eight* untill the said Sum of *Sixty Pounds* ————————————————— with Interest at the Rate of *Five Pounds* ——— per Centum per Annum, shall be repaid, such Proportion of all the Tolls, Rates, and Duties arising by Virtue of the said Navigation, as the said Sum of *Sixty Pounds* ———————— ——————————————— shall bear to the whole Sum advanced on the Credit of the same. Dated this *Sixteenth* Day of *March* in the Year of our Lord One Thousand Seven Hundred and *Sixty Eight*.

George Crowe

Edw: Lau

John Talbot

John Hardcastle

Matt: Dodsworth

Miles Stapleton

Jim: Scroope

Tho: Raper

Jos: Butler

9. A Linton Lock subscription certificate of 1768

working on the Bedale Beck works. He had also to cope with the maddeningly variable changes of river level which several times damaged the works, as on 15 June 1768 when he refers to 'the great efforts and Strugles that were made for upwards of six hours with the auxiliary help of a whole Barrel of Ale'.[51] A 25-ton timber-carrying boat was ordered at Selby, and in October it got up to Topcliffe. Before then, John Smith had chosen the site of another lock at Leckby, about 200 yards above the mouth of the Cod Beck. By November, however, the commissioners were starting to dismiss staff and recognize the money difficulties they were facing. Nevertheless, on 25 January 1769 Jackson wrote:

'The Earth and Sheeting remov'd and taken away, and the Water let into the Cutt, the Lower Gates being open'd, the Keel* run into the Lock wch being fill'd wth Water by opening one of the upper Sluices, was soon done, the upper Gates being then open'd, the [Keel] with our Navigation colours flying (and amidst the Loud Huzza's of the People there met) saild thro' the first Swale Lock wch without vanity it may be said if not the very best, yet one of the best and compleatest Locks in England'.[52]

The following day a timber keel from Malton reached Topcliffe bridge, and with another passed through the lock on the 27th. John Jackson then resigned, but in March 1769 the commissioners agreed with William and John Peacock to build Leckby lock, and tenders were sought in May for timber to be delivered there and to another lock-site at the mouth of the Wiske, near Kirby Wiske. Some work was probably done at Leckby.[53] Heavy calls were made on subscribers during the summer and new people sought who might be willing to lend. Then on 28 November 1769 it was announced that the hauling path was completed from the mouth of the Swale to that of the Wiske, and that the river was navigable in 'freshes' to Morton bridge. Tolls were therefore fixed, of $\frac{1}{2}$d per ton/mile on coal and stone, 1d on merchandise.[54] A month later, when about £11,400 had been spent on the Swale and Bedale Beck, work stopped for lack of money,[55] though several subscribers, while refusing to provide cash upon the security the commissioners could offer, agreed to put up more in exchange for the right to a 10 per cent dividend. Meanwhile work had also ceased upon the Bedale Beck; a wharf had been built at Bedale, part of a lock below it, and a completed one at Leeming.

John Smith having estimated that £25,000 was still needed, and

* That built at Selby.

successive advertisements in the *York Courant* having produced
no offers of loans in the current recession conditions, subscribers
now formed themselves into The Company of the Proprietors of
the River Swale and Bedale Brook Navigation, and contributed a
3 per cent call towards the cost of an Act. This,[56] passed in 1770,
gave them power to raise as much by shares as they needed, and
borrow £30,000, though still to take the same tolls, for they did
not think the trade would bear an increase. Money already subscribed, and interest owing on it, was to be converted to shares.
The right to a higher dividend was included, but, consciously
following the Calder & Hebble Act of 1769, they bound themselves to a reduction in maximum tolls of one-eighth for every £1
of dividend over 10 per cent in any year. Existing loans were to
be converted to shares, to receive 5 per cent interest until completion. This Act also provided that nothing in it should impede
the making navigable of any other tributary of the Swale between
the Ure and Morton bridge, or of the Swale itself above that
point. The original Act was repealed.

The new company seems never to have got going: perhaps the
Swale was too liable to floods to be made navigable. In September
1771 a 10 per cent call was made to settle accounts,[57] a year later
the company were wondering how to get their arrears in, and
finally, Christopher Appleby, who ought to have been getting
50p a week as overseer and superintendent of stores, wrote an
open newspaper letter that he had been forced to buy necessities
on credit and was being threatened with prison. He went on to
say that unless he had his pay he would have to sell some stores
to provide for his family.[58] He probably did, as did others who
advertised from time to time that unless they were paid for
damages they would sell stone and timber that had been delivered
for lock construction. In 1780 a meeting was advertised[59] for
those who wished to promote the navigation to Bedale, at which
there was to be an engineer's report. But no further work was
done, though when conditions permitted, craft navigated some
3 miles of the Swale to a coalyard at Helperby'.[60]

The Linton Lock Navigation struggled to survive. In 1775
Ralph Rainforth and his partners were complaining that they had
not been paid for stone delivered in 1770,[61] and three years later
they repeatedly tried to find a lessee of the tolls, though they
hopefully advertised that 'This Navigation is in an improving
state'.[62] Then in 1783 the lock weir became so dangerous that the
river level had to be lowered, and tenders sought for a major

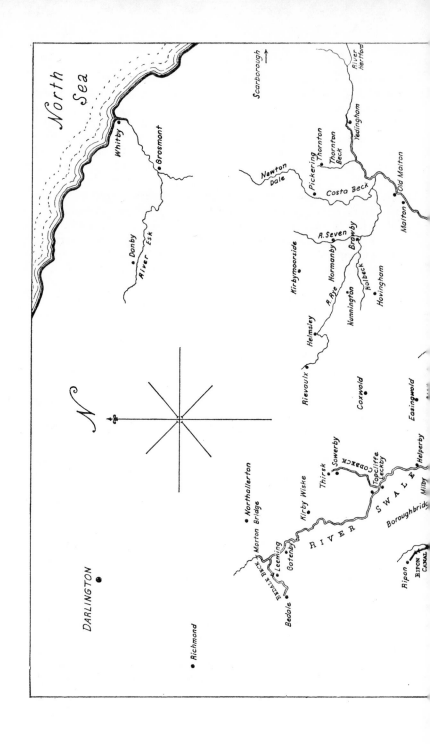

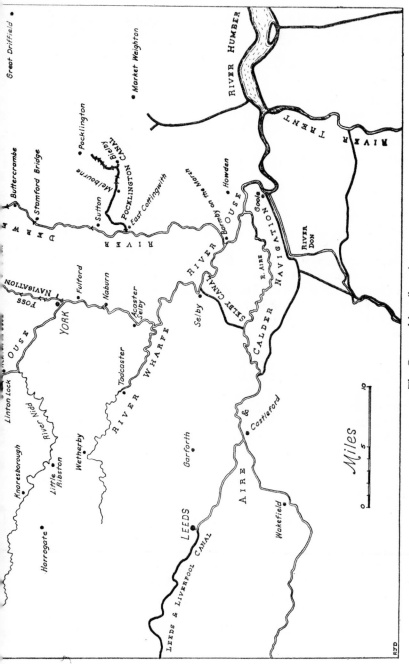

10. The Ouse and its tributaries

repair,[63] which caused 'an extraordinary Sum of Money' to be 'immediately laid out in the supporting it'.[64] The commissioners' debt eventually reached £13,046, the sum upon which dividends were later to be paid.

Much of the Navigation's business was through to the Ure; but on its own line, there were in 1794 landings at Newton upon Ouse, Aldwark bridge for the Ouseburns, and Aldwark,[65] as well as at Linton lock itself. (*To continue the history of the Linton Lock Navigation, turn to Chapter XV*.)

The Cod Beck

A second Act of 1767[66] authorized the making navigable of the 5-mile long Cod Beck, which leaves the Swale below Topcliffe and runs to Thirsk. The same long list of commissioners as for Linton Lock and the Swale was empowered to execute it, with power to raise money by borrowing or annuities. Richard Firth in Parliament had proposed to build four locks to overcome a fall of 42 ft 8 in;[67] later five locks were intended.[68] Authorized full-length tolls were 1s 6d (7½p) for coal and stone, 2s 6d (12½p) for merchandise.

A News item of May 1767 reads:

'Thirsk, May 30th. Last Thursday, being the day appointed to return thanks to Lord Granby, and Mr Bell, for obtaining the Act for making the brook Codbeck navigable from the Swale to Thirsk, the morning was ushered in with the ringing of bells and firing of patteraroes, which continued almost without intermission that day and the next. On Thursday evening Mr Bell, accompanied by the Gentlemen and Tradesmen in town, were elegantly entertained'.[69]

Work was done on the Cod Beck at Thirsk,[70] where a basin and wharf were built in 1768. Thence the Beck was deepened and straightened down to the only lock that was built, at Sowerby.[71] Some work was probably also carried out on the proposed lock at Dalton bridge near Topcliffe, for which tenders were invited in May 1769.[72] Then the money ran out, and no more was done, though a newspaper of 10 July 1770 reported[73] that two new 40-ton vessels had reached York from Thirsk, the first two cargo-carrying craft to make the journey. They were probably also the last. Nine years later workmen who claimed they were owed large sums of money were trying to call the commissioners together.[74]

The Ure Navigation and Ripon Canal

On the same day in 1767 as the Act for the Swale, another[75] was passed to make navigable part of the river Ure from its junction with the Swale upwards past Boroughbridge to Ox Close, with a cut to Ripon. There were now to be two locks, Milby below Boroughbridge and Westwick on the river section, an entrance lock to the canal at Ox Close, and two others at Ripon, to take keels 58 ft × 14 ft 6 in. The estimate was £9,000. Commissioners were appointed, and empowered to borrow whatever money was necessary. Interestingly, the only case I have seen, they were given powers to regulate freight rates on the navigation, analogous to the contemporary authority of the Justices to regulate road transport charges.[76] Full-length tolls were granted of 1s 6d (7½p) a chaldron of 32 bushels for coal and lime, the same per ton for bricks and stone, and 3s (15p) a ton for merchandise and timber.

The line seems finally to have been surveyed by William Jessop, then a very young man, and built by him under John Smeaton's supervision, with John Smith as resident engineer and Joshua Wilson of Halifax as masonry contractor. Work began as soon as the Act had been passed, and on 31 October 1769 the line was announced as open to the tail of Westwick lock. Charges for passing Milby lock only were fixed at 6d (2½p) per chaldron for coal and per ton for stone and bricks, and 1s (5p) for merchandise, but there must have been protests, for these were hurriedly lowered three weeks later to 3d on everything. Cutting of the canal itself seems to have begun early in 1770, and the whole to have been opened early in 1773 at a cost of £16,400,[77] the excess seemingly raised not by additional calls, but by giving landowners rent-charges on the tolls.[78] In February 1773 three firms advertised jointly that they were starting a service of vessels regularly leaving Ripon twice a week for York.[79] In that year also the commissioners began to let the tolls. In 1777 a new regular service through from Hull to Boroughbridge was announced:[80] by 1781 warehouses were available there and at Ripon.[81]

As completed, the navigation was 10¼ miles from Swale Nab, including a 1,105 yd cut from Milby to Boroughbridge, one of 616 yd at Westwick, and the 2¼ miles of canal to Ripon, this last being supplied with water from the streams of the Laver and the Skell. The tolls of the Boroughbridge and Ripon turnpike road were immediately affected. Here are figures.[82]

Date	Tolls	Date	Tolls
	£		£
1766	140	1772	62
1767	124	1773	67
1768	112	1774	60

T. S. Turner in his history of Boroughbridge[83] tells us that flax for the Knaresborough linen industry, timber and coal came up the navigation. Movement was often slow in those days: in December 1785 three Aire & Calder craft each carried 16 waggons of coal from Selby to Ripon. Two of them took 16 days for the return journey, the other a day less. Coal moved steadily from the Aire & Calder—at least three coal merchants were handling it at Ripon in 1788. In 1789 the Aire & Calder company bought property there 'for the Use of the Navigation', presumably for a wharf.[84] In 1792 the undertakers were prepared to sell this property—then valued at £220 or so, though they had paid £315 for it—and for which they were receiving £14 p.a. rent. However, it then seemed possible it 'might become useful as a Coal Staith' and the sale was postponed.[85] In this year the Aire & Calder claimed that they supplied nearly all the coal used at Boroughbridge. (*To continue the history of the Ure Navigation and Ripon Canal, turn to Chapter XV.*)

Kyle Navigation project

The Ouse and Swale schemes probably engendered a proposal, made to an Easingwold meeting, to make a navigation from Newton upon Ouse to that town, using part of the river Kyle and a tributary brook towards Tollerton and Alne.[86] The scheme was revived in 1772, to run now to Raskelf mill some 2 miles west of Easingwold, possibly combined with a drainage scheme.[87] But it went no farther, and later Easingwold would have been more easily reached by way of the Foss.

Farther north, there were three short canals, two medieval ones at Rievaulx Abbey, and one at Whitby, and also a navigation level at Little Punchard Gill.

Rievaulx Abbey Canals

Stone to build the abbey was carried on short canals built in the twelfth or thirteenth century. The stone from Bow Bridge was carried from a dam across the Rye at Penny Piece, by a cut along the hill bottom on the left flank of the valley to a point near the abbey site. That from a quarry at the foot of Hollins Wood ran to the east of the abbey, and this seems to have had a means of changing level, perhaps a half-lock.[88]

Whitby Canal

An undated Whitby map of about 1811[89] carries the legend: 'Granary, was formerly the Mill at Ruswarp belonging to Mrs Cholmley. Line of Canal made about Sixty years ago by Nathaniel Cholmley Esq, to Facilitate the Communications between the Harbour and Ruswarp Mill'. The mill, built in 1752, stood on the edge of the Esk estuary, and was only accessible by water on spring tides. The canal, beginning near Water Lane End, cut off the river bend below. With a long barge which he had built locally, Cholmley could now get corn to the mill at neap tides, and flour back.[90] The mill account books begin in 1753, and carry only four relevant entries:

7 June 1754	'Thos Swales 2 Boat Load of Gravel 4s'
23 Feb 1754(5)	'To Robt Coates for Lighterage of Wheat 12'
3 May 1756	'Delivering & loading Boat 6d'
2 March (1756(7)	'a Man for delivering Boat 1s'[91]

Cholmley gave up the mill about January 1766: I do not know when the cut ceased to be used.

Little Punchard Gill Navigation Level

There was a boat level, closed in 1860, in Little Punchard Gill in Arkengarth Dale, above Richmond in Swaledale. Driven up into the Cocker vein, and then to cut the Bishop's vein, which ran north and south, a boat was used to convey lead ore.[92]

In County Durham and Northumberland there were abortive navigation and canal schemes.

Tees Schemes: the Stockton & Darlington Canal

The river Tees was naturally navigable to Yarm, which in 1743 claimed that 'great Quantities of Lead, Butter-firkins, Corn, Tallow, and other Commodities . . . [were] shipped for London, and other Places'. She claimed to be the shipping point for Richmond, Bedale and higher points in Swaledale and Wensleydale, and opposed alike navigation projects on the Ouse tributaries and the turnpiking of the Great North Road between north and south Yorkshire.

The expansion of coal-getting demanded more. Probably in the 1760s, George Dixon planned

'to carry coals from Cockfield Fell Colliery (which he rented from the Earl of Darlington), by a small canal, without a lock, to the top of Raby Bank, near Keverstone, and then to convey them in waggons down an inclined plane, to the foot of the bank, the loaded waggons to draw up the empty ones: from the foot of the bank the coals were to be conveyed in another canal, without a lock, to near the top of Grant Bank,* where they were to be taken up by the carts from Yorkshire, that came over Pierse Bridge and Winston, &c. He cut a short piece of canal upon Cockfield Fell, and had a flat-bottomed boat upon it, to prove to the late Earl of Darlington the practicability of the scheme; but his Lordship refusing to advance any money, the scheme was abandoned'.[93]

Cockfield Fell is a few miles west of Bishop Auckland. This seems to have been the only canal actually cut in Co. Durham.

The inventive George Dixon also cut an experimental flume on Cockfield Fell, by which coal could be moved by a water current and eventually deposited in containers at the flume's lower end.[94]

The growth of the colliery area of south-west Durham between Bishop Auckland, Barnard Castle and Staindrop led to talk of a canal to carry away the coal. A meeting on 1 December 1767 at Darlington, called to discuss a possible navigation from Stockton by Darlington to the collieries,[95] appointed a committee which included members of the Pease and Backhouse families. Darlington was an agricultural town, and also an important centre of the linen industry. A survey was ordered, of the Tees to Croft and then of the river Skerne, upon which Darlington lies, and in December it was reported that the plans were to be put into execution in the spring.[96] Brindley was applied to, and sent Robert Whitworth, £861 being raised for expenses. His survey done in September and October was checked by Brindley, and a joint report dated 19 July 1769 was put before a Darlington meeting. It proposed a 25-ton narrow boat line 26⅞ miles long to

* Grant or Grants Bank is just outside Gainford, some two miles west of Piercebridge.

by-pass the winding Tees on the north side, running from Stockton (now part of Teesside) above Yarm, Darlington and Piercebridge to Winston, with 41 locks to overcome a rise of 328 ft. Level branches were proposed to Yarm (1⅞ miles), Croft Bridge (3⅛ miles) and Piercebridge (1¾ miles) from each of which there was access to the south over the Tees bridges. The cost was put at £64,000. Linked with this plan there seems to have been talk of a cut from the Tees to the upper Ouse, which is said to have encouraged the Cod Beck scheme.[97] It must be remembered that much of the North Riding then drew its coal from the southern part of County Durham.

George Dixon of Cockfield Fell once more revived his earlier scheme, proposing a winding lockless 10-ton tub-boat branch from near Bishop Auckland past various collieries to Cockfield Fell, whence the coal would be carried down a self-acting inclined plane to join the main canal near Staindrop. The branch was surveyed and estimated at about £8,000. An alternative, based on Dixon's original scheme, for a canal from Cockfield Fell to Keverstone and a plane thence to the main line near Staindrop, is also shown on a 1770 plan.

Money did not come in because of doubts about profitability, and though these were said to be 'pretty well over' when an article and plan appeared in the *Gentleman's Magazine* in August 1772, nothing was then done to take the scheme further.[98] (*To continue the history of the Tees schemes turn to Chapter XV.*)

Wear Schemes

The river Wear seems always to have been navigable from the sea to Biddick Ford near Washington, and higher when there was enough water. In 1716 an Act[99] appointed commissioners for 21 years empowered to improve Sunderland harbour; they were given additional powers by a second Act[100] of 1726. This envisaged that they should continue the navigation upwards to New Bridge (Chester-le-Street). In 1737 a plan of the river downstream from New Bridge was prepared,[101] and in 1747 a third Act[102] said that the river had not yet been made effectually navigable between Biddick Ford and New Bridge, and that commissioners were to remove shoals and impediments, and make it navigable to carry 'Boats, Keels, and Vessels, of the Burden now used upon the said River'. They were given power to borrow, and to levy a toll on coal loaded.

Just before the commissioners' 21-year powers ran out, their engineer, Joseph Robson, in June 1758 did an estimate for extending the navigation to New Bridge;[103] then in December Durham corporation sought support for a Bill they proposed to introduce, to make the Wear navigable from Biddick Ford to Durham. London's Court of Common Council supported it, and were told by a grateful Durham that 'Nothing can more contribute to frustrate the opposition of our Adversarys than the petition you have been pleased to present'.[104] The Act[105] was passed in June 1759. It said that nothing had been done above Biddick Ford, authorized a navigation from Biddick Ford to Durham, and repealed the powers relating to the Biddick Ford–New Bridge stretch given in 1747. Commissioners were appointed, with powers to borrow money on security of the tolls, and toll rates were granted. A parallel Act strengthened the commissioners for the section below Biddick Ford, which thenceforth was considered part of the port of Sunderland.

John Smeaton, who had appeared on the Bill, was asked to make a survey, and produced a plan[106] for building 12 locks and a number of short cuts, the longest about a mile. The map shows two coal staiths just above Biddick Ford, and, just below it, Mr Lambton's new coal staith. Below that, and 1,267 yd from Biddick Ford, a little north of the river, is Mr Lambton's engine. The bottom lock is placed just above this engine, and the top one at Keeper mill about ¾ mile below Durham. Seemingly no action was taken because of Sunderland's opposition and perhaps owing to the difficulty of building locks and weirs in a rapid river. J. Thompson, who in 1795 was supporting a canal from the Tyne towards Cumberland, says that about 1765, he thought advantage might have been taken of the party feeling about 1760 that was caused by Sunderland's opposition to build a canal from the Tyne by way of the Team valley to the Wear, Durham 'and as far towards Barnard Castle, as might be found practicable'.[107] (*To continue the history of the Wear schemes, turn to Chapter XV.*)

Tyne Schemes

In 1710 there had been a Parliamentary petition in support of extending the navigation of the Tyne upwards from Newburn to Hexham, John Errington having said he would bear the cost of making it if he could have the profit. A Bill was introduced, but dropped after second reading.[108] A tentative scheme proposed by

Captain Bainbridge for a canal to by-pass the river from Stella*
upwards along the south bank to nearly opposite Wylam, a
stretch briefly surveyed by John Smeaton in 1778,[109] also came
to nothing. (*To continue the history of the Tyne schemes, turn to
Chapter XV.*)

* Stella is on the Tyne some four miles above Newcastle, and a little below
Newburn.

H

PART TWO—1790-1845

CHAPTER VI

The Aire & Calder Flourishes

EARLY in 1792 the company had foreseen major improvements to their navigation to accommodate a growing trade; a year later these had shrunk to minor works. This was, one assumes, because the undertakers, their consulting engineer William Jessop, and their chief officers, had all got involved in promoting the Barnsley Canal (see Chapter VIII) at a time when 'the Scarcity of Money and the Advance of Interest thereon'[1] were making money so difficult to raise that new cash borrowed tended to be matched by old loans withdrawn.

In 1795 great floods damaged banks, carried sludge on to the towpaths, and created new shoals. An insurance list of late 1797 shows the company owning five warehouses at Leeds, one especially for cloth, and two at Wakefield, one being for corn. Loyally, the company had fitted out a gunboat, the sloop *Ouze*, carrying two 9-pounder guns and a 32-pounder carronade. After her maiden trip in July 1798, they offered her to the Government[2] and were much dashed when she was refused. Sadly they sold her in 1800.

A main preoccupation of the undertakers was their carrying trade. The Humber keel[3] was to be, for the period covered by Part II of this book and beyond, the basic trading craft, working between the Humber and its vicinity and the waterways that depended from it, and occasionally to sea: a sailing boat that could carry a good cargo in proportion to its size. Keels were not all of the same dimensions. These were regulated by the waterways on which they traded: they were Sheffield size, Barnsley size, Driffield size and so on. They had leeboards and a single mast carrying a square sail, with sometimes a topsail also, and occasionally other variations. The mast could be lowered. It became the practice for keels entering the Aire & Calder at Selby and later Goole, for masts to be lifted out, and sails and rigging taken ashore and stored. These could then be picked up again on the return journey.

On the tideway, sloops commonly worked between Humber ports and Selby, Goole, the Market Weighton Navigation and up the Don and the Aire & Calder. Built like keels, but differently rigged, they sometimes went to sea, as did the older billyboys—resembling keels, but with a sharp bow and generally rounder lines. A newspaper of 1796, for instance, advertises seven sloops, 45 to 50 tons burthen, used in the trade from Leeds or Wakefield to Hull, 'three of them registered for coasting at Sea, and may be sent to Lynn, Wisbech, or such places in the Corn Trade, occasionally, as required'.[4]

Before 1793 the undertakers had built about two craft a year for their own trade. Then in May 1795 they agreed to buy the Hull and Selby sloops owned by the consortium of which they were a part (see p. 40) and integrate them into a single carrying service from Hull 'to Leeds, Wakefield and other places up the Rivers Aire and Calder'.[5] The company paid £396·25 for each of the consortium's seven sloops and £651·40 for a bigger one, £3,425·15 in all, and then decided to add sixteen boats* and sloops to the four already being built. Of these twenty, four were built at Knottingley, one at Allerton, three at Hunslet, four at Methley, three each at Howden Dyke and Horbury bridge, and two at Mirfield. By 1804 they had 48 carrying craft.†

In 1797 the old and experienced William Martin died; he was succeeded by William Rooth as manager and accountant. A review revealed that from 1784 to 1793 the company had probably lost about £993 p.a. on their carrying trade, with an average annual turnover of £7,581, not counting the amounts paid by their craft in tolls. From 1795, however, the position had improved, and in 1796 a profit had been made, as well as £8,097 paid in tolls, over one-sixth of the total. There had been general freight increases in 1793 and 1796 to meet rising costs, but now they decided to increase freights on bale goods, yielding about a quarter of the tolls. About half this business was to and from Manchester and Rochdale, either by the Trent or the Calder & Hebble, the rest from Halifax, Leeds and Wakefield. They reckoned the increase might cost business, but 'the Preference (is) to the Calder Navigation on account of its superior Expedition, and which will certainly be the cheapest Conveyance from Man-

---

* Boats meant craft used upwards from Selby on the Aire & Calder.
† A few of these might not be operated directly, but hired to other carriers.

chester to Hull when the Rochdale Canal is opened'.[6] They were comparing it with the Trent & Mersey route. Bale vessels usually carried general merchandise, sometimes coal, as a return cargo. By 1804 the company's carrying trade turnover was £52,196 and their profit £1,785.

As the canal system extended, so did Aire & Calder carrying, until in 1806 their craft were working to Barnby Bridge on the Barnsley Canal, Manchester on the Rochdale, Huddersfield on Ramsden's, and over the completed portion of the Leeds & Liverpool.[7] Longer runs were done by independent or contract vessels: in 1811 the *Alliance*, one of the latter, made a record passage from London to Leeds in five days.[8]

In 1796 a case was heard at York assizes. The sloop *Foster* from Selby sank in March 1795 as a result of hitting a wreck as she entered the Hull River.[9] Her owners, defending, disclaimed liability for the cargo, pleading act of God, but the judge held that the immediate cause of the accident was within the responsibility of the owners, and gave it as his opinion that carriers by water were equally liable with those by land to make good any damage. Judgement was given for the plaintiffs.[10] The verdict, which was upheld by the Court of King's Bench, created panic among the tideway and coasting carriers, including the Aire & Calder company. First the company advertised that they would only carry if exonerated from claims arising 'by the danger of Water Carriage & ffire'.[11] then those affected thought of getting an Act to restore the old position. Finally, on 5 August 1797 the Aire & Calder called a general meeting of sloop owners. They agreed to announce that in future they would not be responsible for losses above £5 per ton unless by prior arrangement an insurance premium of 3s (15p) per £100 were paid. This in turn led to national action and a Relief Act in 1798, and the adoption of a safeguarding clause in bills of lading admitting liability only for wilful neglect, and then only for 10 per cent of the value of the goods up to the value of the ship.

In 1798 a private dry dock was built by John Foster at Selby, linked to the canal. In August of that year the undertakers took a cool look at the cost of having their craft privately repaired at Selby. They decided that 'It w^d be much to the Interest of the Undertakers to have their Vessels built and repaired by Carpenters in their own Employ in a convenient Yard—there w^d then be no temptation to make Use of unfit Timber, or to do the Work slightly'.[12] This raised in their minds the need for their own yard.

Lake Lock is on the Calder below Stanley Ferry, and below it the navigation curved round a big bend, nearly two miles long, to Bottom Boat, less than a mile in a direct line, before continuing to Penbank and Methley. In 1779 and again in 1792 the undertakers had thought of making a cut from Lake Lock to Bottom Boat to cut off the bend, but had not followed up the idea. Then in 1799 their engineer Elias Wright reported that he hoped to build a depot at Lake Lock with 'Workshops and other Conveniences for depositing the different Articles used in the Repairs of the Rivers'.[13] At first they thought of combining this with a cut to Bottom Boat, but, being advised they would need an Act, they decided upon a new lock and short cut to avoid the shoaling at the old ones. And so began the great Lake Lock controversy.

Sir John Goodricke had sold land at Lake Lock to William Fenton, who in turn parted with it to John Lee and Shepley Watson, Wakefield solicitors who had gone into the colliery business. These two had promoted the Lake Lock railroad which ran thence past Lofthouse Gate to collieries at East Ardsley.* Lee, then an Aire & Calder committeeman and shareholder, and Watson agreed in 1800 to sell the necessary land for the depot, and for a new lock and cut, the works being also intended to improve the coal-loading facilities at Lake Lock.

The agreement made, Lee and Watson started being so difficult about it that the company considered alternative sites for their yard at Heath and elsewhere. However, Elias Wright preferred Lake Lock, and the depot, on a short arm of the intended longer cut to the new Lake Lock, was opened in 1802. By 1804 Elias Wright proudly reported that better work was now being done more cheaply. There were 9 carpenters, 4 blacksmiths, 4 sawyers, 1 blockmaker with his boy, 1 sailmaker and an assistant: 'a better set of Workmen are not to be found in any Yard in the Kingdom, not only as to their ability in their Profession but also for their Industry, Sobriety and good Conduct'.[14]

Meanwhile Lee had in 1801 sold his holding in the Aire & Calder, and in 1803 he and Watson had reconstituted their railroad as the Lake Lock Rail Road Company, roughly two-sevenths owned by them, its line now open to the public. In 1804 at their own expense they extended the railroad to a new terminus at Bottom Boat, so saving themselves 2 miles of river toll, putting

---

* It was opened in 1798, replacing an earlier line of the 1780s. Another railroad, Fenton's, nearly paralleled it in the 1820s to end at Bottom Boat.

an extra mile of railway tolls into their own pockets, and costing the Aire & Calder £500 p.a.

The Aire & Calder, having built their depot, made the new lock cut, but not the lock. Instead, Lee, having extended his railway to Bottom Boat, revived the idea of making a cut thence from Lake Lock, with the new lock at Bottom Boat. When Wright approached Lee and Watson to ask their terms for allowing the Aire & Calder company to build this cut, the two proposed to seek powers to make both lock and cut themselves. These would enable the Aire & Calder company to collect their existing tolls for the longer mileage from craft using the cut, while Lee and Watson also took a separate toll 'so as to be equivalent to the Expences they have been at in making their Rail Road and the value of their Wharfage'.[15] This presumably referred to the cost of their recent extension of the Lake Lock Railroad to Bottom Boat and the building of wharves there. They would be unnecessary were the cut to be made, for the railroad would then end at Lake Lock. I take it that Lee and Watson then envisaged the river navigation being abandoned, so that all craft would have to take the new cut, for Wright advised the shareholders to oppose the idea: 'to suffer any individual, or set of them, to have the Power over the Water, would be the total Ruin of the Navigation'.[16]

An alternative was put to Lee and Watson, that the undertakers should make the long cut, charging the original mileage, but giving Lee and Watson a special rate. It was refused. The Aire & Calder then told Wright to build the lock at Lake Lock. This he did in 1807. At the same time the Aire & Calder built a coal-shipping basin for Lee and Watson there, intended to be served (it never was) by a branch off their railroad. After more argument, Lee and Watson gave notice of a Bill in September 1810 to go ahead with the cut without Aire & Calder agreement, and extend their railroad inland. However, Lord Cardigan objected to the latter passing through his land, and it went no farther.

The irrepressible Lee and Watson themselves eventually built the long cut (though not to full depth), and a lock at Bottom Boat, about 1819, without the agreement of the Aire & Calder, and after having tried to eject the company from their depot. But in the absence of Parliamentary power they could not connect the cut to the navigation, or charge tolls, and without reaching agreement with the navigation company they could not get the power. So the cut remained unused, and Lee and Watson bided their time.

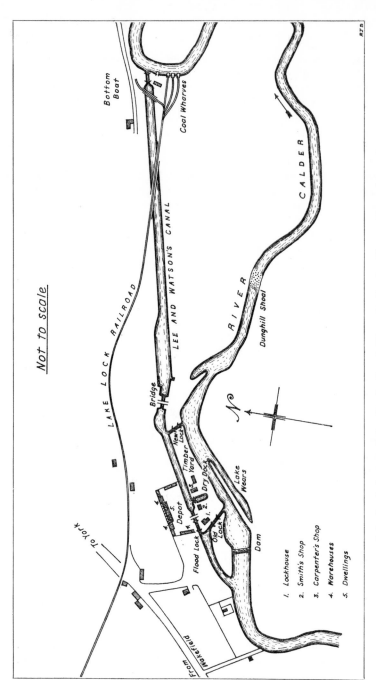

11. Lake Lock depot and the plan for Lee & Watson's Canal to Bottom Boat, about 1809

We must now return to 1800. Business was increasing and dividends rising, but a period of war inflation was not one for rapid expansion. The company carried on, pursuing those who evaded tolls, settling for damaged goods, in August 1803 offering their carrying fleet to the Government in case of invasion,* coping with the introduction of income tax, and in 1804 taking on a law clerk who was to become a well-known name in their affairs, Samuel Hailstone. Late in 1804 the company ordered a new lock to be built at Knottingley, encouraged by the great increase in their trade, and maybe also by the opening that year of the Rochdale Canal and so of waterborne trade with Rochdale, Manchester and Liverpool by way of the Calder & Hebble. In 1805 they began talks with the latter company about a new cut, wharf and dock at Fall Ing, Wakefield, where the two lines met. By November the two companies had agreed to make improvements at shared cost, these to be vested in the Calder & Hebble. Land was bought, and eventually the new works were opened in 1812. They had cost the two companies about £5,000 each. At this time the whole Aire & Calder line was 31 miles long.

In 1807 Elias Wright their engineer told shareholders: 'On the Navigation of the general Line of the Rivers, I think I may be permitted to say, it improves every Year, and is at present better than at any former time'.[19] In that same year, in agreement with Lady Petre at Selby, the company told Wright to build a lock and dock there 'fit to receive large Vessels, the Lock to be not less than Twenty four feet wide'.[20] But negotiations with Lady Petre came to nothing, and the dock was never built. Improvement, including lock widening, went on; the new Lake lock had been completed in 1808, and in 1812 Wright could report that only two more locks, at Penbank and Altofts, had to be dealt with before craft of 18 ft beam could reach Wakefield.† Penbank was rebuilt in 1813 and Kirkthorpe in 1815, so opening an 18 ft line to the warehouses at Wakefield reached through the new Fall Ing cut to the Calder & Hebble. The old cut to Wakefield by way of the mill goit was, however, retained.

The Leeds & Liverpool Canal had been opened throughout in

* Fear of invasion went with fear of privateers. In July 1803 a firm running contract ships from Thorne to London advertised that they were fitting out each of them with 'two Carriage Guns, one Swivel, and Small Arms, and Men in Proportion, for the better Security of the Trade'.[17] The fear was real: 'The Fly, Asquith, of Knottingley, with coals for Lynn, is taken by a French Privateer, and carried into Flushing'.[18]

† So Wright said, but Haddlesey remained at 14 ft 6 in and Selby at 15 ft.

1816. To a hoped for increase in trade from it was added 'great pressure of business at Leeds which is not adequately provided for by the present Wharfs and the natural Bank of the river',[21] which meant that craft had to wait out in the stream until they could get berths. Thomas Wood, who had been Elias Wright's assistant, succeeded him as engineer in 1816, and soon put up plans for improving the Leeds cut and building a basin there. These were approved, the basin was opened in 1818,[22] and the improvement reported complete in 1820.

This year of 1816 was, perhaps the last of the second period of the Aire & Calder's history, which had begun with the Act of 1774. Here are average figures[23] from 1794:

			Tolls			
	Coal	Stone & Lime	Corn	Misc	Tota	Dividends
	£	£	£	£	£	£
1794–96	11,569	5,305	6,611	20,950	44,435	32,666
1797–99	14,520	4,361	7,671	21,770	48,322	34,000
1800–02	18,253	7,193	10,522	26,299	62,267	38,000
1803–05	20,301	9,001	8,886	27,060	65,248	43,333
1806–08	20,721	9,991	8,408	24,670	63,790	48,000
1809–11	22,020	10,815	9,641	25,431	67,907	48,000
1812–14	22,586	11,481	9,620	26,687	70,374	44,800*
1815–16 (2 yrs)	22,863	10,320	8,556	29,570	71,309	45,600*

* A 10 per cent property tax was deducted at source from 1813 to 1815.

On 18 June 1813 'a great concourse of spectators were assembled on the banks of the Aire, near Leeds, to witness the progress of a boat, which was put in motion by a steam engine erected in it, by Messrs Fenton, Murray and Wood. It went down the river and up again with astonishing velocity, to the admiration of the assembled multitude. This boat we understand is to be employed as a packet boat on a canal',[24] said the newspaper. Towards the end of July she was reported at Hull on her way to Yarmouth 'and from thence to Norwich, she is to be employed on the canal. . . . She makes 7 miles per hour in smooth water, without either sails or oars'.[25] She was a portent. So was the first iron sloop, launched at Hunslet in 1818.[26] So was Joseph Priestley from the Wilts & Berks Canal, son of the Leeds & Liverpool canal official of the same name, who in October 1816 was appointed 'Head Clerk' in place of Rooth at £500 p.a. and a house; so also was Daniel Maude, one of the undertakers, in 1817 appointed salaried auditor in charge of finance. Maude and Priestley were new brooms, and were to sweep clean; steamboats, too, were to sweep old ideas aside.

First result of Maude's and Priestley's reforms was an overhaul of the company's finances: £27,027 of bad debts were written off in the 1817 accounts, fortunately at a time of buoyant revenue. One result of their investigations was to establish an arbitrary capital of £20,000 as invested in the company's carrying business, and that £2,000 had been lost on the year's working: 'Notwithstanding your Vessels have been fully and actively employed and a considerable saving made' in wages and running costs.[27] They added that the loss 'abundantly proves the fallacy of former Accounts upon that head, and . . . in a great measure determines a much agitated and controverted question'. They meant, whether the company should continue to carry. But there were more important matters to decide, and for the time this one was laid aside.

All the traffic of the Aire & Calder was funnelled through the river section between Castleford and Haddlesey, and then by the Selby Canal or the lower Aire, including some craft running direct between Leeds and London.[28] The company had found it difficult to keep the lower Aire sufficiently dredged. Between Knottingley and the entrance of the Selby Canal it was about 5 ft deep in 1820, while below that, 'from Haddlesey to Airmin the River is in a most wretched state, being not only exceedingly crooked but full of Shoals—insomuch that in Spring Tides it requires two Tides to carry a Barge from Airmin to Haddlesey and in Ordinary Neaps four Tides'.[29] However, 'altho' the Ouze from Selby to Goole is a much better Navigation . . . it is by no means a good one and does not fulfil the object required, namely The Wants of the Trade'.[30] Nevertheless, about four-fifths of the traffic went by Selby. But the Selby Canal was too shallow and too narrow, while Selby, with its single lock into the tidal Ouse, had no docks: 'it has been found requisite to provide Basins and Wharfage of considerable extent, for the accommodation of Barges; but the want of Docks suitable for the reception of Brigs has been much complained of', Leather wrote in 1822,[31] when proposing dock accommodation at Goole.

Another factor had an urgent bearing on the situation, the growth of steam packet services with a tendency to encourage road transport.

On 5 August 1815 the *Hull Advertiser* carried a notice for a steam packet, probably the *Humber*, from Hull to Selby and adjacent towns, with a room for ladies only next to the best cabin. The following year the *Waterloo* was advertised to run three times a week between Hull, Selby and York,[32] and by 1818 we find such packets also working from Hull up the Trent past Keadby to Gainsborough, and the Dutch River to Thorne. By 1819 the *Caledonia* was leaving Selby at 9 a.m. every Tuesday, Thursday and Saturday 'after the arrival of the Leeds and Wakefield coaches', the fare being 6s (30p) best cabin and 4s (20p) second cabin. Such craft carried fast freight also, the owners announcing that they had 'fitted up the Packet, in a most complete manner, for the Accommodation of Passengers, as well as for the secure conveyance of Bale Goods, &c', adding that goods from Manchester, Halifax, Huddersfield, Bradford, Leeds, etc., could be sent by it.[33] These packets ran non-stop. Passengers joining along the route had to hire a boat to take them out to meet the ship, or use a ferry boat to do so.

Steam packets offered speed and, ultimately, reliability. Flyboat services started to connect with them, using faster and perhaps narrower craft than ordinary boats. So did coach and road carriers, the last-named taking the sort of goods upon which the Aire & Calder were earning high tolls. In the company's report for 1819 shareholders were told that some 80 tons a week of merchandise which would have paid 7s a ton, as well as 'large Quantities of Wool' travelled weekly in this way because of the 'very active operation of several new establishments for the expeditious conveyance of Goods from Manchester and Leeds to Hull by means of Waggons and Steam Packets'. In 1821 a carrier unsuccessfully asked the Calder & Hebble to be allowed to pass on Sundays because of 'the increasing Dispatch with which Goods are sent from Manchester to Leeds by Land & thence Per Fly Boats & Steam Vessels to Hull':[34]

The development of canals in the Midlands and south of England was another factor: it encouraged goods, for instance from Manchester, to travel all the way to London by the Trent & Mersey–Grand Junction canal route rather than by canal to Hull to be shipped coastwise. In 1817 the undertakers referred to the two 'Bugbears of rival parallel navigations and inland southern communications'.[35]

A better and more direct route from the Rochdale Canal and Wakefield, and the Leeds & Liverpool and Leeds, was urgently needed. So was a direct connection with the Dutch River and so with the Stainforth & Keadby Canal, for the Trent trade. If the undertakers did not build them, someone else would. This was the danger when in July 1817 they first heard of the proposed Aire & Dun Canal from their navigation at Knottingley to the Dutch

River at Newbridge, with a branch to the Don at Doncaster (see p. 212). This was soon followed by another, the Went & Wake-field, to run from the Barnsley Canal at Cold Hiendley down the Went valley to the Don a little above Newbridge.

The year 1817 had been financially encouraging, the toll revenue of £82,092 being £10,000 more than the average of the previous six, and producing a dividend of £54,000 in 1818. It was clear that business was waiting, and that money could be raised. So in September 1818 the undertakers gave Parliamentary notice of a Bill to build a canal from Haddlesey on the Aire to the Dutch River, and asked the engineer George Leather to help their own Thomas Wood with the preliminary survey. Then, faced with a serious threat from the Aire & Dun scheme, John Rennie was asked in October to survey for a line, not now to the Don, but to the Ouse.

On 6 January 1819 Rennie's report proposing a line from the Knottingley cut to Goole* with a cut back into the river at Bank Dole† to give access to the Selby Canal, and a branch to the Dutch River at Newbridge, at an estimated cost of £137,700 was approved by a shareholders' meeting. By using a site lower down the Ouse, they hoped on the one hand to attract vessels trading to Hamburg, the Baltic and other Continental districts which had not been able to reach Selby, and on the other a transhipment trade to and from the Don. This meeting decided to go for a Bill which should also amend existing Acts, especially to make the undertakers a corporate body, though this part was later dropped. In September, Leather was asked to survey a possible branch to Womersley and the limestone quarries that had already attracted the Don (see p. 214). The Aire & Calder's Parliamentary petition, on 1 December 1819, was followed by Lee's for the Lake Lock–Bottom Boat canal on the 7th and the Don's on the 9th for a canal from Sprotbrough to Newbridge, with branches to Womersley and the Don below Wilsick House, which was followed by one against the Aire & Calder's Bill on the 30th. This opposition, some of it led by their old enemy John Lee, compelled the company to agree to what it had every intention of doing anyway, to main-tain the Aire down to the Ouse junction and also the Selby Canal,

* The big bend south between Great Heck and Newbridge was put in to get the canal as far as possible away from Lord Downe's mansion at Cowick Park. Rennie did not suggest that the new canal should itself join the Dutch River because of its difficult navigation. At Goole the canal was to lock straight into the Ouse.

† The lock at Bank Dole was given a pair of flood gates above the upper lock gates to prevent the river flooding upwards into the canal.

and to charge no higher mileage tolls on the new cut than they were at present taking.

In January 1820 the proposed branch to the Dutch River was deleted from the Bill at the request of landowner Lord Downe, and in 1824 the line was altered to begin at Ferrybridge. The Act[36] authorized the borrowing of £200,000 for the main canal and the Womersley branch. It also modernized the Aire & Calder's constitution, though the concern was still not a body corporate, and on 20 July J. H. Smyth presided over the first shareholders' meeting under the new Act. The old committee was now reconstituted as a board of a dozen directors and four trustees.

George Leather was given charge of construction, Joliffe & Banks took the principal contract, and the first stone of the Goole works was laid on 28 September 1822. It was not until July 1821 that Rennie had proposed to a board meeting that there should be 'an intermediate Basin & Locks' at Goole, 'instead of locking directly from the Canal to the River Ouze'.[37] * They agreed, and asked him to make plans and estimates. Four days later, they proposed a 7 ft instead of a 6 ft depth in the canal, to take 100-ton craft, and Rennie in turn agreed. However, no one seems to have told John Timperley, the Aire & Calder's resident engineer who in the 1820s rebuilt other locks with only 6 ft on their sills. He had to go, but it may not have been his fault. A few months later Rennie was dead, and it was George Leather who in February 1822 produced plans not only for a barge basin, but for a ship dock also. They were approved, and he was told to execute them 'with all dispatch'.[38]

If the new canal were to be properly used, clearly the navigation above Ferrybridge must also be improved. Rennie had in 1821 recommended deepening the Ferrybridge–Castleford section to 7 ft depth, and also doing such improvements on the Leeds line as could be afforded, given that the main expenditure would be on the new canal. Action here was also needed because of objections to the illegal height the company were keeping the river level, made by the Leeds Water Works Company and others, the company alleging that it was hindering the working of their waterwheel. Francis Giles worked on alternative schemes based on Rennie's plans, and the work was done by John Timperley, who had replaced Wood as the company's engineer, under Leather's supervision. Thwaite and Leeds locks had been rebuilt to 18 ft width by the end of 1823, and a new lock and flood-lock were

* The deposited plan had shown a simple barge basin and a single lock.

Page 133 The Aire and Calder: (*above*) Leeds in 1829; (*below*) Stanley Ferry aqueduct. In front is the semi-circular structure that protects the low-lying aqueduct against flood debris; beyond, the old Stanley basin, terminus of the railway

Page 134 An age-old practice: (above) discharging at Goodman Street wharf, Leeds; (below) unloading overside from ship to canal craft in Goole docks

built at Knostrop. A widening of the flood-lock in Crier Cut
followed in 1825.* The result was a patchy improvement. The
available accommodation at Leeds was also becoming over-
crowded, and from 1823 the company began to buy land and
provide more storage space for the wool and corn trades. Old
buildings were replaced by new ones, and in 1829 they were told
that their big new warehouse 'has been nearly filled with Corn
brought up the Navigation during the early part of this Season.
This depot for Grain has added considerably to the convenience
of the Corn Factors'.[39]

While the Bill of 1820 was being prepared, the undertakers had
been considering how to develop a new town and port at Goole;
they were strengthened in their ideas after they had approved
Leather's dock plans early in 1822, for it was now clear that much
transhipment hitherto done at Hull would be transferred to
Goole. The company had bought land there which, after the level
had been raised by warping, that is, by allowing the river to flood
and so deposit mud on it, was to be laid out as a town. Building
plots were to be leased for 99 years at low rents, subject to
approval of structure by a building committee. Leather was told
to make a town plan and to lay sewers along the streets he proposed. But a report a year later sadly noted: 'The Ground set
apart, at Goole, for building upon, has not, yet, been disposed of,
notwithstanding the elapse of another Season'.[40] The company
then decided to do the building themselves, reporting for 1824
that such work 'may be delayed by the utter impracticability of
procuring workmen to execute the Buildings now laid out' in the
boom conditions prevailing. Meanwhile a newspaper had reported in September 1822: 'The projectors of the New Dock at
Goole, seem to be carrying that work on with great spirit. A
Steam Boat has been obtained from London, for the purpose of
pumping as the excavation proceeds, and for the greater convenience of the workmen employed, a considerable number of
cottages have been built in the immediate vicinity'.[41]

Meanwhile the steam packet services had been growing, from
Selby, Thorne and Gainsborough to Hull, whence passengers and
goods could move to the coastal steam craft running down to
London or up to Scotland. An advertisement of March 1822, for

* This left one of the two Leeds locks (1822–3), the two Knostrop locks (1822–3
and 1822), Thwaite (1821–2), and one of the two locks at Castleford and the flood-
lock 18 ft wide, with four others, Woodlesford, Fleet, Methley Flood and Castleford
Old, between 14 ft 3 in and 15 ft.

I

instance, says that the Hull & London steam packet runs weekly each way, being served by 'a daily line of carriage . . . by Steam Packets and Coaches to Hull'. Freight charges are given for bales and cases of linens and woollens, hardware and heavy goods, furniture and light goods, glass, pictures and parcels.[42] These services, of course, attracted not only West Riding trade down the Aire & Calder, but that from farther inland. Selby was flourishing, and there were those at Hull who seriously feared that, were it to be made an official port and helped by the current harbour and docks congestion at Hull, much of Hull's trade would move there.[43] They were right, though it was to be to Goole, not Selby.

In 1823 'An elegant new packet called the Calder, of 32 horse power, commenced running between Hull and Selby . . . in conjunction with the Aire Steam packet',[44] and by 1825 a week's excursion was being announced on the *Lowther*, with 100 berths, from Selby to Rotterdam, returning via Yarmouth, at a fare of £3 3s (£3·15).[45] By now the Aire & Calder Steam Packet Company were running four packets daily between Selby and Hull, the *Aire, Calder, Duke of Wellington* and *Caledonia*. The company's *Graham* ran daily to Grimsby, the *Lowther* weekly from Selby to Yarmouth, another twice-weekly from Hull to Scarborough.

In 1820 Clough & Godfrey, who had shares in steam packets running between Selby and Hull, asked for preference at locks to be given to their narrower and fast fly-boats running to Selby with goods for the packets. The directors agreed. In that year they decided in principle to give up carrying, and wisely began to sell the older sloops from their fleet, which had been 33 craft in 1819. This was wise, for the newer packets were beginning to replace them.

Then they changed their minds; perhaps Clough & Godfrey's request had given them the answer. In March 1821 they decided themselves to run fly-boat services between Leeds and Selby, and Wakefield and Selby, to connect with the packets, and ordered four to be built immediately 'upon the most eligible and approved construction'.[46] The service from Leeds began on 18 June.[47] The report told shareholders that increased revenue from merchandise 'may in a great measure be attributed to the system of Fly-Boats, by which, many Goods have been diverted into this Navigation from the Trent':[48] these would be goods for Manchester and Liverpool now using the Pennine routes instead of the Trent & Mersey Canal. Six more fly-boats were ordered in 1822, and in 1823 the carrying trade made a profit of £3,522, more traffic being taken from the Trent. At the end of 1823 cuts were made in Aire & Calder carrying charges and a corn drawback granted. Thereafter the company energetically worked their carrying business, but their profit of £748 was the last they were to make for very many years. During the resultant rate war, there were usually losses of £2,000 p.a. or more, against which the company could take credit for the tolls their boats paid. Competition was not only against bye-traders, but with road transport. In the slump of 1826, for instance, the annual report complained of 'great competition with Land Carriers, thrown out of Employment in other Quarters, eager to find Employment'.

The picture is now like this: from Leeds, fly-boats left every evening except Sunday for Selby, taking about 12 hours, and connecting with the morning steam packet for Hull, arriving there in the afternoon. The Union Company's boats ran from Leeds via Castleford, Wakefield and Sowerby Bridge to Manchester, while for very fast transit in 60 hours, goods went from Leeds by light van to Dewsbury on a newly-opened turnpike, and then fly-boat on the Calder & Hebble and Huddersfield Canal. Finally, daily fly-boats on the Leeds & Liverpool took four days to transit that canal.[49]

The bye-law of 1821 giving fly-boats a general precedence had been questioned in the courts, and such craft had sometimes been attacked. It was upheld by the Pontefract Quarter Sessions in April 1824, after which Maude and Priestley observed that they hoped the matter was settled, to 'leave this improved system of Navigation, to convince the Public, of the great advantages to be derived from it: a self-evident result, when it is considered that, in connection with Steam boats, goods are now regularly delivered, at Leeds, or Wakefield, on the third day after their departure from London: for about one half of the Charge by land carriage'.[50] Tolls received on merchandise in 1824 were £47,359, against £30,818 in 1819: this seemed justification enough for the fly-boat system. In this year, 1824, W. M. Maude (who was no relation) succeeded Daniel Maude, but policy did not change. In 1825 a famous name was added when Thomas Hamond Bartholomew was appointed Surveyor and Clerk of Works: in other words, engineer.

Nothing had been done about the Womersley branch, though the proposed railroad had been switched to it from the Don, but in November 1825, hearing that the line was now to run straight to Heck, the directors agreed both to oppose it and to begin work on the branch. However, their opposition to the Bill having failed, they assumed the railway's success and ordered work to stop again. They examined the project again in 1829, but did nothing, and in 1830 their powers lapsed.

Between 1815 and 1818 two Haxbys, brothers, with other local quarry-masters built a cut some 300 yds long from the Aire & Calder across Brotherton Ings to the drain which ran at the foot of the limestone ridge. Having bought tramplates in 1819 from the Low Moor Co, they built railroads and worked the quarries. In 1829 the business went bankrupt, and the canal became disused.[51]

Probably about the same time Staniland's Canal was built, perhaps by E. & W. P. Watson, lime merchants,[52] who later became E. Watson & George Staniland. The canal is shown on Greenwood's map of 1817–18, and, with kilns along it and continued by a tramroad through a tunnel at the quarries, on the first edition of the 6-in. O.S. map, where it is marked as Staniland's Canal. G. A. Staniland died in 1845, and later it seems the tramroad was continued along one of the canal's embankments to the river. The quarry was still being worked in 1871.[53]

In 1824 the Fairburn Canal, planned in 1821, was cut for some ½ mile from the navigation, and then continued by tramroad tunnels to quarries belonging to Lord Palmerston. It was probably disused by 1849–50, for the 6-in. O.S. map, though showing lime-kilns at its head, does not indicate tramroads.[54]

The Aire & Calder's shareholders now began to read in their newspapers little puffing paragraphs: 'railroads, worked by the loco-motive steam engine, have so decided a superiority, both as regards time and expense, that . . . they will be generally adopted whenever a new line of conveyance has become necessary, either from an increased trade, or from the exorbitant demands of canal proprietors',[55] followed in January 1825 by a notice for the forming of a Leeds & Hull Rail Road Company[56] and, later, by other railway proposals. However, on 28 July 1825 a party of directors proudly travelled in 'one of their boats . . . from Ferrybridge, where their new canal joins the river Aire, along the whole line, into the docks at Goole; this being the first vessel which has made the voyage'.[57] It was then thought hopefully the whole might be open 'ere the setting in of winter'.

As the opening date for the new canal approached, the boom ended and slump, patched with local bank failures, followed. It was in an atmosphere only slowly beginning to improve that lock-keepers and a harbourmaster were appointed. Drought and so

Opening of the Goole Canal.

𝔑𝔬𝔱𝔦𝔠𝔢 𝔦𝔰 𝔥𝔢𝔯𝔢𝔟𝔶 𝔤𝔦𝔟𝔢𝔫,

THAT THE

New Canal

FROM GOOLE TO FERRYBRIDGE,

Will be OPENED to the PUBLIC,

FOR THE

Passage of Vessels,

On Thursday next, the 20th Instant.

N. B. All Vessels which enter the Lock at Goole *upwards*, or at Ferrybridge *downwards*, on Thursday the 20th, Friday the 21st, and Saturday the 22nd Instant, will be allowed to pass, upon payment of the same Tolls as by way of Selby :—afterwards, they will be charged agreeably to the Rates under the Act of 1st. Geo. IV. for making the Goole Canal.

NAVIGATION OFFICE, WAKEFIELD, July 13th, 1826.

R. NICHOLS, TYPOGRAPHER, WAKEFIELD.

12. The Goole Canal opens

delay in filling the new cut delayed the opening, but at last, on 20 July 1826 the great new canal and basins were opened in an embryo town on a cold and showery day. Coach-loads of passengers came from Leeds and other parts of the West Riding, the *Graham** packet steamed in from Hull on a special trip, and packets, too, came from elsewhere.

Those who were there saw, looking at Goole[58] from the Ouse, two entrance locks, on the left a barge lock 72 ft 6 in. × 22 ft, on the right a ship lock, 120 ft × 33 ft 9 in able to take vessels of between 300 and 400 tons. These locks both led to a basin some 276 ft × 220 ft, and 17 ft deep, for craft drawing 15 ft, from the far sides of which an inner barge lock led to the Barge Dock some 900 ft × 150 ft, from which the canal led off at the far end, and an inner ship lock to the Ship Dock. This was about 600 ft × 200 ft, and also 17 ft deep. The two docks were linked by a short cut, and there was a tramroad to carry stone from barges to ships. They

* Some say the *Lowther* from the same stable.

would have seen a multi-storey warehouse built over a basin off the Barge Dock, where fly-boats were to be unloaded under cover, and beside the Ship Dock, a big bonding warehouse was rising. Offices, and some houses for the staff, had also been built near the docks. As for the town:

'A large and commodious Inn, called the Banks Arms Hotel,† is already opened, and fitted up in capital style. On the north of it, is to be a spacious market place, 220 yards square. Several streets are staked out, in parallel lines, branching west from the Ouse; some of these are 60 feet wide, with flagged causeways already laid. . . . The houses in three or four of these streets are already built, and many of them occupied;—when the whole, now contracted for, are completed, they will amount to about 120. Those of the lowest class are finished in a style of neatness very unusual.'

Ferrybridge lock was opened about 10 a.m. After

'about 50 sail had been admitted, the principal officers of the establishment, with their friends, set forward in a Fly Boat, splendidly fitted up, followed by three others with goods and passengers. They . . . came within sight of Goole about half past three. . . . Flags were displayed from the buildings and the shipping in the river. The vessels, on nearing the town, advanced at a brisk pace. The foremost of them was decorated with a large union jack and a profusion of colours, among which were four blue banners bearing the inscriptions— "Agriculture and Commerce", "Prosperity and Plenty", "Jolly Tars and Cheerful Swains" and "Success to the Port of Goole". . . . The whole party then proceeded through the Barge Dock into the Harbour, the music performing "Rule Britannia", the multitude cheering, and the firing being kept up by the vessels, and great guns—about five o'clock, a number of gentlemen sat down to an excellent dinner. . . . The Company then adjourned to witness the entrance of the Lowther Steam Packet by the proper lock into the Ship Dock, which, after some delay, was effected'.[59]

The newspaper added that: 'Several roads, communicating with the port, have been opened and improved, and others are in contemplation'.

---

† This had been built and paid for by Sir Edward Banks. It was bought by the company in 1828; after his death in 1835 its name was changed to the *Lowther* to commemorate the company's chairman at the time the Goole Canal was opened, Sir John Lowther.

The canal itself was $18\frac{3}{4}$ miles long, 60 ft wide at top, 40 ft at bottom, and 7 ft deep. There were entrance locks at Ferrybridge (a flood-lock) and Goole, and intermediately at Whitley and Pollington, 70 ft × 19 ft. Craft could still use the old route down the Aire, or reach the Selby Canal, by locking out of the Goole Canal through Bank Dole lock at Knottingley.

A week before the opening, advertisements began to appear for Mr J. M. Harvey's 'Fly Packets (with suitable Cabins)' that would begin to run on 21 July daily 'between Ferrybridge and Goole, *in three hours*, for the Conveyance of Passengers and Parcels'. These would connect with the Aire & Calder Steam Packet Company's *Aire* running a daily return trip from Goole to Hull for passengers and goods. The *Aire* was replaced in 1827 by the navigation company's own craft the *Eagle*, bought secondhand after having been taken off the Gainsborough and Hull run. At Ferrybridge passengers from Hull and Goole would 'meet the Coaches for Pontefract, Wakefield, Barnsley, Huddersfield, Bradford, Halifax, Leeds, &c; . . . by this Route . . . the constant and long delays of the Steam Packets in their uncertain passage between Selby and Goole, occasioned by their getting and remaining aground for Hours together, for want of Water, will be avoided'.[60] It looks as if the canal packets were not initially profitable, for very soon after opening the board told their officials to make arrangements with the packet owners concerning 'the conveyance of Passengers in order to encourage their continuance'.[61]

The company then moved its own carrying craft running to Hull from Selby to Goole. Selby, of course, suffered by Goole's opening, as boat captains had to move house, hauliers to make new arrangements, and shops found their custom falling away. It took some years for the transfer to become fully effective.

The new port became a minor tourist attraction. On 3 August the *Royal Charter* steam packet took nearly 150 passengers from Barton upon Humber to see it: 'The proceeds, £15 11s were generously devoted by the Proprietors to the fund for the relief of the distressed Manufacturers'.[62] *

The Treasury was petitioned to give Goole the status of a port with its own Customs facilities. This was granted in 1827 in spite of strong opposition from Hull; Selby was also transferred to Goole from being part of the legal port of Hull, and the first week of April 1828 was fixed for 'opening the Port of Goole for Foreign Trade', officials being told 'to provide Steam Power to

* Workmen engaged in the manufacturing industries.

NEW PORT OF GOOLE.

THE Public are most respectfully informed, that the Aire and Calder Steam-Packet Company have arranged with the Proprietors of the " Ferrybridge and Hull Fly Packets" to run one of their STEAM PACKETS every Morning from GOOLE to HULL, on the immediate Arrival of the Fly Packets from Ferrybridge.

That well-known Packet, THE AIRE, will commence plying from GOOLE to HULL, on FRIDAY NEXT, the 21st Instant, at Ten o'Clock in the Morning, and return from Hull the same Evening.

☞ Further Particulars will be given after the Opening of the Port, which takes place on the 20th Instant.

RICHARD CLAY, Jun. Agent, Goole.

13. Steam packets start running from Goole

assist Vessels in and out of the Port'[63]—the 50 h.p. *Britannia*, which worked between Goole and the sea. It cost them £2,330. On 6 April the brig *Stapler* left for Hamburg[64], and at the end of August the first ship from the Mediterranean arrived, the *Camilla*, 'with a cargo of Gallipoli oil' for Leeds.[65]

The cost of the Goole Canal and port works to the end of 1826 had been £361,484 Of this, £221,350 had been borrowed and added to the Company's previous small debt of £38,250, the balance found from their own considerable resources. Remarkably, they had financed the new works and also managed to increase their demands from £58,000 in 1820 to £70,000 in 1826.

CHAPTER VII

Growth after Goole

✦

THE opening of Goole during a trade depression intensified the impact of the new inland route. Road carriers were hard up and hungry for work. Rates were low, and some water carriers, unable to pay the tolls of the new canal, continued to use the cheaper though longer Selby route. Competition being so keen, the Aire & Calder for a time maintained their own carrying services on both lines, which helped to produce a loss on this activity of £2,568 for 1827. In that year company's craft were taken off the Hull and Selby run, and by mid-1828 'very little business' was 'being done through our medium'[1] there, only one clerk being retained.

Coach services changed. In the middle 1830s there was still a coach service from Leeds to Selby to link with the steam packet to Hull, but others ran to Knottingley to connect with the two-horse canal packet-boat thence to Goole, and also to Castleford for the steam canal packet. Coaches from Wakefield also connected with these, and others from as far west as Huddersfield, with connections from Manchester.[2] Most of the Hull steam packet trade in goods and passengers transferred to Goole. Selby was, however, still well enough situated for the promoters of the Leeds & Selby Railway of 1830 to end their rails at the river, whence passengers and goods would be transferred to the packets. This happened from the opening on 22 September 1834, but only until the completion of the Hull & Selby Railway in 1840. After that Selby became, and remained, a very minor port compared with Goole, though a steam packet service serving it was still running in the 1860s.[3]

Meanwhile the board had in 1824 suspended further piecemeal changes and commissioned George Leather to recommend improvements that would be needed once the Goole Canal had been opened.

In August Leather reported on a piecemeal development plan
for the Leeds to Castleford line, then went outside his brief to
recommend a 7-ft canal all the way, using most of the existing
cuts. The company liked this idea, and sent Leather to look also at
the Calder. They also called in John (later Sir John) Rennie, who
confirmed what Leather had already said, that the line was 'far
from complete to enable vessels of only 5 feet draught of water to
navigate at all times; in fact, what Mr Smeaton thought necessary
to secure a navigable depth of water of 3 feet 6 inches at all times
has scarcely yet been obtained'.[4] On the Calder Leather proposed
the same 7-ft depth, with a cut out of the river below Wakefield
and back into it. His line then left the river again above Kirkthorpe lock and as a continuous canal ran north of it all the way,
crossing the Aire above Castleford and again just above Ferrybridge, whence it extended on the west side to join the Goole
Canal. Leather did not, however, like or recommend the Castleford–Ferrybridge canal, and was pressed (so he said in 1828) to
use the river course instead.

In November the company ordered a Bill to be prepared
covering the improvements to both lines, in January 1825 resolv-
ing in principle to build a Ferrybridge–Leeds canal to avoid the
'interruptions and imperfections' of the existing line.[5] In November Leather reported on the whole Leeds–Wakefield–Ferrybridge
canal project, and a plan was deposited. His estimate was £196,686
or £240,626 depending on certain alternatives.

In November 1825, the board changed their minds, deciding to
wait for the following session. They themselves later said that
they had done so because of the heavy expenditure they were still
incurring on the Goole Canal 'and the extraordinary pressure of
the times and scarcity of Money'.[6] Doubts about the Castleford–
Ferrybridge line may also have been a reason for delay; so
probably also was a notice by Lee and Watson of a Bill to complete and open their canal from Lake Lock to Bottom Boat, and
take tolls. As usual, the Aire & Calder board decided to oppose it.
No action followed, until in October 1826 the board were horrified
to read not only another Lake Lock notice, signed now by
Thomas Lee and Edward Hemingway (who was later to replace
his uncle Shepley Watson in his Wakefield solicitors' firm), but
also another for an entirely new canal from Wakefield mill dam
direct to the Aire at Ferrybridge. This also was signed by Lee and
Hemingway, as well as by a London firm of solicitors. The course
ran on the north side of the Calder for 12 miles from a basin at

Wakefield, where branches were provided to Wakefield Ings and the Barnsley Canal. It took in Lee and Hemingway's land and their unused cut between Lake Lock and Bottom Boat; then, just below Penbank, crossed the river on a two-arched aqueduct to run through Whitwood and south of Glass Houghton to Ferry-bridge.[7] It had neatly adapted Leather's proposal for the Calder to Lee and Watson's need to make use of their unopened cut, and made the Aire & Calder appear dilatory into the bargain.

The prospectus,[8] dated 17 January 1827, was short and not particularly informative. It offered a canal at a cost of £180,000 to take seagoing craft of 18 ft beam which, it promised, would not be 'subject to the various and vexatious delays and impediments, nor the wear and tear of the Craft, and tackle, nor the great expence of haling, which must prevail on every navigable River', nor would seagoing craft have partially to unload their cargoes before they could get to Wakefield. Traders, landowners and occupiers, it said, had long complained of the state of the Aire & Calder, 'but no effectual relief hath been provided'. It implied that mileage tolls would be the same as upon the Aire & Calder, except that reductions might be made upon merchandise, so that savings to traders would be one-third of tolls and freight because of the shorter distance. No estimate of revenue other than the promise of 'very ample remuneration' was given. The prospectus was signed by ten promoters, John Lee and Watson among them.

The board naturally accused the promoters of having taken over their idea, for which plans had been deposited, for a Calder canal, and resolved:

'that the project . . . if carried into execution by the Promoters of it will be ruinous to the rights interests and Property of this Navigation and will tend to the total annihilation of the River Calder as a Navigation which together with the Navigation of the River Aire (being Freehold Property) has been a subject of Family Settlements amongst the Undertakers for nearly a Century and a half'.[9]

A special sub-committee was set up to conduct the opposition, shareholders were circularized, their engineer was told to check the proposed line and its levels, and representatives were sent to interview landowners affected. The Bill was brought in early in 1827. It became a cause to which all those with a grievance against the Aire & Calder could attach themselves. Heavily supported by 52 petitions, including the Rochdale and Calder & Hebble companies and many traders, the Bill was narrowly defeated on second reading by 133 votes to 130, and that only after the Aire & Calder had pledged themselves to introduce a Bill to improve the Calder line. Their opposition had cost them some £2,000.

They then employed Thomas Telford to re-examine both the Wakefield and the Leeds routes in the light of Leather's existing proposals. He reported in outline in July, the navigation's engineer being then told to do further work on details. Telford chose a different and more radical line for the main Calder improvements, and in turn borrowed the idea of an aqueduct crossing from the rival scheme. He proposed a cut from the same point above Kirkthorpe lock as in 1825, to cross the river on a 6-pier aqueduct at Stanley Ferry having a cast-iron trough with overhead trusses, and run south of it to Fairies Hill beyond Penbank where three new cuts would shorten the river's course to Castleford.[10] In October Telford's plans for the Calder were finally chosen, Leather's for most of the Aire, and a Bill prepared. And then the board learned that Lee and Watson were renewing their Wakefield & Ferrybridge Canal application.

Their Bill contained an unusual provision: that after a certain percentage dividend had been paid—stated as 7 per cent—the balance of distributable profit should be divided between shareholders and landowners in proportion to the length of canal through their estates. Lee and Watson, as landowners, were taking out an insurance. One subscriber at any rate was disgruntled at their behaviour: 'we, the shareholders, are fighting their battles, and that of the other landholders; and if we lose, we pay the bill, and if we win, they divide the profits'. As for the line, only 500 yd shorter than the revised Aire & Calder proposal, 'Does it not go out of the direct road to take in the estates and canal of Mr. Lee and Mr. Shepley Watson, for 2½ miles'?[11] Apparently Thomas Wood, the Aire & Calder engineer who had been dismissed in 1820 for malpractice, had gone over to Lee, taking some early but confidential information with him. He is probably referred to in a newspaper letter of February 1828, which refers to 'the dismissed and disgraced clerks of the Aire & Calder Company, in the pay of the projectors', and the 'purloined accounts published'.[12]

Another Parliamentary battle followed. Lee and Hemingway lost their Wakefield & Ferrybridge Bill more decisively this time by 179 to 91, in spite of an even larger shower of petitions, from which, however, the Rochdale and Calder & Hebble companies had judiciously absented themselves. The pair of belligerent solicitors would probably have claimed their intervention had compelled the Aire & Calder to modernize their line. They now opposed the Aire & Calder's own Bill, however, on the grounds that the navigation had contracts with them binding the company to maintain their old line to serve the Lake Lock Railroad. A clause had to be inserted giving them the right to compensation, partly for the prospective removal of the Lake dam and so for lowered water levels, and eventually the Aire & Calder paid an arbitration award of £13,074 damages and £6,318 costs, though the tonnage carried on the railroad had fallen from 109,050 tons in 1806 to 53,438 tons in 1826.

The company's Act[13] passed in June 1828. It authorized Telford's proposals for the Calder line and Leather's for that to Leeds, as well as a railway from Stanley Ferry to Lofthouse Gate and dock extensions at Goole. Tolls, and the mileage on which they were to be calculated, remained as before, in spite of the shortenings in practice. Finally, a 5-ft depth was to be maintained in the Selby Canal. The improvements, which would enable 100-ton craft to reach Wakefield and Leeds, were estimated at £313,570 and the Goole works at £148,850; altogether the company were empowered to borrow up to £750,000. Very much had happened since 1818.

We may here glance at the navigation's financial position. Dividends had risen from £35,000 in 1800, £52,000 in 1817 and £60,000 in 1822 to £70,000 in 1827. Apart from loans, the original capital was now £29,667 (the original £26,700 plus the one-tenth added for Peter Birt in 1774); on which to 1828 over £2,250,000 had been paid in dividends. Of the shareholders, the two biggest in 1826 were Richard Fountayne Wilson, who in 1826 received £9,322, and Sir William Milner, whose share was £7,843. The Aire & Calder had proved a most judicious investment.

The 1828 Act passed, the company began work on the new Castleford cut just below the junction of the rivers, and then on the Leeds line, but found themselves compelled also to give effort and money to the Selby Canal. They had tried to placate that town by starting work on a new lock there, to replace the old semi-ruinous one, just after the Goole line had opened, and now hoped to maintain the statutory depth of 5 ft under the 1828 Act by keeping the dam boards at Haddlesey and Beal higher than the law allowed. But, having been convicted at Quarter Sessions, they had to start widening and deepening the canal. That done, 'the Inhabitants of Selby . . . expressed their dissatisfaction with what had been done, and threaten an Action for the purpose of compelling further Improvements of the Selby Cut'.[14] They took it, and the cut had to be further widened and deepened in 1832 and 1833.

At the end of 1833 traders at York, Malton and elsewhere asked for the Selby Canal to be made deeper than 5 ft, and other improvements made. These were refused. In 1836 a 'new wharf wall, founded so deep that fully laden Vessels may lie close to it'[15] was built at Selby to replace the old and mainly collapsed one. The same policy of keeping the dam boards higher than allowed was followed elsewhere while the improved line was being built. It helped traffic but annoyed landowners whose land was sometimes flooded. These landowners in turn did not willingly rally to the navigation in time of such need as opposition to the Leeds & Selby Railway Bill. The dam boards were briskly lowered at Castleford, however, when the chairman himself, Sir John Lowther, complained of injury in August 1830, then raised again, and lowered after another complaint from Lord Mexborough in 1834.

The improved line to Leeds was finished in April 1835, when 'a continuous line of Canal is formed from Hunslet to the River Aire near to Allerton Bywater',[16] giving a 7 ft navigation all the way from Leeds to Goole. Work had been somewhat delayed because it was 'considered advisable to secure the slopes of the new Works in a more substantial manner than was first intended, to enable them to withstand the effects of Steam Navigation, which the Rivalry of Rail-Roads will require to be adopted in future'.[17] The improved line saved 2 miles; it was 10 miles long and 7 ft deep from the junction with the Leeds & Liverpool Canal at Leeds to Castleford with seven 18-ft locks. 'The long vistas of water, wide and straight, bounded by graceful elliptical bridges in the distance, the lockhouses, ornamental buildings, the solid masonry at the sides, whether by slanting planes of paving-stone, or low perpendicular walls, altogether form a pleasing exhibition of modern art and excellent taste'.[18]

In 1840, the Aire & Calder bought 13 acres of land at Leeds for £27,000 for a new dock. Designed by George Leather and built by T. H. Bartholomew, the work began in 1841; it was finished in 1843, and 'cannot fail to be of great advantage to the Trade of Leeds, by supplying the accommodation which from the crowded state of the River at certain seasons, has been so frequently pressed on your attention', as the 1842 report said. The dock was at first mainly used for the potato and stone trades.

The improved line* of the Calder, with four 72 ft × 18 ft locks, took the company and their engineer Leather much longer than that to Leeds. In mid-1833 the lower part was opened to the river at the Penbank pond through Altofts, Fairies Hill and Foxholes locks, but the main work, the iron tied-arch aqueduct at Stanley Ferry and the deepening of the river beneath it not until 8 August 1839, when 5 miles were taken off the former distance of 12½ miles from Castleford to Wakefield. Foxholes now became a side-lock to give access to Bottom Boat and Lake Lock depot. Both the aqueduct and the river deepening had caused difficulties: the aqueduct in establishing the foundations and in carrying and erecting castings, some of which weighed 17 tons; the deepening by floods. In their 1837 report the company said sadly: 'the deepening of the River at Stanley Ferry seems to be an interminable Work, the great flood of December last (1837) having nearly filled it up again'. Soon after opening the aqueduct was indeed tested, when the biggest flood for twenty years caused the river actually to flow into the trough. It was undamaged, and 'the subject of admiration to all the professional Gentlemen who have been to look at it'.[19] The contractor who had built not only the Calder line, but much of the Leeds line improvement and the Ouse dock and lock at Goole, was Hugh MacIntosh.

The aqueduct—perhaps the least known of the major canal aqueducts of Britain—seems to have been designed by Leather, whose 1827 plan[20] shows a tentative suggestion of a lattice structure with an iron trough and six piers. In 1828 Telford said that he had first approved this, but later, when the nature of the river had become known, Leather and he had rejected it, implying that the new design would have a single arch. In April 1834 the board told Leather to prepare plans for it, and in November he let the contract for a cast-iron structure to MacIntosh. The foundation stone was laid on 12 May 1837, and the aqueduct built by William Graham & Co of Milton ironworks, Elsecar, upon foundations provided by MacIntosh. They lost heavily on it, and in 1840 were given an *ex gratia* payment of £2,000.

Beside the aqueduct the company had built a basin capable of shipping 500 tons a day, and to it their own coal-carrying 3 ft 4 in. gauge Stanley Railway which crossed the Lake Lock line and ran to Lofthouse Gate. It began by the Leeds to Wakefield road, and

* This ran to Fall Ing at Wakefield, the junction with the Calder & Hebble. Opposite Fall Ing, the old lock leading to Wakefield old wharf had not been enlarged.

Page 151 The Barnsley Canal: (*above*) Barnsley aqueduct about 1906;
(*below*) barges pass towropes near Heath

ran thence for 1¾ miles to Stanley Ferry. The Lake Lock line itself closed in December 1836. The lower part of this Stanley Railway was opened on 1 January 1840 and 'immediately adopted by the Proprietors of the Grove Colliery, and others',[21] the whole in June 1843. The old river was still navigable to Lake Lock depot, and by an agreement with the successors of their old enemies Lee and Watson the company dredged between Lake Lock and Bottom Boat, work which, of course, also served their own depot at Lake Lock. In 1840, ironically, the undertakers were offered the Lake Lock Railroad, and in 1841 the whole Lake Lock and Calder property. Except for one farm, they refused it. Farther down the Calder, the line as it now exists through Woodnook lock (duplicating Altofts and Fairies Hill) was opened in 1842. The cost of the main rebuilding of the Leeds and Wakefield lines, the Stanley Railway and other works authorized in the 1828 Act, was some £510,000, not counting later additions.

In early 1834 a steam packet service was started from Goole to Hamburg. It revealed both Goole's inadequacy for handling Continental trade and over-optimism in forecasts. At first the company thought of building a wharf on the Ouse, but instead decided to let a contract for the additional Ouse or Steamship dock, 490 ft × 360 ft, together with a new lock entrance to it from the river, 210 ft × 58 ft, the great width the result of the contemporary use of paddle-steamers. The works were designed and built by Leather, who had James Abernethy as his assistant— Abernethy's first important job—and Hugh MacIntosh as contractor. Sir George Head wrote that 'the cast-iron gates of this dock, and the lock, will, when finished, be, it is said, the largest in England'.[22] They were opened in 1838. Meanwhile, the Hamburg service was short-lived. It was restarted in 1838 with the *City of Carlisle*, but did not flourish, for Richard Clay was asking for company help in continuing it. They offered £500 on conditions. The service probably ended soon afterwards, and efforts in the 1840s to revive it came to nothing.

So the improvements begun with the 1820 Act were completed: here are some figures of takings attributable only to the Goole Canal, which show steady growth in spite of toll-cuts from 1834 onwards:

	£
1828	20,834
1830	20,061
1832	27,128

K

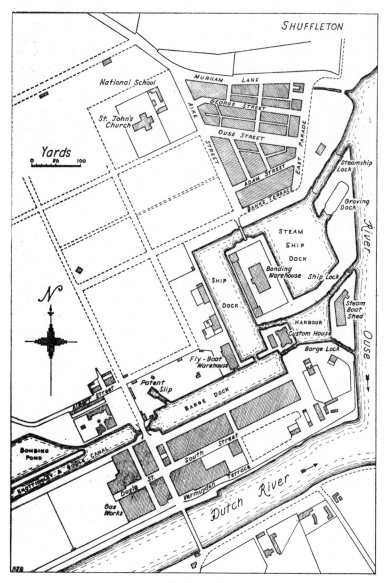

14. Goole in 1845

£

1834	26,768
1836	31,143
1838	35,213
1839	38,531

The population of Goole, 508 in 1821, had by 1841 increased to 3,629.

All these works had been financed by borrowing and out of profits, no fresh share issues having been made. In 1835 the debt was £341,100, of which £264,605 had been spent under the 1828 Act. But it had not proved possible to keep dividends to the £70,000 p.a. level reached in 1824 to 1826. From 1827 to 1829 the figure was £60,000, and in 1830 it was dropped back to £54,000, where it remained until 1839.

The improved line had been built just in time, for the railway age was approaching. In 1824 a Leeds & Hull Rail Road Company had been promoted, with George Stephenson as engineer. Joseph Locke did a survey, but there was doubt whether the line could be worked with locomotives, and no action followed. In 1828 merchants and bankers at Hull who were worried at Goole's growth allied themselves with others in Leeds who feared the Aire & Calder's power. A railway was now proposed from Leeds to Selby, whence steam packets would carry passengers and goods to Hull. Ralph Walker surveyed it in 1829 and supported locomotive working, it was authorized in June 1830 after opposition from the Aire & Calder and landowners, a part of whose expenses the navigation company paid, and opened on 22 September 1834, having cost £340,000, much the same as the Goole Canal. Goods traffic was carried from 15 December. At the directors' request, James Audus of Selby built two iron steamers to run thence to Hull. As opening day approached, the company offered cheap rates between Leeds, Selby and Hull, causing the Aire & Calder to make wide-ranging toll cuts averaging some 40 per cent on 1 October, and further cuts three months later. At the same time they extended their carrying business. However, a plea by the Aire & Calder to the Calder & Hebble and Rochdale companies also to make reductions went unrewarded.

The Leeds & Selby were only moderately successful with their price-cutting policy, for in September 1836 Newman Cash of the railway told the navigation committee that they had raised their rates and hoped the canal company would do the same. The Aire & Calder did not: their position was strong, and their income had rapidly recovered. Railway dividends of 1½ per cent in 1836 and 1837 were followed by nothing in 1838, and then by 4 per cent, at which figure the line was in 1840 leased to the York & North Midland, who bought it in 1844.

In August 1834 the Hull & Selby Railway Company was formed. In its prospectus of November[23] it emphasized that the distance from Hull to Selby, 50 miles by river, would be 30 by rail, and made a good propaganda point of the varying times of sailing of the steam packets because of the tides, their unpunctuality, the danger of their grounding on ebb tides during neaps if they sailed at fixed times, as at Selby, and the troubles of frost and fog. All were true,[24] none as true as all that. The line from Hull to Selby was authorized in 1836 and opened on 1 July 1840. Leeds was now linked to Hull by rail as well as by water, and the days of the packets were almost done. In 1845 the York & North Midland also leased the Hull & Selby Company.[25]

Meanwhile, in December 1830, the board had received a deputation from the proposed Sheffield & Goole Railway pro-moters. The Aire & Calder raised no objection to the line being built to the borders of their Goole estate, if they themselves could build, and pay for, the rest of the line to the ship dock, and receive a proportionate revenue.[26] It got no further, but the company followed the same policy with later schemes.

Before we follow the Aire & Calder's efforts to come to terms with railways, we must go back to other sides of the navigation's story.

After the Goole Canal opened, the company continued to reduce the number of their own vessels running to and from Hull. By 1828 only 17 of these were left, some unserviceable. In addition they had 15 working on the navigation, mostly fly-boats. The experiment was then made of paying captains a proportion of their earnings instead of wages; these dated from a time when trade was being developed, and boats had to sail regularly, whether loaded or not. Competition remained keen, between water carriers and between water and road transport, and the company's fleet continued to fall. They had 27 craft in 1830. In 1831 they ceased to carry to Wakefield, the trade there being transferred to Buckley & Co, who themselves only held it for a year before returning it to the Aire & Calder. Craft were down to 22 in 1832, due partly to competition, partly to the company having given up the direct Hull trade, instead using fly-boats to Goole, ships or contract steam packets thence to Hull.

Steam had been used for many years on the Ouse and Humber. In late 1831 the company were still profitably running *Eagle*,* carrying goods and passengers between Goole and Hull, but losing money on *Britannia*, towing vessels between Goole and the sea. In 1831 the company put on a steam tug to haul fly-boats on the Goole–Leeds run (it meant that they had to protect the Goole Canal banks), a second a year later, and a third in 1834 'in order to complete the system of towing boats by steam on the Navigation'.[27] Other steam tugs were also at work: Hamer, Bromley & Co had more than one running at the end of 1833. All were probably paddle-driven. Then, early in the 1840s, the first four iron fly-boats were put on.

In 1833 fast packets were running between Goole and Castleford 'at the rate of six or seven' m.p.h.; a steam packet seems also to have been working on the canal in late 1832, for there were complaints of her severe wash compared with the 'Horse Boat Packet' which 'is so sharp built and delivers its water so well'.[28] Two horse-boats ran from Goole to Knottingley until 1834. Built at Wells in Norfolk in 1830, each was a remarkable craft: twin-hulled, like a catamaran, intended to run at 8 or 9 m.p.h. without creating a surge,[29]

'gaudily . . . decorated and painted, exhibiting, among other embellishments, a gigantic portrait of Queen Adelaide† on her quarter; it was, in fact, a floating house, with seven windows on each side; and affording to those passengers who preferred an airy seat, a flat roof for the purpose, as well as comfortable benches thereon . . . those who occupied the cabin enjoyed the usual accommodation of a steam-boat'.

She was hauled by four horses, each on a separate line, in charge of three postilions, 'each a small boy, under six stone, and dressed in a light blue jacket, with red collar, and a white hat'.[30] By 1835 two paddle-steamers, running right through to Leeds and carrying 100 passengers each, were supreme: but not for long. In October they were offered for sale, presumably in face of the threat from the Leeds & Selby Railway.[31]

The carrying improvements came just in time, for in 1834 heavy price-cutting and the diversion of some traffic marked the opening of the Leeds & Selby Railway. Takings fell, but the cuts increased the number of craft using the Goole Canal from 12,164 in 1834 to 15,659 in 1835, and the coasters clearing from Goole

---

* She was replaced about 1845 by a new *Eagle*.
† The other craft was the *William IV*.

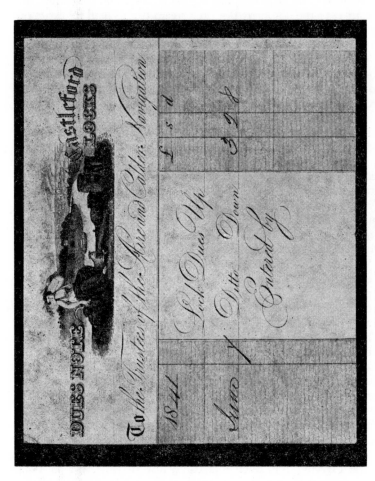

15. Toll ticket issued at Castleford lock

from 2,048 to 2,639. Dock dues fell from £1,215 in 1832 to £1,049 in 1834, and it was then decided temporarily to waive them upon 'the large Steam Vessels trading to Goole'.[32] To meet the railway, the company increased their own carrying, and on 1 December 1834 cut their competitive wool, bale goods and groceries' rates by nearly 60 per cent. By doing so they carried more tonnage, but received less money. Coal and corn tolls were unaffected. Their toll revenue for 1835 was therefore £114,935 against £130,719 for 1834, and their carrying loss increased by some £2,500. Railway competition induced a more generally co-operative attitude. When in 1833 the York traders had asked for night working at Beal lock, they had been told its hours were those of the Goole Canal. The same request in 1835 brought an order to the Beal lock-keeper to comply.

Competition also developed in warehousing, each concern of course regarding storage as a service linking customers to its own form of transport. In 1838 the company reported of Leeds that 'The Accommodation to the Trade of the Town is greatly increased by these large Erections, but no adequate remuneration is derived from them. Competition induces our Rivals the Railway Companies to afford Warehouse Room gratis, to which we are also in great degree compelled to submit', and in 1844: 'As some of the Floors which had been let in the Great Warehouse at Leeds, are lately given up, and as the Railways offer great accommodation, it may be feared that new Tenants will not easily be found'.

Nearly all the coal that moved on the navigation was used along its lines, or was conveyed up the Ouse to York or beyond, or into the canals and harbours of the Humber estuary. Little moved coastwise, still less was exported. In 1818, 16,475 tons had been sent coastwise from Hull, and 1,179 tons exported.[33] The sea-going trade was in stiff competition with seaborne coal from the north-east. In 1824, when winter floods hindered traffic on the Aire & Calder, 'the Consumers, on the Eastern coast, were compelled to have Recourse to Sea borne Coal, for their Winter Supplies'.[34] Reductions in the coastwise duty also helped the sea-coal.

In the twelve months June 1825–6 the coal tonnage brought to Hull by river craft was 109,588.[35] Once Goole was opened, it, of course, became a convenient shipping port for coal because of its nearness to the collieries. To help the sea-going trade, the Barnsley Canal company in 1830 suggested a toll reduction on Silkstone coal exported at Goole for London or abroad. The Aire & Calder agreed to reduce by one-third on all coal shipped coastwise if the Barnsley company also reduced, whereupon the lowered tolls* came into operation. All the same, in 1833 the company had to report that 'Goole is unable to cope with the present very low prices to which Coals have been reduced in the Northern Ports'.[36] The drawback much annoyed other waterway administrations, such as the Witham, who received their coal from the Aire & Calder by canal and not by sea. In 1833, interestingly, Thomas Wilson of Silkstone colliery was given permission to carry his coal in waggons on boats to Goole to avoid breakage without paying toll on the waggons, one instance of waggon-carrying boats. Others worked from Waterloo colliery near Rothwell to Leeds.

By 1836 the general trading situation had partly stabilized: toll revenue was increasing again, and by 1838 had exceeded the 1834 total. The company felt strong enough in 1836 to increase the Goole–Leeds freight rate for wool from 6s 8d (33½p) to 8s 4d (41½p). The 1840 report said that two-thirds of income was hardly affected by railway competition, which indeed was worse from 'certain competing lines of Navigation', presumably the Don, the Dearne & Dove and perhaps the Trent & Mersey. It was a brave statement, for toll revenue was to fall heavily thereafter, from £145,511 in 1840 to £114,654 in 1845. The company followed up their point in their 1846 report, which regretted they were unable to command the coal traffic, and 'meet the reductions which were made on the line of the Don Navigation, by a corresponding decrease in the Dues on the Barnsley Canal'.[37] Though at the time they were not being forthcoming in their negotiations to lease the Barnsley (see p. 187).

For the two years 1836–7 the export figure was averaging only 10,934 tons a year from Hull and 3,830 from Goole, compared with the near half million of Newcastle; but the coastwise figure from Goole, 101,599 tons average, though tiny beside the 2¼ million of Newcastle, was large compared to Hull's 11,113 tons, and showed how successful Goole was becoming as a coal shipping port, though one must remember that coal shipped at Thorne on the Don came through Goole port.[38] She was already twelfth in the coastwise league. Comparatively little coastwise coal went to London from the Humber, for the billyboys of 80 to 100 tons, in which it was carried, could not compete with the

---

* In 1855 the drawback was extended to coal reshipped at Hull as well as at Goole.

300-ton Tyne and Wear craft, nor could they readily break into the London factors' ring. Instead, the Humber coal went to such smaller ports as Louth, Boston and King's Lynn. Competition in the early 1840s was with Newcastle coal carried by sea, coastwise and to London; this led to price cuts by the Yorkshire coalowners, and the Barnsley and Aire & Calder companies. There was also steep competition from the Dearne & Dove and Don line after the Dearne & Dove cut its tolls by one-third in 1841. This competition led into that from the northern railways.

Here are some figures for coal tonnages carried on the Goole Canal:

	Tons
1827	140,853
1834	200,802
1845	313,449

Whereas between 1827 and 1845 coal carryings had not much more than doubled, those of corn had greatly increased, as had stone and lime. Merchandise, for which we only have a toll receipts figure, was probably higher in tonnage, but not in yield:

	Corn tons	Stone and Lime tons	Merchandise toll recs £
1827	36,017	36,338	9,863
1834	59,884	55,066	11,332
1845	126,357	129,675*	7,803†

* Includes 'other minerals'.
† Tonnage figure for 1845, 131,294 tons.

Here we must remember that about the middle of the century Wakefield was second only to Mark Lane, London, as a grain market, and had enormous storage capacity in its thirty corn warehouses.[39]

In 1836, taking up a suggestion made by the Stainforth & Keadby Canal company in 1833 and then turned down, the board seriously thought of building a short cut and lock near Newbridge to connect the Don to the Goole Canal, bought land for it, and indeed let a contract to MacIntosh in October. The cut was, however, dropped when the company learned that the Don proposed either to buy the Stainforth & Keadby Canal or build a new outlet to the Ouse for themselves at Swinefleet (see p. 219), and the policy of having a navigation railway at Goole was substituted.

In January 1839 John Atkinson, a Leeds solicitor, put before a board meeting a prospectus and plan prepared by Leather for a Leeds & Armley Navigation, to extend wharfage facilities for craft drawing 7 ft into the new manufacturing areas above Leeds bridge, and to reach Armley mills higher up the river. The board were non-committal, and the scheme did not survive long, being partially replaced in 1845 by the Arches lock branch of the Leeds & Liverpool Canal.[40]

In 1841 W. M. Maude resigned as auditor or accountant-superintendent, and was succeeded by Thomas Wilson, who served until 1875. The changeover was the occasion to institute a Finance Committee, and to tighten up procedures in line with the progressive Victorian times. After consideration in 1842 of whether the head office at Wakefield and the central toll-collecting centre at Castleford should be amalgamated at Castleford, it was decided that no economy or increase in efficiency would result. In 1842, too, old Samuel Hailstone, who was 74 and had been law agent since 1804, resigned. Behind the minute book entry probably lies the story of an elderly man, not poor, who did not want to give up. He was not replaced, John Hope Shaw of Leeds being appointed the company's attorney instead.

In 1840 the company reached its maximum toll revenue, £145,511, compared with £110,328 in 1826 when the Goole Canal had opened. The dividend was £66,000, less than the £70,000 of 1825 and 1826, the highest paid, but still a very creditable figure. Here are average figures from 1822 to 1845:

Years	Tolls £	Dividends
1822–24	102,446	64,667
1825–27	112,526	66,667
1828–30	118,742	58,000
1831–33	127,633	54,000
1834–36	123,360	54,000
1837–39	136,009	56,000
1840–42	126,812	64,000
1843–45	111,691	60,000

We must always remember, as background to the navigation's history, the company's preoccupation with the many mills of all kinds—flour, seed-crushing, flint or bone grinding, dyewood crushing, paper and whitening among others—they owned or rented, mainly in order to control the water, but also to absorb the passage tolls, usually 1s (5p) per loaded boat, the mills' occupiers could take as compensation for loss of water. These rents were quite lucrative, yielding £3,900 p.a. in 1824, but the mills needed constant repairs, capital outlay and attention. In 1840, when the company agreed to buy Nether Mill near Leeds and its surrounding property for £31,239, their report said: 'You have hereby secured an Interest in every Mill on the River, and the complete control of the Water of the River Aire'. But the situation was about to change. Joseph Priestley wrote in 1846: 'what is very singular, I am informed by the Millers, that some of them have even given up Grinding, because they can do better by purchasing American Flour, than they can by grinding English Wheat'.[41] In 1848 he reported that a reduction in duty on foreign oils had killed the oil (seed-crushing) mills. The result was a fall in mill rents, and later of course, partial disuse of the mills,* so that they no longer constituted a threat to navigation.

On 5 January 1836 the promoters of the proposed Manchester & Leeds Railway had asked the Aire & Calder, along with other interested canal companies, to receive a deputation. The Rochdale and Calder & Hebble agreed, and eventually came to agreements which they regarded as satisfactory, but though the Aire & Calder arranged a meeting for 16 January they did not send a senior official, and it was not a success. Leather, jun., wrote after it 'announcing the decided hostility of the Aire & Calder Company, as resolved upon at their meeting on Saturday the 16th Inst',[42] and in April the railway's chairman said that 'The Aire and Calder Company still continued immoveable in their opposition, and he was sorry that he could not hold out to the Meeting, any hopes of bringing this Company, once considered to be so powerful as to have acquired the name of "the fourth Estate of the Realm" to any thing like reasonable terms, out of Parliament'.[43] However, immediately after this speech further offers were made, and in Parliament protection clauses were agreed, and a payment of £12,325 to the Aire & Calder for adjustment to the navigation near Broad Reach in the railway's interest. In 1836 the Aire & Calder found itself opposing in Parliament the Manchester & Leeds, North Midland, York & North Midland and Great Northern (not the 1846–7 company) Railways. They were especially bitter about what they considered favouritism shown to the North Midland: committee hearings held on the same day as the Manchester & Leeds; 'every statement of the Promoters . . .

---

* Two, Thwaite and Castleford, still work by water.

acquiesced in and every Opposition to it disregarded'; their committee hearing 'opened when never more than five, and frequently only four were present—and *not one* paying any Attention whatever, but writing Letters!'[44]

In March 1841 the Manchester & Leeds Railway met Bartholomew of the Aire & Calder to ask for an interchange point. The latter strongly recommended Broad Reach where the line crossed the Calder just below Wakefield, and said that it would cost £2,000 (Gooch of the Manchester & Leeds Railway thought much more) and could be ready in two months. Talks went on, and in May the Aire & Calder quoted rates at which it would carry from Wakefield to Hull. At the same railway meeting the board considered a letter from Hudson suggesting a meeting to discuss 'rates for the Hull traffic in order to compete with the present low rates per Canal'.[45] Gill, the managing director of the Manchester & Leeds Railway, brought the Aire & Calder's suggestion for an interchange point to be made by them at Broad Reach before the board, but himself recommended one at Wakefield, not to be made by the Aire & Calder. However, two months later Capt. Laws, the superintendent, and Gooch both recommended the board to have Broad Reach as well as Wakefield, 'as the latter would be required for the corn trade alone and would be unsuitable for the quick dispatch of goods from the want of sufficient room and the time required to pass the locks'.[46] The board agreed to have both, and to urge the project forward.

In September a plan of the proposed junction at Broad Reach was approved, though the board thought the £5,000 or £6,000 proposed to be paid to the Aire & Calder if the interchange station was abandoned was too much. In November the Aire & Calder decided they would not undertake so great an expense without a guarantee that it would be used, which the railway would not give. The Broad Reach junction was never made, but an hydraulic lift gave access to Thornes wharf and the corn trade at Wakefield in the 1850s.

Railway problems multiplied. Those caused by the construction of the North Midland Railway, as, for instance, damage to Woodlesford paper mill, were solaced by agreed deviations, and by the £20,000 paid to the Aire & Calder, the old annoyance over their Parliamentary treatment during opposition in 1836 being replaced by 'the most perfect Harmony'[47] between the navigation and the North Midland. That line was opened in 1840 from Derby, where it had London connections, to Leeds, and was to have not only immediate effects, but to begin a revolution that substituted rail transport to London for the old route from Manchester, Leeds, Wakefield and Goole by sea. Another Hudson line, the York & North Midland, had been opened to connect with the Leeds & Selby at Milford in May 1839, and to join the North Midland near Normanton with a curve at Methley junction to allow through running from York to Leeds in July 1840. Taken with the Great North of England line, this seriously affected the Aire & Calder's trade with the Ouse. Finally, in November 1840, the York & North Midland leased the Leeds & Selby, and the Aire & Calder found itself fighting a great Hudson empire. In November 1840 the York & North Midland were quoting a through charge from Altofts (near Normanton), their junction with the North Midland Railway, to Selby and thence by steam tug to Hull of 7s 6d (37½p) a ton.[48]

The Manchester & Leeds at first tried 'to buy the Water Carriers off the Navigation'.[49] Failing in this, they published very low rates for Manchester–Hull traffic, and for two months extreme price cutting took place, the canal carriers being supported by the three water companies. Then in June 1841 agreement was reached on a compromise which left the water carriers with a fair proportion of the traffic.[50]

On 1 March 1841 the Manchester & Leeds Railway started to carry goods over its whole length to Normanton and so by the North Midland to Leeds. The pressure was such that in October representatives were sent to meet the Calder & Hebble and the Rochdale companies to consider whether the Aire & Calder tolls should be reduced from 1d to ¾d, 'and . . . upon the plan of carrying goods by the Undertakers and to reduce the freight if necessary'.[51] A meeting of the three companies at Normanton in November, though strongly united in theory, was inconclusive in practice, the Aire & Calder considering the first step to be agreement on common mileage tolls over all three navigations, and the second to be reductions. But action was difficult to concert,[52] though the need was great. Indeed, in October 1842 a memorial with 210 influential signatures came to the company from Goole, complaining of depression at the port, partly caused by railway competition, and asking for changes. The depression was real enough: the company opened a soup kitchen there in February 1843.

Heavy toll reductions had to be made by the Aire & Calder against this railway, competitive with the whole water line to

Manchester. The position became even worse when the Manchester & Leeds Railway gained temporary control of the Calder & Hebble in 1843, and for a time fought a bitter rate-cutting war with the carriers on the Rochdale Canal. By 1845 the Aire & Calder had lost almost all the bale (finished textile) goods traffic, 'practically excluded . . . by the power which the Manchester & Leeds Railway Company exercise over the charges on the Calder & Hebble Navigation'.[53] Laws of the Manchester & Leeds Railway wrote nervously to Hudson of the York & North Midland on 20 December 1844: 'I am told the Aire & Calder and Rochdale and Huddersfield Canals intend Bale Goods to go next year . . . 6d p ton, or a nominal Toll', being himself in favour of a rates agreement. Hudson, however, replied that he did not wish to increase rates to Selby in any case: 'I have an objection to these combinations with water companies, they are generally injurious to the public interests, & seldom of advantage to the parties making them'.[54] The Aire & Calder managed to make a provisional rates and traffic agreement with the Manchester & Leeds Railway in 1845, having first acquired the promotion of the proposed Horbury Bridge & River Calder Railway from the Flockton collieries to the navigation to give them *locus standi* in Parliament, in order to put pressure on the railway, then withdrawn when they got agreement. This did not last, but another of August 1846 governed the Manchester and Hull traffic.

The Aire & Calder, though wealthy and fully modernized, was finding life difficult as the railway mania year of 1845 began. In it yet another problem first seriously showed itself, the attraction for railway companies of Goole itself. (*To continue the history of the Aire & Calder Navigation, turn to Chapter XVI.*)

The Heck & Wentbridge Railway

The limestone deposits round Womersley and Wentbridge were for a time thought to be commercial prizes. Transport for the quarries' products would have been provided by the Aire & Dun or the Went & Wakefield Canal schemes of 1817–19, and a related Don plan of 1819, for all were planned to run down the Went valley. They were superseded by the Aire & Calder's 1820 Act for the Goole Canal, which itself authorized a canal branch from near Knottingley to Womersley. Naturally, therefore, the navigation company opposed independent schemes of 1821, 1822 and 1824 to build a railroad from Womersley to the Don (see p 214), which were in part answers to the Dearne & Dove Canal Company's contemporary proposals for a tramroad towards Thurgoland. But, busily building their own canal, they did nothing about the branch.

In 1824, however, Enoch Taylor, a local man from Sandal near Wakefield who had been engineer to the earlier railroad scheme, prepared a new plan for a line some 4 miles long from Wentbridge past a 300-yd tunnel to Womersley to join the branch. Then, the branch not appearing, he laid it out afresh from Heck. At this point the Aire & Calder gave orders that their branch should be started. But the railway was authorized in May 1826[55] as the Heck Bridge & Wentbridge,[56] and in August the earlier orders were countermanded.

The line was 7½ miles long. The company were given power to raise £11,300 in shares, and borrow a further £2,800 if necessary. The proprietors seem at first to have intended to tranship on the canal bank, but a shipping basin was added in Parliament. They therefore had to get a second Act[57] in 1827 to raise another £7,600 and acquire the land to make a cut and basin at Heck, as well as to provide wharves and other accommodation.

The railway, engineered by Enoch Taylor, was opened in 1827–8, and in 1828 the shareholders were optimistically talking of extending the line to Barnsley, Thurgoland and the Worsborough valley to get into the coal business[58]. However, the line was far from being a success. Seemingly it had been intended to ship the limestone, thought more suitable for building than for burning lime, to London and other towns, but it proved too poor in quality. In 1829 the Aire & Calder claimed that, having examined the railway, 'there is no Limestone fit for agricultural purposes . . . on any Part of that Line, or in the vicinity of it',[59] whereas their proposed canal branch to Womersley, which they now thought of reviving, would tap deposits as good as those, now almost worked out, at Knottingley.

In October 1828 the line was working* at Kirk Smeaton, for a waggon loaded with three tons of limestone and gravel ran over and killed a donkey and his rider,[60] but by January 1831 the railway was described as disused.[61] Then the Barnsley Canal Company, who had had a canal line surveyed from their canal towards Goole and maybe thought they could get some cheap land, asked Francis Giles, acting for the Exchequer Bill Loan Commissioners

---

* It had probably just been opened, for in August the company were hoping to finish the dock and basin within a few weeks.

who had lent it money, how much it would cost.[62] In 1832 Giles offered it to the Aire & Calder, who declined it.[63] In the same year the Dearne & Dove Company were trying to get support from the Aire & Calder, Don and Barnsley companies for a plan to buy and then destroy it, presumably because it might compete with limestone coming from their own lines. Only the Don seems to have thought it worth any money at all. After one or two more inquiries from the Barnsley company, mention of the railway dies out of the canal records, until in 1845 the Exchequer Bill Loan Commissioners took possession of it for unpaid debts. They sold the basin and 10 acres of adjoining land to the Aire & Calder for £440—a bargain.

Today it is still possible to trace much of the track. Heck basin itself is used as a base for pleasure cruisers.

CHAPTER VIII

The Barnsley Canal

◆◆

IN the later eighteenth century the Don Navigation had encouraged the growing trade by road between Swinton and Barnsley. Then in the early 1790s the quickly-growing demand for coal led to a shortage: so much was being used by industries and townspeople round the collieries that not enough was left for distribution elsewhere. Indeed, coal traffic on the Aire & Calder and the Don was tending to fall. In September 1792, for instance, the Aire & Calder said of coal: 'at times, when it can be had, there are considerable Quantities sent Coast-wise'.[1] This demand and the incentive of the canal mania caused both companies, and the Calder & Hebble also, to seek to develop the rich coalfield north of Barnsley.

The first off the mark were the Aire & Calder, for in 1790 William Martin, their manager, was seeking a colliery on the Earl of Cardigan's estate north-west of Wakefield, and projecting a canal to it which John Gott surveyed. This scheme was dropped, partly through opposition by the Duke of Leeds, but in July 1792 Martin was told to get a plan and estimate made for a canal from 'the neighbourhood of Barnsley' to that of Wakefield.[2] His activity quickly alerted the Don committee, who on 9 August recommended their next shareholders' meeting to consider making the river Dearne navigable to Barnsley and its neighbourhood. Three weeks later the shareholders decided to promote a subsidiary company to build what became the Dearne & Dove Canal (see Chapter XII).

Two days before this Don shareholders' meeting, the Aire & Calder had held theirs. A well-rounded resolution presented the need throughout Yorkshire for coal, and the case for building a canal that would bring it from near Barnsley. That town's manufactures would also be carried downwards, and, as back carriage, Knottingley lime to improve the land. They tried to discourage the Don scheme by emphasizing that their own route to Hull was 'much better and more certain (it is presumed) than any other way because [on] that from Selby . . . to Hull, there is always a sufficient Depth of Water to Navigate Vessels, even at the lowest Neap Tides, which is not the case with any other Navigable River that a Canal from Barnsley or near it, can possibly be connected with'.[3]

William Jessop, William Martin, and their two resident engineers, John Gott and Elias Wright, were therefore asked 'without loss of time' to survey a route and estimate it, preliminary to a public meeting. Jessop had also been asked to survey the proposed Dearne & Dove, but was then too busy to do either. The Aire & Calder's men therefore surveyed the Barnsley line from the Calder to Barnsley and thence 'in or near the Township of Silkstone'.[4] Jessop was, however, present at a meeting on 20 September. He reported that he had looked at various lines the three had surveyed, and thought that from near Wakefield to Barnsley and Silkstone 'will be Practicable, be a very eligible Line to be Adopted and that the Expence upon a cursorary View wou'd not exceed the Sum of Fifty Thousand Pounds'.[5] He and his three colleagues were then told to prepare a definitive plan and estimate. The Aire & Calder undertakers decided themselves to subscribe for £20,000 worth of shares, the balance to be allocated to landowners on the line, and 'to such Gentlemen, Merchants and others, as are likely to trade on the Canal, or reside in the Vicinage', no person to have more than eight shares. In other words, the undertaking would be controlled by the Aire & Calder, as the Dearne & Dove was intended to be by the Don. Meanwhile men were despatched to organize the usual petitions: Thomas Shay got them at Ripon and Boroughbridge, William Martin jun. at Hull, Beverley, York, Market Weighton and Howden.

A public promotion meeting was appointed at the White Bear at Barnsley on 15 October. The Don company, wanting the key section of canal from Barnsley to Silkstone for their own Dearne & Dove, sent a delegation to argue their case. The meeting, with John Smyth of Heath, prominent in the Aire & Calder, in the chair, thought both lines to Barnsley from Don and Calder alike would be beneficial, and agreed that they should connect. The estimate for the Barnsley Canal, which, the meeting thought, 'affords a fair prospect of Profit to the Undertakers',[6] was now £60,000, subscribed by 86 people, to build a canal 15 miles long

from Heath, John Smyth's home, on the Calder just below Wakefield past Barnsley to Barnby bridge, 1½ miles from Silkstone,
whence the original plan shows a proposed waggonway to Norcroft Bridge towards Silkstone.[7] There were to be flights of locks
at Agbrigg and Walton in the first 3 miles, and at Barugh on the
coalfield section. The Don company agreed that the Barnsley
should build this Barnsley–Barnby section, in return for the safeguarding of the river Dearne's water, important to the proposed
Dearne & Dove Canal and the Don itself. The Barnsley company
at that time proposed to pump their own water up the locks from
the Calder.

A branch 2½ miles long from the coalfield section at Barugh to
Haigh bridge was also added to the Barnsley scheme at the Don's
request, this involving 7 rising locks and a fourth steam engine,
and agreement reached that the Dearne & Dove's tolls should
be the same as those agreed at the promotion meeting on 15
October for the Barnsley, both companies binding themselves
not to reduce them without the consent of the other. At the promotion meeting James Hebdin was appointed law agent, and
William Martin, also of the Aire & Calder, treasurer.

The money was raised easily enough, the eight shares limitation
being maintained except for Walter Spencer Stanhope,[8] a stock-
holder of the Aire & Calder and the man who owned much of
the land above the Silkstone coal. He became a trustee of the
river company on the day William Martin was first ordered to get
a survey made, and was allowed 16 shares.* He was chairman
during the whole time the canal was being built. Two committeemen of the Don Navigation also appeared in the original
subscribers' list. Five tramroads to points on the coalfield were
surveyed and included in the Bill that was then prepared.

Difficulties began. On the one hand, Jessop re-estimated the
main line together with the proposed new Haigh bridge branch,
and produced a revised figure of £82,080. Originally he had
estimated for three steam engines at Agbrigg near Heath, Walton
and Barugh; now he proposed to have a reservoir instead of the
first two, which would add £3,000 to capital expenditure but
save £350 p.a. Other reasons for the higher figures were additional
land costs of £8,700, which included £5,000 to finance a clause
that had been inserted in the Bill ordering the company to level
soil they had excavated; £3,000 for more puddling than had
originally been thought necessary, and generally rising prices.[9] So

* The limitation was not enforced after the initial subscription.

the promoters had to raise another £22,000. Some was taken up by the Aire & Calder shareholders, the rest by local landowners and others.

A rival scheme appeared in February 1793. This was promoted by G. W. Wentworth and Thomas R. Beaumont, a member of the Barnsley's committee and a promoter named in their Act, in opposition to the Aire & Calder, and was for a canal from the Calder & Hebble at Horbury to Haigh bridge and Barugh (with a branch to Barnby bridge for Silkstone) to join another planned to run to Barnsley and along the Dearne valley north of Wath-on-Dearne to the Don at Conisbrough, with branches to Worsbrough and Cobcar Ing (Elsecar).[10] This extension to the Don was promoted as providing a 'communication from the port of Gainsborough to Halifax, Huddersfield, and all the trading populous country adjacent, for the raw material of the woollen manufactory, which the counties of Lincoln and Nottingham produce', independent of the Aire & Calder, 'the expence upon which river admits a competition by land carriage of upwards of fifty miles', and also of the Don-supported Dearne & Dove scheme.[11]

The Barnsley–Don section of the scheme was probably not serious, but designed to get Dearne & Dove support, but the Haigh bridge–Horbury section, which would have served Beaumont and Wentworth estates, went to a Bill, naturally supported by the Calder & Hebble and opposed by the Aire & Calder. The line had been surveyed and estimated by John Hodskinson: it was to be $3\frac{3}{8}$ miles long from Horbury to Haigh bridge, $5\frac{7}{8}$ miles to Barugh, with 23 locks and a $1\frac{1}{2}$-mile tunnel, and cost £53,335 plus £6,000 from Haigh bridge to Barugh.[12] It was argued that it would shorten the carriage of Silkstone coal to Heath from 15 miles by the proposed Barnsley Canal to 11 miles, and make available Haigh bridge and Bretton coal, 'nearly the same quality as the Silkstone'.[13] The Barnsley committee, led by Stanhope, stood firm on their own line, at the same time seeking support from the Aire & Calder and the Ouse and Humber navigation towns, and were strong enough to close their subscription list in March. But, assisted by the closure about this time of Haigh furnace, they compromised. They abandoned their own Haigh bridge branch, and clauses in their Act (120–2) provided that should Beaumont and the Calder & Hebble subsequently apply for an Act to build a canal from Horbury to Barugh, the consent of the Barnsley would not be required, discriminatory tolls could not be imposed, and existing tramroads north-west of Barugh would be closed. Jessop, Gott and Wright estimated the 6-mile-long but difficult cut at £72,115. For a few months the Calder & Hebble thought of going ahead; but the coalfield on the Haigh bridge side proved poor, and nothing further was done.

The Dearne & Dove and the Don were protected by clauses in the Barnsley's Bill which provided for a junction stop lock to prevent loss of water in either direction, this to be under joint control, and for both companies to maintain a level, on penalty of having traffic stopped. The Barnsley company were also to take no water from the river Dearne.

The Act,[14] passed at a cost of £2,610 on the same day as that for the Dearne & Dove, authorized the company to raise £72,000* in £100 shares, and £25,000 more if needed. The committee of 13 elected at the first shareholders' meeting on 3 September 1793 included a majority who were connected with the Aire & Calder. William Martin, confirmed as treasurer, was given £210 for his trouble in promoting the company. On 27 September several committeemen, with the treasurer, engineer and contractor, local dignitaries, and a band, went to Heath Common, where Martin (perhaps as recognition of the concern's origin) dug the first sod[15] to the accompaniment of prayers. Cash was then distributed to the workmen, and the crowd returned singing 'Rule Britannia', 'God Save Great George our King', and 'Britons Strike Home'. 'The company afterwards sat down to a good dinner, with plenty of excellent wine'.[16] The contractor was John Pinkerton, and the resident engineer, Samuel Hartley. Pinkerton ran into unexpected difficulties, especially in the Cold Hiendley cutting, and in coping with rising prices. Hartley lost confidence in him, and there were frequent disputes, which went on after the canal was finished, and were only settled after a lawsuit, in 1812.

The canal was opened from the Calder to Barnsley on 8 June 1799: 'On which occasion the Proprietors of the Aire & Calder Navigation, ordered two of their sloops completely rigged, and furnished with men, guns &c. to attend. These sloops left the River Calder about nine o'clock in the morning with cargoes of yarn and other merchandize, and proceeded to Barnsley, amidst a vast concourse of spectators, miners, & manufacturers, who expressed the most lively joy'.[17] Tolls were not collected until the 17th. The upper part of the line, however, needed more work and

* A reduction of £10,000 on the estimate because the Haigh branch had been taken out.

more water; it was not begun until late in 1798, nor finished until the beginning of 1802, when Jessop reported it complete. Its partner, the Dearne & Dove, was not opened throughout until late in 1804. The company did nothing about tramroads, however, until in January 1805 they ordered 'the railway from the Bason at Barnby bridge or near thereto, to Norcroft Bridge, and from there thro' Silkstone to Silkstone Cross to be immediately staked out', at the same time having in mind to lease it to get rid of the construction cost.

The Barnsley Canal was 11 miles long to its junction with the Dearne & Dove near Barnsley, or 15 to its end at Barnby basin. The entrance lock to the Calder at Heath was at first set at the end of a deep cut, but this collected rubbish when the river level rose, and a new cut and lock at the river were built in 1816 to replace it. Beyond it, there were two locks at Agbrigg, and a flight of twelve at Walton, after which the canal ran level to the junction. Finally, five locks at Barugh took it to Barnby. Two important engineering features were the long and deep cutting at Cold Hiendley, and the five-arched masonry aqueduct over the Dearne near Barnsley, upon which Jessop decided in June 1794 instead of an embankment and culvert. The canal was built to a 5-ft depth, water being eventually obtained not by pumping from the Calder, but from a reservoir at Cold Hiendley (also called Haw Park or Wintersett), with a Low Moor pumping engine ordered in 1803, and another Low Moor engine of 1801 at Barugh to pump back up the locks. Total expenditure had been about £95,000.

As the coalfield developed, the predominant trade was coal downwards, to the Calder and the Dearne & Dove. But manufactured goods also moved down, while up came lime and limestone (this from Brotherton and Knottingley) for land improvement, notably on the moorlands north and west of Barnby, and linen yarn for the mills. Kilns to burn the limestone were built at Barnby basin and Barugh. Agricultural produce, seed, slates, building and paving stone, and, of course, groceries were normal traffics also.

Water supply was a constant problem. Some was got from the Dearne & Dove; the reservoir was enlarged in 1807, and another steam engine provided in 1806. A worse problem was to get traffic, especially coal. By 1801, the Low Moor Company had won a colliery at Barnby Furnace to mine the Silkstone coal; they built a ½-mile long tramroad from it to the canal head at Barnby basin, and began to move coal in 1802. By 1804 they were despatching 10,000 tons. The Dearne & Dove having opened throughout some three months before, in March 1805 the Low Moor Company advertised that they were 'now selling COALS at 14s a waggon, delivered on board the Vessels', and invited customers to send craft up the Barnsley Canal or the Dearne & Dove. The Silkstone coal, they claimed, had 'superior Quality in Point of Heat and Durability'.[18] Indeed, demand outran supply, helped by the poor road that linked the colliery to the canal; as for increasing supply, 'it is impossible to do it with Carts either as to Quantity or the Price'.[19] The result was 'a great discouragement to Vessels going from the Calder up the Barnsley Canal for Coals'.[20] In any case, about half the coal loaded on the upper section of the Barnsley Canal went down the Dearne & Dove after 1804.

By 1807 the company was in difficulties. The original capital had been spent by the end of 1797. Then some shareholders had put up about £20,000 as calls of £33 on shares that were then converted to loan stock, and £3,000 was raised by mortgage, which brought the company near their legal limit of £97,000. The crises came when the Barnby colliery failed (it reopened in 1810–11), and lost the canal three-quarters of its coal traffic, so that coal tolls, £1,616 in 1804, were expected to be only £500 for 1807. What was needed was the authorized tramroad to Silkstone, for the use of that colliery and others which nearby owners were waiting for transport to open. In January 1805 Samuel Hartley, the company's engineer, was ordered to lay out this line of some 2½ miles, to cost £4,000, but there was no money. The company could not afford to make it, efforts to get a further call on shares got little response, and Jonas Clarke of the Silkstone colliery refused to build it and repay himself out of the tolls. By 1807, owing a good deal and with little money in hand, the committee told the shareholders that 'the Company's Affairs are at present exceedingly embarrassed and that their difficulties are increasing'.[21] Poor Benjamin Shillito, lock-keeper, felt the effects: his pay was cut from £54·60 to £36·40 p.a. A Bill was therefore promoted, and passed in March 1808.[22] This granted some toll increases, though the Dearne & Dove insisted on a clause that there would be no preferential rate for coal carried the full length of the Barnsley, and empowered the company to raise £43,200* by calling £60 on every £100 share, and also £10,000 on mortgage. Tolls and wharfage charges were lifted at once, and the whole

---

* But this sum included the subscription loan of £33 per share, now reconverted to equity capital, and arrears of interest on it, for 603 out of 720 shares.

£43,200 called in one instalment, which caused some panic selling of shares to avoid paying the call. Priestley says some shareholders sold out for £5. Some, more prescient, bought. William
Rooth, treasurer since 1797 and a committeeman, had 2 shares in
1800, 12½ in 1807, 30 in 1810 and 35 in 1815*. In fact, only two
shares were forfeited because of the call.

Though in April 1808 they ordered negotiations to start with
landowners on the Silkstone line of railway, even now the company seem to have hesitated, for in November the Dearne &
Dove wrote to the Don company to ask the latter to help them
put pressure on the Barnsley to build the Silkstone tramroad.[23]
Then the Low Moor Company's tramroad from Barnby basin
towards Norcroft bridge, built some years previously, was
bought and utilized, rails obtained, and the new line laid as a
plateway from Barnby basin to Silkstone Cross to serve Jonas
Clarke's (Robert Coldwell Clarke's from 1822) colliery. It cost
some £4,500. Barnby basin was also enlarged, and the whole
opened in 1810. By then, a first dividend of £1·50 per £160 share
had been paid for the second half of 1809. Samuel Thorpe had a
branch from the main line above Barnby furnace to the pits near
Banks Hall, and another to Norcroft bridge was built in 1812 for a
new colliery worked by Richard Stringer & Co.[24]

Tonnages

Years	Corn qrs	Coal tons	Iron tons	Lime tons	Lime-stone tons	Tim-ber tons	Sundries tons
1800–02	4,129	5,093	773	2,848	6,842	462	2,123
1803–05	1,363	25,052	1,334	2,300	12,649	465	2,613
1806–08	1,320	30,365	1,976	3,025	15,355	589	5,518
1809–11	2,529	47,900	1,599	2,280	17,413	489	7,637
1812–14	7,532	76,208	1,329	2,689	23,681	593	10,148
1815–17	12,643	95,104	1,132	1,880	21,087	688	10,610
1818–20	20,874	95,062	1,282	2,102	22,980	802	10,670
1821–23	36,107	109,945	1,029	1,443	19,337	1,267	11,935

Coal traffic now rose steadily: in May 1809 Benjamin Shillito's
pay returned to £54·60 p.a., and in September 1813 the company
were happy to appoint a man at a similar salary 'to count the
Waggons of Coal delivered into the Vessels at the Bason'[25] from
each colliery. Counting was not enough: in 1815 a weighing
machine for the waggons was ordered. Coal contributed not only

* He had 9 in 1824. When he retired in that year, the company said in future no
servant of the company should be a shareholder.

16. Silkstone colliery ticket

greater total figures, but an increasing proportion of the company's revenue. Limestone and lime were also steady trades, and corn a growing one as Barnsley expanded, and as the practice grew of bringing corn up and taking coal back. Here are averaged toll figures from 1800 to 1823:

Tolls

Years	Coal	Other	Total canal tolls	Tramroad tolls	Total tolls
	£	£	£	£	£
1800–02	239	587	826		
1803–05	1,211	817	2,028		
1806–08	1,344	1,120	2,464		
1809–11	1,968	1,471	3,439	527	3,966
1812–14	3,812	1,996	5,808	1,431	7,239
1815–17	4,992	1,916	6,908	2,086	8,994
1818–20	4,927	1,946	6,873	2,086	8,959
1821–23	5,924	1,725	7,649	2,094	9,743

The canal tolls can be split. The first column in the table that follows shows tolls taken at Agbrigg, and therefore on Aire & Calder traffic; the second at the Dearne & Dove junction; the third mainly at Barugh. Given that the Dearne & Dove traffic passed only a few miles on the Barnsley, though at a higher toll for coal than was charged between the junction and the Calder, the tonnage interchanged was considerable. Here are averaged figures:

Years	Agbrigg	D & D Junct.	Barugh etc.	Total
	£	£	£	£
1809–11	2,777	625	37	3,439
1812–14	4,590	1,203	15	5,808
1815–17	5,358	1,537	13	6,908
1818–20	5,024	1,838	11	6,873
1821–23	5,611	2,024	14	7,649

The company had one keel in 1807, and later bought two more. They sold three in 1823, however, and do not seem to have done any carrying thereafter.

The Barnsley Canal formed part of a transport system that extended from the Trent to Hull, the Yorkshire Ouse and over the Pennines. Therefore the pattern of carriage was exceptionally varied. Here are a few examples of cargoes carried, part-way at

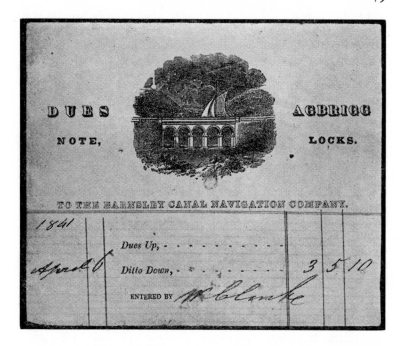

DUES NOTE, **AGBRIGG LOCKS.**

TO THE BARNSLEY CANAL NAVIGATION COMPANY.

1841

April 6

Dues Up, · · — · · — · · —

Ditto Down, - · ·. , · — · — · 3 5 10

ENTERED BY

17. Toll ticket issued at Agbrigg. Note the picture of the Barnsley aqueduct

any rate, by the company's own craft between 1809 and 1815: yarn from Leeds to Barnsley and the Dearne & Dove; oak bark from Worsbrough (Dearne & Dove) to Leeds and York; iron from Barnsley, Elsecar (Dearne & Dove) and Sheffield to Wakefield, Leeds, York, Rochdale and Manchester; ironstone and limestone to Elsecar; malt to Manchester; coal to Hull, Boroughbridge and Ripon; millstones to Leeds, York and Manchester.

The Barnsley company, always in need of water, often tried to divert some of that feeding the Dearne, though this was denied them by their Act. In 1803 the Don company had to 'request them to cause all the Waters which ought to run and flow into the River Dun, to be turned into their proper Channels, and that all Obstructions which have been made to turn those Waters into the Barnsley Canal be immediately removed'.[26] After hoping the Don would then forget about it, the Barnsley did the work. But a few years later they were diverting the Silkstone stream, and again had to be stopped, though the Don tried to make a bargain that if the coal toll down to the Dearne & Dove junction were reduced to 1d a ton/mile, they would not enforce their rights. But the Barnsley then wanted the money more, and eventually in 1812 the Don allowed them to have some surplus water. In 1820 the committee told Hartley to enlarge the Cold Hiendley engine, and in 1821 employed John Rennie to survey for an additional reservoir in the Silkstone valley, though this was never built.

In November 1819 the company were approached by the promoters of the Went & Wakefield Canal, a scheme for a line from the Barnsley Canal by way of the Went valley to the Dutch River (see p. 213). The promoters asked for permission to make a junction near Cold Hiendley reservoir. In turn, the Barnsley wanted to know whether the projectors would compensate them for loss of tolls on craft using the new canal instead of the Aire & Calder, and so travelling a shorter distance on the Barnsley, and for loss due to the competition of coal worked on the proposed line with that from Silkstone. The scheme got no further, being in practice superseded by the Aire & Calder's Goole Canal.

In October 1820 the company heard of a possible Dearne & Dove Bill for a railroad from Worsbrough bridge, at the end of the Dearne & Dove's branch, 'to Tomroyd [Wood] in Thurgoland', where there was coal-bearing land. Having told the Dearne & Dove that they and the Aire & Calder would oppose it, they sought support from landowners and dissident Dearne & Dove shareholders. At the same time they employed George Leather to survey for an extension of the Silkstone tramroad into the Worsbrough valley, or a new tramroad direct thence to the upper level of their canal. Rennie was also to be asked his opinion on these lines. He gave it, and reported that two tramroad routes were possible at a discouraging £8,000 or £9,000 a mile. He thought such a line essential if the Barnsley company were 'to preserve their present Tonnage in Coals' and forestall the Dearne & Dove's advance into the Stainborough valley, 'where it is said a very large quantity of Excellent Coal lyes unworked'.[27]

After abortive negotiations with the Dearne & Dove, the latter in 1821 gave notice of a Bill for making a railroad from Worsbrough bridge to Thurgoland and Oxspring bridge, and the Barnsley set about organizing opposition. Upon which the Dearne & Dove dropped the scheme, though about this time a 3¼-mile line was privately built from Worsbrough bridge on a rather more southerly line by Rockley to Top Pit Wood, with a branch to Pilley.[28] The Barnsley company do not seem to have regarded it as a threat. However, to make their active rivalry clear, in 1823 they resolved that a boat coming up the canal from Heath empty, loading between the junction lock and Barnby, and then going down the Dearne & Dove, should pay £1 as well as tolls; and an empty boat going straight to the Dearne & Dove, £2·25.

In November 1823, at the request of the Rochdale Canal Company, the latter were given a bonus of 6d (2½p) a ton (they had asked for 1s (5p)) upon 'all Grain and other Articles' shipped at Sheffield, Rotherham, etc., or coming from the Trent and passing into the Rochdale[29] or vice versa, therefore by way of the Dearne & Dove and the Barnsley.

In February 1823 Joseph Atkinson was appointed resident engineer in place of Hartley and, a year later when William Rooth the elderly accountant who had succeeded William Martin in 1797 was asked to retire on pension, chief clerk and book-keeper also. Atkinson was to have a new house, in which offices and a committee room were also to be provided. It was built at Sandal, and demolished in 1965.

The year 1826, later described as 'unprecedented', combined hard frost in January, which closed the canal, with a summer drought which hit the upper levels of the Dearne & Dove so badly that many coal vessels could only carry half cargoes from Silkstone, and were loading instead at Elsecar or Worsbrough. Because of the hot weather also, demand for coal was low, and 'a large proportion of the Coal Vessels are employed in the Lime Trade'.[30] From 2 March to 27 October the canal was supplied solely from the reservoir, until Atkinson the manager got the disused engine of Barnby colliery to work. This, and the use of lightening boats, enabled the canal to continue working until 2 December, when rain came. The engine was then kept as a stand-by.

Early in 1828 the Barnsley company supported the Aire & Calder's plans to rebuild the Calder line, on the undertaking that current tolls would not be raised in the Bill. In January and July Atkinson said he was raising and altering some bridges on the canal, and recommended raising the others, 'to enable that Description of Sea-going Vessels called Billy-boys to navigate up the Line', a type of craft that stood high when empty. He added that he thought many such craft would enter the trade to carry Silkstone coal coastwise.[31] A few months later he had died, to be succeeded by W. T. Hall, who took over the company's house after Mrs Atkinson had been recompensed for the water closet and the marble chimney piece she and her husband had installed. In January 1830 Hall announced that, bridge-raising being finished, 'all BILLY BOYS, COASTING and other VESSELS of not more than 14 Feet 10 Inches Beam, may now pass along the whole length of the Canal for Silkstone Coal, Merchandise, &c'.[32]

The year 1829 saw trade depression and so increased competition: the company had to cut tolls on malt, corn, coal and slack. The following year they suggested to the Aire & Calder that the two companies should reduce coal tolls on the trade to Goole. The Aire & Calder and Barnsley eventually agreed early in 1831 that each should give a drawback of one-third current canal and tramroad tolls on coal destined for the foreign and coastal trades. They found, however, that this was not enough to encourage the coalowners to begin such trades, and decided to increase the allowance; in 1832 coal used by steam vessels was also given the drawback.

Oddly, the first time national railway schemes touched the Barnsley, in 1831, the projects were for horse tramroads. Mr Skelton of Middlewood Hall near Sheffield wrote about schemes for a horse line from the Peak Forest Canal to Sheffield via Penistone, and a 'Canals Junction Horse Railway' from the heads of the Barnsley and Dearne & Dove Canals to the Peak Forest at Marple, 'with a Branch into Stephenson's Railway from Manchester to Sheffield'. These did not excite the committee, though Hall was asked to look at the plans and report. A few months later at Skelton's request they sent representatives to meet the Peak Forest and Ashton-under-Lyne Canal companies at Woodhead to discuss 'a proposed Horse Junction Railway on Telford's Line to connect with these Canals'.[33] In this year also Hall was employed in surveying for a canal eastwards towards Goole—perhaps a precaution in the light of the Sheffield to Goole railway via Doncaster that had been promoted in the autumn of 1830 (see p. 217). It may be that this survey was to see whether such a line to the Goole Canal might make the Heck & Wentbridge Railway (see p. 167) worth buying. They decided it was not, then in 1834 inquired the price, and afterwards took the matter no further.

In 1831 Thomas Foljambe, clerk of the Barnsley, wrote to the Don to ask whether they had any objections to the company building without Parliamentary powers a new reservoir in Banks valley near Silkstone, as Rennie had earlier recommended, to be supplied by a stream in which the Don had an interest under the 1793 Act. The Don replied that they would like 'a clear understanding respecting the priviledges the Barnsley Canal Company now enjoy from the Silkstone Water as it is understood that the Barnsley Canal Company give greater Advantages to Vessels proceeding down to Agbrigg* than those to the junction of the Dearne & Dove'.[34] The company replied denying any preference, and offering a small annual payment for 'the privilege of taking the Silkstone Water which would not injure this Company'.[35] In 1837 the town of Barnsley itself promoted a Bill to supply the town with water using some of the streams that supplied the Don. However, protective clauses were agreed. Then, once again, in 1841, the Don and Barnsley companies exchanged letters about the Silkstone and other streams that were being diverted to the canal, until the Barnsley agreed to pay an acknowledgement.

Railways were now taking much of the company's attention; it may have been the promotion of the North Midland line which made the committee in July 1835 reduce the charge for empty craft from Wakefield going through to the Dearne & Dove from £2·25 to £1·50. A few months later they were opposing that railway's Bill in order to force railway bridge dimensions over their canal equal to those on the Goole Canal in case they wished later to enlarge it. In September 1836 they ordered that their canal depth should be increased forthwith to 7 ft by raising the banks and lock-walls. The Cold Hiendley reservoir embankment was also raised to increase its capacity, and in 1839 the company decided the reservoir should be extended if reasonably-priced land could be got.

They were doing well, paying £13 per £160 share dividend (8⅛ per cent), and hoping to keep it that way. In 1837 their toll revenue reached its peak of £16,687, £13,688 from the canal and £2,999 from the tramroads. It was to remain much the same until 1840, and then start to fall, at first slowly, then increasingly fast.

The North Midland Railway opened from Derby to Leeds in 1840, but in June 1838 Clarke of Silkstone's agent wrote asking for a cut of 2d per ton on the tramroad tolls 'as Mr Clarke expected soon to be the only person using the railway when his opponents would be placed in a more favourable situation, and he should want some assistance from the company by a reduction

* The toll-office at the Calder end of the canal.

of dues on the road to enable him to lower the price of coal in order to promote his trade'.[36]

In 1838 the committee decided to buy two canal shares if they could be got at not more than £280 each (against the nominal £160), as a few other canal companies were rather short-sightedly doing about the same time. They bought them, I do not know at what price. At the end of January 1840 the coal drawback on sea-going coal and for use in steamers was withdrawn, but the Dearne & Dove stepped in to capture the trade. The drawback was therefore reinstated in August 1841. In March 1842, unusually, navigation and railway companies—the Aire & Calder, Barnsley and Dearne & Dove, the Manchester & Leeds and the Sheffield & Rotherham Railway—met to oppose a projected railway connection from the line at Penistone to the North Midland in Felkirk, promoted by the Sheffield, Ashton-under-Lyne & Manchester Railway, on the grounds that 'such project would be injurious to the existing Lines and ought to be opposed'.[37]

By July 1842 competition of railways in the coal trade was increasing. The one that then affected the Barnsley most was the Great North of England Railway from Darlington to York, opened at the beginning of 1841. By it 'a considerable quantity of Coal has been sent into the neighbourhood of Ripon, Boro'-bridge, York etc which was formerly supplied by Mr. Clarke's Silkstone Coal to the extent of about Fifty thousand Tons per Annum'.[38] Coal tolls were maintained for the time being, but at the end of 1842 those on burnt lime were cut from $1\frac{1}{8}$d to $\frac{1}{2}$d 'when the vessel carrying the Lime shall return loaded with Coal'.[39]

Here are average toll figures:

Years	Canal tolls £	Tramroad tolls £	Total tolls £
1824–26	9,978	2,172	12,150
1827–29*	10,323	2,174	12,497
1830–32	10,737	2,483	13,220
1833–35	10,375	2,638	13,013
1836–38	12,460	2,813	15,273
1839–41	13,239	2,811	16,050
1842–44	11,248	2,111	13,359

* 1827 and 1828 only.

The dividend for 1842 had to be dropped from £14 to £12 per £160 share, and in his report in July the company's manager, W. T. Hall, told shareholders of 'the depressed State of trade in the country' and the competition in coal being experienced from the Great North of England Railway. Early in 1844 the company met the Aire & Calder to discuss what to do to meet a cut in charges recently made by the G.N.E.R. and the Durham colliery owners, which produced a railway rate of $\frac{1}{4}$d a mile, but failed to agree on cuts to be made. Meanwhile, the coal tonnage sent to York and the upper Ouse continued to fall.

Back in March 1842 we saw the canal company allying themselves with the Manchester & Leeds Railway and others to oppose a railway from Penistone to the North Midland. This scheme came up again in December 1842; then, the following autumn, the Barnsley company had some idea of making a Silkstone–Penistone line. Early in 1844 they agreed to oppose what had now become the Barnsley Junction project, from the Sheffield, Ashton-under-Lyne & Manchester Railway at Penistone (later Oxspring) to the North Midland near Royston. They were backed in this by the Manchester & Leeds Railway. Then, in February 1845, the Manchester & Leeds said they had decided to give up their opposition to the Barnsley Junction and offered to refund the canal company's expenses of opposition. The latter then sought to agree protective clauses. In March the railway refused these, and the canal company then decided to petition against the Bill. In April they agreed with the Manchester & Leeds jointly to oppose the Bill, and also, should the Barnsley Junction not be made, to seek a Bill themselves for a Penistone–Silkstone railway according to plans already deposited. In April they gave a drawback of $1\frac{1}{2}$d a ton per mile on coal on the Silkstone tramroad.

The company were now heavily involved in the railway mania, in May assenting to the Wakefield, Pontefract & Goole Railway Bill, a move that cannot have endeared them to the Aire & Calder, and sending a deputation to meet the Huddersfield & Sheffield Junction promoters to discuss a branch from the Silkstone tramroad—when the Don Navigation stepped in. The Wakefield, Pontefract & Goole project was heavily supported by the Manchester & Leeds Railway, and the Barnsley company's friendliness with this company may have been a motive with them.

Representatives of the Barnsley and Don companies met in May 1845, and quickly came to the agreement dated 31 May. The Don were to lease the Barnsley Canal for a year from 1 June at £12 per share (except on the two the company owned) or £8,616, the rental to be paid in two half-yearly instalments. Then,

M

on 1 June 1846, the Don would buy the Barnsley for £240 a share on 718 shares or £172,320, settle some minor debts, and give a golden handshake of five years' salary to the Barnsley's officers. The Don's motive was to prevent Silkstone coal supplies from falling into railway hands. The provisional agreement made—it was ratified by the Barnsley shareholders in November—the Don immediately offered to transfer the Barnsley to the Aire & Calder and themselves acquire the Dearne & Dove, so safeguarding both water outlets from the coalfield.[40] In August the Aire & Calder stockholders agreed to buy the Barnsley for up to £185,000 if agreement could be reached. However, they stipulated for the right to withdraw the necessary authorizing Bill 'in case any limitation of their present powers should be introduced in its progress through Parliament',[41] this presumably because Lord Shaftesbury had been prominent in Lords committees in trying to remove old rating and other privileges as the price of granting canal companies new powers. The Don broke off negotiations, alleging this stipulation would leave them uncertain for too long, but probably also because they had begun to negotiate with the promoters of the South Yorkshire Coal Railway, itself planned to give rail access to the Barnsley coalfield. In September the Aire & Calder commissioned a survey for a railway or canal from the Barnsley coalfield direct to Goole, at the discretion of the same sub-committee that was negotiating with the Barnsley and Don companies, perhaps as a hint that there was an alternative to purchase. By October the Don had agreed to acquire the Dearne & Dove, proposing to bring both canals into the amalgamation they were now arranging with the projected South Yorkshire Railway. This, of course, threatened to remove all Barnsley coal from the Aire & Calder, and led that company strenuously to oppose the resultant Bill. However, a special general meeting of Barnsley shareholders in November 1845 were quite prepared to stick to the agreement with the Don, and arrangements were made for the first instalment of rent to be paid out of cash already in the Barnsley company's hands.

In January 1846 the Don, foreseeing that the amalgamation Bill would not pass, and now regarding their agreement to acquire the Barnsley as being firmly linked to their own agreement with the South Yorkshire promoters, wrote that they did not consider the leasing agreement made the previous May was valid, because the Barnsley company were not empowered to lease. They also thought that to complete the purchase on 1 June 'would be attended with great if not insuperable difficulties', and suggested instead a three or five years lease followed by purchase,[42] for which they intended to seek powers. One gets the impression that the Don were trying to back out of an exposed position, fearing that the Coal Railway Bill would fail, and that they could not quickly raise the purchase money. However, the Barnsley company still kept firm, offering a lease either for one or twenty-one years from 1 June 1846, subject to an Act to authorize sale.

The Don, driven into a corner, rejected the lease offers, whereupon the Barnsley notified them that they considered the original agreement to be in force—that is, they expected the purchase to be completed on 1 June. This gave the Aire & Calder their chance. With much moral indignation they pointed out that on the Barnsley Canal higher tolls were charged on one part than another;* that anyway the tolls on coal were too high and should be reduced to $\frac{1}{2}$d a ton as on other navigations in the public interest, and therefore that the meeting would 'oppose by every means in its power the Amalgamation of the Barnsley Canal with the South Yorkshire Railway Company in order that the Interest of the Public may not be thereby sacrificed'.[43]

In early July the Barnsley company approached the Aire & Calder about a possible sale. The latter told them to get clear of the Don first. Since the South Yorkshire Bill had failed in Parliament, and the future of its successor was unknown, the Don were agreeable, and late in July concurred in considering the agreement at an end. Rather annoyingly, the Barnsley company told them that their 1808 Act did, in fact, contain powers to lease for up to 21 years, which suggests that the Don's clerk had earlier not done his homework properly. Therefore, early in August the Barnsley were once more open to an Aire & Calder offer and were asked what terms they suggested. They replied asking what the Don had offered. Thereupon the Aire & Calder said there was no prospect that they would offer so much, and emphasized the point by refusing a Barnsley offer to cut coal tolls on cargoes for York and the Derwent if they would do the same.

The Aire & Calder came back with the offer of a lease for seven years at £10 a share, or £7,200 p.a., with the option of a further seven at £8,000, subject to the Barnsley losing none of its sources of water during the lease, and to any improvements made by the Aire &

---

* Higher between Barnsley and the junction than thence to Agbrigg; this gave Elsecar and Worsbrough coal a competitive advantage at Goole and eastwards over that from Silkstone.

Calder during the lease being paid for at the end. The Barnsley company rejected both the water clause and the proposed length of lease—presumably they wanted 21 years—whereupon the Aire & Calder broke off talks, and for the time being the Barnsley remained independent in a dangerous world.

Here is the company's dividend record, averaged in three-year periods:

Years*	Dividends per £160 share				Dividends per cent
	£	s	d		
1809–11	2	0	0		1·25
1812–14	5	6	8	(£5·33½)	3·33
1815–17	7	0	0		4·38
1818–20	8	0	0		5
1821–23	10	13	4	(£10·66½)	6·67
1824–26	14	0	0		8·75
1827–29	13	0	0		8·125
1830–32	11	6	8	(£11·33½)	7·08
1833–35	12	16	8	(£12·83½)	8·02
1836–38	13	10	0	(£13·50)	8·44
1839–41	14	0	0		8·75
1842–44	11	13	4	(£11·66½)	7·29

* Year ending 30 November.

CHAPTER IX

The Calder & Hebble

✦✦✦✦✦✦✦✦✦✦✦✦✦✦✦✦✦✦✦✦✦✦✦✦✦✦✦✦✦✦◆✦✦✦✦✦✦✦✦✦✦✦✦✦✦✦✦✦✦✦✦✦✦✦✦✦✦✦✦✦✦

WITH Acts passed for the Rochdale and the Huddersfield Canals, the Calder & Hebble's prospects, already good, seemed even better. By 1796 business justified a bigger warehouse at Salterhebble, and substantial pay increases to the Fall Ing toll-collector and the Cooper Bridge lock-keeper; in 1797 a new warehouse was built at Sowerby Bridge. Capital improvements went steadily on, these always being paid for by making small calls (not, however, compulsory) on shares and not out of revenue. This policy, followed in order to increase shareholders' income without exceeding the legal 10 per cent dividend, meant that between 1782 and 1799 calls of 27 per cent had been authorized, each, of course, on capital enlarged by previous calls. Dividends were also being paid on a steadily increasing total. A specially important improvement was the building of the extensive Thornhill Cut about 1798: this replaced the old line of navigation through Dewsbury.

As the opening date approached for the first part of the Rochdale Canal—it was opened from Sowerby Bridge to Todmorden on 24 August 1798 and through to Rochdale on 21 December—the company became concerned lest there would not be enough boats to carry the traffic. In February 1798 they wrote to the Aire & Calder to ask whether 'a sufficient Number of Boats to take down regularly, all Goods that shall come to the Company's Warehouses at Salterhebble and Sowerby'[1] would be made available. They also pressed ahead with increasing wharfage, stable and warehouse accommodation at Sowerby Bridge for carriers and the Rochdale company. Important upwards traffics going west were timber and corn, with textiles downwards.

By the end of 1799 business was good enough for the company to decide 'That a Table of Rates be formed agreeable to the Clause . . . of the Act, for regulating the Dividends, and stating the proportionate Reduction to be made in the Rates, when the

Dividends exceed 10 per cent'.[2] Tolls were therefore reduced from the beginning of 1801. It was a time also when the old customary weights and measures were causing increasing fraud: in coal the former practice of measuring coal by counting so many waggons to the ton was superseded when the committee ordered all waybills to show the tonnages as well as the variable waggon loads and in 1815 stone began to be charged by weight and not measurement.

On 21 December 1804 the Rochdale Canal was opened through to Manchester. This and another toll-cut from the beginning of 1804 further increased business. A new station was opened that year at Elland, to supplement those at Sowerby Bridge, Salterhebble, Cooper Bridge, Horbury bridge and Wakefield; the main toll-collecting point being Fall Ing lock. A new office for the company at Halifax was ordered to be ready in 1805 at a cost of £1,000. In 1805, too, they put in a weighing machine at Sowerby Bridge to check cargoes suspected of being overweight. So many were found that three years later they used the powers of their Act to compel gauging marks to be put on boats, and built a gauging dock at Horbury bridge where the marking could be done. Between 1805 and 1808 a new cut and lock were made at Brookfoot near Brighouse, and at the beginning of 1808 there was another toll reduction. In 1815 the upper cut at Elland was extended to link with the Sowerby cut.

Trade between Leeds and points east of Sowerby Bridge tended to pass by road from Salterhebble to Leeds, rather than go round by the Aire & Calder. In 1810 Job Cogswell, a carrier between Liverpool, Manchester and Sowerby Bridge, suggested that he should extend his carrying down to Wakefield. He was encouraged, in the hope that the overland trade would move from Salterhebble to Wakefield. However, he did not seem 'equal to the Undertaking',[3] and a few months later the company's support was transferred to Thomas Knott & Co, running contract boats between Liverpool and Salterhebble, who agreed to extend their service to Wakefield with the same object.

In 1811 the company got involved in a tremendous legal threat. It began in 1806 with a suggestion from the Aire & Calder that a new cut and pair of locks having falls of 5 ft and 4 ft 6 in. should be built in a better position than the existing Fall Ing single 9 ft 6 in. lock and cut higher up the river. The Aire & Calder offered to pay half the cost on condition that they could build wharves and warehouses at Fall Ing, access to which would be toll-free. Then in early 1808, having made an agreement with the Aire & Calder, our company were offered, and refused, Sir Thomas Pilkington's soke corn mills at Wakefield. Having done so, they began to buy land for the new cut, at the same time, quite unrelatedly, preparing a Bill to amend and modernize their powers.

The first hint of trouble was a notification from their Parliamentary agents that a 'violent opposition from the Town of Wakefield and other Places is making',[4] whereupon they withdrew it. After consulting the Aire & Calder, and concluding that the agreement they had made was doubtfully legal, they cancelled that too, and told Bradley their engineer to start forthwith on the new works. Whereupon Pilkington (whose lawyer was John Lee, arch-enemy of the Aire & Calder, keen to get money out of the navigation's pockets and into his client's and his own) got an injunction against them on the ostensible grounds that the water supply to his mills would be diminished, though the real motive was probably to compel the company to buy the mills. Jessop, called post-haste from Butterley, was consulted, and negotiations begun with Lee. However, like the Aire & Calder, the Calder & Hebble found he was not a man one could negotiate with. They therefore counter-attacked Pilkington for taking more mill-water than his legal entitlement. He then gave up, and soon afterwards died, but Lee came back to the battle, now representing another property owner near Fall Ing. Much legal huffing and puffing followed, but steadiness paid off, and nothing happened. The cut and pair of locks were opened in 1812, the Aire & Calder working their traffic through at special rates.

Bradley, who had built the new Fall Ing works, was a very respected engineer. He had been taken on in December 1792 at £105 p.a. By 1803 he was earning £400 p.a. and receiving donations from time to time, and in 1819 the company gave him £500 cash 'as some remuneration for his past long and valuable Services', added £100 p.a. to his salary, and promised him a pension of £200 p.a. when he retired.

As on all river navigations, the rights of millers conflicted with the needs of navigation, and often the only solution was to buy the mills. It was reported, for instance, in June 1814 that the owner of Hall mills, Mirfield, had rebuilt them to use more water. The company's engineer was sent to negotiate, but he got no satisfaction. They then went to law, after which less water was taken. They suspended the lawsuit, and the millowner in 1818 thereupon offered the mills for £18,000; they agreed to take them

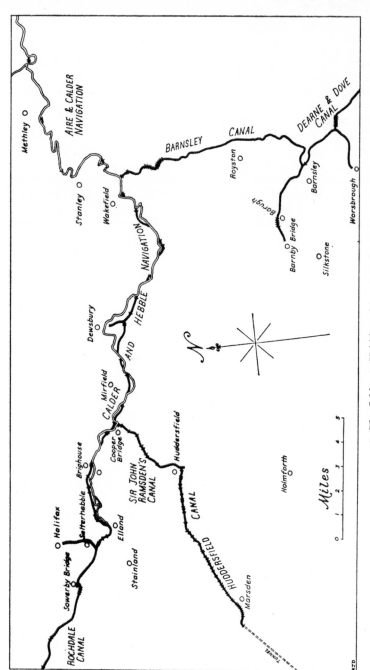

18. The Calder & Hebble and its connexions

at £16,000 (they were subsequently let at £890 p.a.). Meanwhile, in 1816 they had bought the lower mills at Brighouse for £4,500. On the other hand, mills had to be allowed adequate water. When there was 'no more Water in the River than the Mills can Work, without drawing their Dams below the Crown of the Weirs', craft were not to pass drawing more than 3 ft 10 in. in below Horbury bridge, or 3 ft 8 in. above, the company ruled in 1819.[5] Craft going aground then became a problem. In 1823 they decided that 'persons be appointed to perambulate the Line to give Information when Vessels overload so as to obstruct the Navigation'.[6] Later, of course, many mills closed down owing to foreign competition, others went over to steam, and pressure eased.

The opening of the Rochdale Canal and the growth of Manchester's population combined to attract the corn trade of Lincolnshire. In 1817 the Calder & Hebble were asked to give a 2s (10p) drawback on corn from the Trent going to Manchester, to enable the Calder–Rochdale line to undercut that by the Trent & Mersey Canal. It does not seem it was then given, but all the same the route developed as a main supplier of Manchester's corn. In 1825 a corn warehouse at Wakefield was enlarged 'for the Accommodation of the Rochdale Canal Co or the Carriers they are about to establish for the Increase of Trade from the Trent, etc.'.[7] In 1823, also, the Rochdale and Calder & Hebble companies consulted upon how best to attract the very large malt trade from the Trent area north of Newark to their canals and away from the Trent & Mersey. Since that company and the Bridgewater trustees[8] already gave drawbacks, the answer must lie in bigger ones, to which both companies agreed, as they did also to similar encouragements for Sheffield–Manchester traffic.

Business continued good. In 1816 the company ordered Wakefield warehouses to be enlarged and extended. They also paid special attention to efficient dredging, sending Bradley to inspect the Thames and the Trent to see how good their dredgers were, and to meet the engineer Bryan Donkin in London. Donkin had already sent them a plan for a dredger, presumably the one they ordered from him in 1817. Short narrow boats coming off the Huddersfield Canal were not welcomed, because they were extravagant in water if they moved singly, and because of the damage done 'by the Prows or Stems of the numerous Narrow Boats now used upon the Navigation', as they said in 1816 when passing a bye-law.[9]

Calder and Hebble Navigation Office.

HALIFAX, April 10th, 1816.

Pardon Asked.

WHEREAS

I John Crabtree,

Of KNOTTINGLEY, in the County of York, Waterman,

Did on Saturday the 6th Day of April Instant, wantonly and unlawfully break and destroy the Lock or Fastening belonging to the Lock-Gates at Fall-Ing, near Wakefield, in the said County, upon the Line of the Calder and Hebble Navigation, and the Proprietors of the said Navigation have threatened to prosecute me for such Offence as the Law directs, but having expressed my hearty Contrition for such unjustifiable Conduct, they have shewn their Clemency toward me on my agreeing to make a public Acknowledgement of my Error, and to be at the Expence of publishing the same upon the Line of the said Navigation.

Now I the said John Crabtree

Do hereby humbly ask Pardon of the said Company of Proprietors of the Calder and Hebble Navigation for such my wanton and unjustifiable Conduct; do acknowledge their Clemency extended toward me in this respect, and faithfully and sincerely promise never again to be guilty of the like or any other Offence upon the Line of the said Navigation.

As Witness my Hand the Date above written.

HIS

John ✕ *Crabtree.*

MARK.

Witness,

John Bentley.

Printed at Jacobs Office, near the New-Market Halifax.

19. The Calder & Hebble makes an example of John Crabtree

A steady programme of small improvements went on: bettering the towing path, establishing more lock-keepers, raising bridges, building coal staiths, and in 1823 deciding to extend Broad Cut. Another sign of busyness was a request from E. & J. Thompson, the carriers, in 1821, that their craft running between Manchester and Hull might pass on Sundays 'in consequence of the increasing Dispatch with which Goods are sent from Manchester to Leeds by land and thence Per Fly Boats & Steam Vessels to Hull'. However, the committee replied that they 'cannot under present Circumstances consent to so great a Deviation from established Custom'.[10] However, in 1823 they agreed that bale or fly-boats could be given passes to move at any time on weekdays. Two years later the Rochdale & Halifax Merchants' Co started a Manchester–Wakefield fly-boat service. The Rochdale–Calder line was indeed doing so well that in December 1824 the Huddersfield Canal company decided to seek a toll reduction from Sir John Ramsden to enable his and their lines to compete.

At the annual general meeting in June 1824, the company considered the important Halifax trade in wool and corn inwards, and cloth outwards, especially to Hull and London. Some, travelling west, was put on canal at Sowerby Bridge instead of Salterhebble, so losing tolls, or going east, went by land. The company therefore decided to build a branch canal from Salterhebble to Halifax, which Bradley had estimated at £34,533. An Act[11] was passed in 1825, authorizing £50,000 to be raised in shares or loans. It also removed the dividend restriction, but, thanks to Aire & Calder and Rochdale pressure, established much lower tolls than those of the 1769 Act, and somewhat lower than those currently charged. The Aire & Calder were exempted from tolls at the Calder & Hebble's first lock for goods delivered or loaded at their wharves at Fall Ing. The new rates came into force on 1 June 1825, and in the same year a bonus equal to 5 per cent on capital was distributed to shareholders from balances to help them pay the 15 per cent call necessary for the new branch, and a number of wage and salary increases were also given. With the passing of the 1825 Act, the practice of increasing the capital by calls ended.

In February 1827 the Calder & Hebble bravely decided to petition in support of the proposed Wakefield & Ferrybridge Canal (see p. 145), or 'any Measure by which a cheaper, more speedy and certain Communication can be obtained with . . . Hull and particularly . . . the Trent'.[12] With others, they gave

PUBLIC
BALL.

The Company of Proprietors of the Calder and Hebble Navigation will give a

PublicBall

In the New Assembly Rooms,

On FRIDAY the 28th inst.

IN CELEBRATION OF THE

OPENING

OF THE

BranchCanal,

To the Town of Halifax.

Mrs. Waterhouse, Patroness.

Dancing to commence at Eight o'Clock.

Tickets of admission may be had *on or before Monday the* 24th *instant*, at Mr. Whitley's, Bookseller, Halifax, at 5s. each, the Produce of which (without deduction) will be paid over to the Trustees of the

HALIFAX GENERAL DISPENSARY.

N. B. Carriages to set down with the Horses' Heads towards Barum Top, and to take up the contrary way.

Halifax, 15th March, 1828.

N. WHITLEY, PRINTER, CROWN STREET, HALIFAX.

20. The Calder & Hebble celebrates the opening of the Halifax branch

the Aire & Calder a severe Parliamentary fright. In early 1828, again, they petitioned against the Aire & Calder's proposed tolls on their planned improved line between Wakefield and Castleford, and again in favour of the Wakefield & Ferrybridge Canal, 'being of Opinion . . . that . . . the Wakefield & Ferrybridge Canal Co is entitled to a decided Preference as securing a more efficient Navigation, independent of the advantage to be afforded by a lower scale of Rates than that proposed by the Aire & Calder Company'.[13]

Meanwhile, the Halifax branch, which Bradley had been building, was ordered to be ceremonially opened on Friday, 28 March 1828, by the company's committee boat the *Savile*,* followed by one or two coasting vessels and then by some trading sloops. There would be a public ball in the evening at the new Assembly Rooms and a supper for the contractors and workmen, each of the 160 or so men to have an allowance of 2s 6d (12½p) and each 'Master & Contractor', about 35 of them, to have 7s 6d (37½p). The branch was 1¾ miles long, rising 100½ ft by 14 locks to Halifax basin. Water for the summit level was provided by a steam engine,† built by the Low Moor company, pumping from Salterhebble basin by means of a horizontal tunnel 1,170 yds long. A mileage toll double that on most of the main line was authorized for the branch because of its high cost,‡ and short length. Expenditure on the branch had been £58,741.[15] Most of this had been raised from shareholders or from revenue, but some £20,000 was borrowed—the first loans the Calder & Hebble had raised. Two years later, 'Halifax contract boats' were running from Huddersfield, presumably with Manchester goods brought on the Huddersfield Canal.[16] One result of the branch was to substitute coal from mines between Wakefield and Kirklees for local coal with its higher road carriage charges in the Halifax market.[17]

Soon after the branch opening, their engineer reported that the Aire & Calder's improvement plans were 'practicable & would be decidedly advantageous to the Calder & Hebble Navigation'.[18] This enabled the company to get out of its commitment to the projected rival canal by putting the argument on a toll basis

* The original Savile had been rebuilt in 1801; she was replaced by a new one in 1825.

† '. . . a steam-engine on an eminence a little more than halfway between the two extreme points. A shaft is here sunk one hundred and nine feet deep, to the bottom of which a tunnel brings the water from the . . . Canal; it is then raised by the engine to the upper level, whence another aqueduct carries it to the canal-basin in the town'.[14]

‡ In 1893 pumping costs alone were put at £600 p.a.

alone. Their representatives therefore negotiated to get these down to those proposed by the Wakefield & Ferrybridge promoters, 'or as near thereto as may be'. However, the Aire & Calder stuck to their proposals, and squeezed them through the Parliamentary committee by 15 votes to 11. Afterwards, in response to an inquiry, the Calder & Hebble said the cost of their navigation had been upwards of £275,000, of which an average of £10,200 a year had been spent in the previous ten years—this, of course, includes the Halifax branch. Share capital was approximately £160,000. Calder & Hebble stock had proved a good investment: James Lister's £1,542 nominal was in 1826 valued at £7,092.[19] Maintenance was given as some £9,600 p.a., while Priestley gives takings as about £40,000 p.a. About 1830 he described the navigation's traffic as agricultural lime 'to fertilize a sterile and mountainous district', stone, flagstones for London and elsewhere from the quarries on opposite sides of the river at Cromwell Bottom and Elland Edge (where there were wharves), ironstone and coal.

Heavy competition, with each other and with road transport, was now developing on the three canal routes to Manchester, by the Rochdale, Huddersfield or Trent & Mersey Canals. Late in 1829 a Huddersfield Canal deputation came 'to represent the necessity of every limitation being removed as to the hours during which Vessels may be allowed to pass upon this Navigation, either by night or day',[20] with support from Hull and Manchester timber merchants. The Calder & Hebble gave a drawback on timber, agreed to open the navigation at 5 a.m. all the year round, and to allow bale goods and other craft 'on urgent occasions' to pass at any time, but were adamant on Sunday closing. One result was a £30 p.a. rise for the clerk at Cooper Bridge, junction for the Huddersfield line, 'in consideration of the extra night work imposed upon that Station'.[21]

Railways, a still worse potential source of competition, first seriously invade the company's minute books in November 1830, when, after letters had been received from the Huddersfield and Rochdale Canal companies, they agreed to attend a meeting with them 'on the subject of the proposed Railways'.[22] It seems to have been unconstructive. Two months later they sent two officers to London to oppose a Bill for the Leeds & Quarry Gap Railway,*

* The Manchester & Leeds. Originally it was to end at Quarry Gap near Pudsey, where it would join a Bradford–Leeds line which in turn would connect with the Leeds & Selby Railway.

which would, they considered, 'occupy or destroy the whole of Elland Wharf, Warehouse and Houses, and also materially injure the Company's Property at Salterhebble & other Places'.[23] In Parliament the line was shortened to end at Sowerby Bridge, but nevertheless the company continued to oppose, reckoning 'that if the road be made to that point it must be continued down the Calder valley as first intended'.[24] The Bill was, however, defeated.

One consequential was a deputation, this time from the Rochdale company, asking for Sunday opening of the Calder & Hebble for fly-boats (as on the Rochdale), Sunday access to the Sowerby Bridge warehouses, and previous notice of any stoppages for repairs, so that carriers could be warned. The Calder & Hebble agreed to the last two points, but maintained 'that no sufficient argument has been offered to show the necessity of relaxing in the strict prohibition of Vessels passing on the Line during Sundays'.[25] Fly-boats now became frequent enough for a new bye-law of 1834 to establish their precedence.

During 1832 the company at Bryan Donkin's recommendation took on William Gravatt as engineer, nominally under Bradley, now in poor health. However, he could not control the men, and after some months had to be paid off in spite of 'Talents unquestionably of a superior Order', in favour of someone 'of more experience in the management of Workmen in this part of the Country'.[26] He was replaced in May 1833 by William Bull, who lost no time in proposing improvements costing £60,000. The Aire & Calder, had, since their 1828 Act, been rebuilding their whole Calder line. Probably with this in mind, a special meeting in October 1833 agreed that the Calder & Hebble's line needed improvement past Horbury, between Broad Cut and Figure of Three locks. As, however, this would require an Act, the committee thought 'the new powers should extend, to all parts of the Line where Canals can be advantageously substituted for River Navigation'.[27] A shareholders' meeting then decided to divert the line at Horbury bridge under existing powers, and to go to Parliament for authority to improve the current situation by which there were nine cuts of varying lengths between the Aire & Calder and that at Brighouse which was then continuous to Sowerby Bridge. The improvements they thought most important were (a) a cut from Portobello above Wakefield, by-passing Thornes cut and running to Broad cut, Horbury; (b) a cut from the head of Broad cut to Thornhill Lees cut just above Figure of Three locks; (c) a cut from the head of Thornhill Lees cut across the Calder on a four-arched masonry aqueduct to join the Ledgard Bridge cut at Mirfield. Less important were cuts from above Fall Ing locks to Portobello, and from the end of Ledgard Bridge cut to the Brighouse cut.

Before they went to Parliament, however, the company modified their ideas, minuting that

'although it was the original Intention of the Company to abandon the use of the River in those Parts where the new Cuts are intended to be made, yet it now appears that the keeping open of the River for the use of Mill owners & others whose Property adjoins it is indispensable'.[28]

An ambitious Act[29] was passed in 1834, which authorized improvement as far up as Mirfield as a first stage of improvement through to Brighouse. H. R. Palmer the engineer was then asked to report,[30] and suggested larger-scale cuts at a total cost of £83,403 than the committee thought wise; a special shareholders' meeting in December agreed that the new canals should be 7 ft deep and 50 ft wide, with bridges giving a 26-ft waterway width, and parallel pairs of locks each capable of being used as a side pond to the other. These were to be about 70 ft × 18 ft 6 in., and therefore congruous with those of the Aire & Calder and in length also the Huddersfield, though the 58 ft × 14 ft locks of Ramsden's would still intervene. The Huddersfield company had in April sent a delegation to the Calder & Hebble 'to represent to them the propriety of building their locks suitable for the passing of long Boats'.[31] The committee were authorized to borrow £50,000 towards the cost.

Early in 1835, foreshadowing a possible revival of the Manchester & Leeds Railway scheme, representatives of the Aire & Calder, Rochdale, Ashton, Huddersfield and Calder & Hebble met at the last-named's office at Halifax to discuss reducing tolls on bales of woollen and cotton manufactures between Manchester & Hull. The Aire & Calder had just made cuts that would reduce the overall rate by 2s (10p) a ton on both routes by Huddersfield or Rochdale. The salt toll was also reduced, and timber drawbacks to the Rochdale Canal extended. But again Sunday working was refused. This time the Rochdale company showed its impatience by supporting a boatman who appealed against conviction for having broken the chain at Sowerby Bridge on Sunday. The Calder & Hebble reacted by a new bye-law early in 1836 firmly closing their navigation and all its establishments for the 24 hours of Sunday, 'to afford protection to the due observance of the

Verses on the untimely end of John Fletcher
who was unfortunately precipitated into the
canal at Salterhebble. on the 22nd. of October
1843

O pensive muse take up thy pen.
A painful story write.
Another from the sons of men
Has ta'en his final flight.

Grim death has snatch'd a friend away.
Whose fate we now deplore.
And we are all compell'd to say.
John Fletcher is no more.

The fading scenes of autumn now
Speak the declining year.
The season lays its thousands low
And comrades disappear.

But he whose end we now bewail.
Sank not by autumn's blast.
More sudden foes did him assail.
One moment seal'd his last.

In the dark silence of the night.
He trod on dangerous ground.
And thus. before the morning light.
A watery death. bed found.

21. A sampler remains as John Fletcher's monument

Sabbath'.[32] On the other hand, whereas the navigation had formerly been closed daily from 9 p.m. to 5 a.m. in the summer, and 8 p.m. to 7 a.m. from November to February, it was now opened for transit round the clock, with wharves and warehouses open from 5 a.m. to 9 p.m. in summer, 7 a.m. to 6 p.m. in winter.
N

In October 1835 the company minuted that 'Fearnley & Sons of Dewsbury may have the use of one of the Dredging Boats for the purpose of making the Communication between their Mill Canal & the River'.[33] By 'Mill Canal' was probably meant a mill goit that had been enlarged to make it navigable.

At Horbury a new cut was made from the tail of the old Broad cut, then abandoned, straight to Figure of Three locks, so by-passing the stretches of navigation past Horbury bridge. Two new large locks (Broad cut Upper and Lower) were built, and a smaller one on a side-cut provided back into the river just above Horbury bridge. At Thornes, next above Fall Ing, a larger lock was built alongside the older one.

Early in 1836 a deputation of smiling tigers, including George Stephenson, arrived from the promoters of a new Manchester & Leeds Railway Bill. They offered good clearances for bridges, and no interference with the navigation's access to 'Fields of Coal or other Minerals', by 'making Arches under the Railway so as to give every facility of access to the Navigation for the shipment of such Materials'.[34] In spite of the blandishments, the Calder & Hebble decided to dissent.

Immediately afterwards, the Aire & Calder and Rochdale asked the Calder & Hebble to join them in joint opposition to all local railways. Our company, however, was lukewarm towards this proposal, preferring only to oppose what directly affected its own interests in the prospective Manchester & Leeds Bill and that for a Leeds–Huddersfield line. However, the policy of friendliness did not get far. Conscientious effort to get the railway company to accept a line agreeable to the three waterway companies in exchange for an unopposed Bill in 1837 met with flat rejection. All the company got were the usual clauses governing crossings. In January 1838 a deputation from the town of Halifax asked the Manchester & Leeds company to build them a branch from the railway at Salterhebble, but the railway postponed the idea because of the difficult gradient problem, though they decided then to seek powers.[35]

The new works at Horbury were opened in June 1838, when '2s 6d per Head be allowed to the Company's Carpenters, Smiths and Labourers, as a treat on the opening'.[36] They were almost all that was done. The stretch above Fall Ing to above Figure of Three now had locks 67 ft 6 in. long or more, and 18 ft wide. However, the Rochdale company continued to press for the remaining locks to be lengthened.

The opening of the Manchester & Leeds Railway in sections between 1839 and 1841, paralleling the whole of the Rochdale and the Calder & Hebble, led the shareholders' meeting of mid-1840 to seek reductions in expenditure; they refused, however, to cut tolls until the railway had actually opened, and then made limited toll cuts, except on yarn and bale goods where in collaboration with the Rochdale company they reduced rates more drastically. However, by late in 1842 they, the railway, and the carriers were all heavily involved in price-cutting. It was reported in 1842 that shares which two or three years earlier had fetched £525 were then being offered for £180.[37]

In January 1843, the Rochdale having reported correspondence with the railway, the Calder & Hebble wrote that they would 'consider any propositions which may be made to them by the Railway Comy; provided that in the meantime the Railway Company shall make a satisfactory arrangement of their outstanding account with this Company'.[38] The Rochdale, tending to look for an excuse to desert the Calder & Hebble, picked on this remark, and replied early in February that they thought it time to agree with the railway, and if the Calder & Hebble were going to let a private difference with them get in the way, the Rochdale would negotiate separately.[39] This brought the Calder & Hebble to a meeting of canal clerks to concert an approach, and then to one with the railway.

The meeting failed to agree, and it seems that the Rochdale then went ahead on their own. Told by the railway that the latter would follow the canals in either an increase or a reduction, the Rochdale moved their tolls upwards, and were followed by the Manchester & Leeds, and the carriers on the Manchester and Hull run. These things were done without consultation with the Calder & Hebble, who wrote regretting 'the Rochdale Company should have passed a resolution raising their Dues . . . without first conferring with this Company; and that this Committee are decidedly of opinion, that it would be impolitic to make any alteration under present circumstances'.[40] A week later they told the Rochdale that they would now act independently, and four days later again minuted that 'the period has now arrived, when negotiations may with propriety be entered into with the Manchester & Leeds Railway Company, independent of the Aire & Calder and Rochdale Canals',[41] and a negotiating deputation was sent with a free hand. On 20 March they reported that they had agreed upon a lease to the railway for £40,000 p.a. for 14 years from 25 March, 'the working and maintenance of the Canal [to] be entirely in the hands of the Canal Company, subject to such Rates, Rents & Wharfages as the Railway Company from time to time, in compliance with the Act, shall arrange'.[42] On 31 March the Rochdale company offered the railway a lease on exactly the same terms, but this was not then taken up, though the two companies began to co-operate.

On the 23rd Charles Norris of the Calder & Hebble wrote to the railway company that 'the Navigation Company had given the necessary order to commence on the 25th Inst for the advanced dues, the Toll on "Empties" and the closing of the Canal on Sundays,* agreeably with the instructions of this Company at Halifax on Friday last', and on the 27th the railway board heard a report that 'in accordance with the increase of rates of the Navigation Company a corresponding increase had been made this day in the Railway Rates'.[43] The railway then moved in to smarten up the Calder & Hebble, changing the management system and the method of collecting tolls, and getting Capt. C. H. Binstead, R.N., appointed superintendent of canal traffic at £200 p.a. Finally, they moved towards acquiring the Huddersfield Canal. Curiously, the railway lease was not minuted when the shareholders met in June. The financial effect was, however, noticeable enough, as 8 per cent half yearly dividends succeeded those of 5 per cent paid in December 1842 and June 1843.

Here are averaged dividend figures to 1844:

Years	Dividends per cent	Years	Dividends per cent
1795–99	12	1825–29	18†
1800–04	12·4	1830–34	18
1805–09	13·6	1835–39	18
1810–14	14	1840–44	15·35
1815–19	14		
1820–24	14		

† One half year's dividend conjectured.

The Manchester & Leeds had been too precipitate. By leasing the Calder & Hebble and negotiating with the Huddersfield, they thoroughly frightened the Rochdale, who probably saw their negotiating strength being weakened. They also antagonized the

* This was already the practice, but in June, after continuing Rochdale protests, they allowed bale vessels only to pass on Sundays.

powerful Aire & Calder by making them nervous also. By early 1844 the two were combining to cut tolls heavily against the railway, and in October the Aire & Calder, supported by the Rochdale, complained to the Board of Trade of the railway lease of the Calder & Hebble, arguing that it was illegal because unconfirmed by an Act of Parliament. The railway countered by cautiously offering the Rochdale a pooling agreement, whereupon the canal company, conscious of being courted, strengthened their position by getting James Thomson to survey for a possible conversion of their own line to a competing railway. Thomson, in his report, recommended against this, but, perhaps on his own initiative, perhaps not, suggested a new canal to by-pass the Calder & Hebble.

The Rochdale thereupon approached the Aire & Calder to join them in a survey for such a new canal. Meanwhile the railway were being asked whether they intended to bring in a Bill to legalize their lease of the Calder & Hebble. In reply, the Aire & Calder minuted:

'the Aire & Calder . . . is most anxious to set aside the Arrangement between the Manchester & Leeds Railway Company and the Calder & Hebble Navigation Co., either by legal proceedings, which it thinks should first be tried—or by some counter project:—But the Aire & Calder Navigation cannot consider the present project sufficiently matured to enable it to decide whether it is, or is not, expedient to join the Rochdale Canal Co in making a Survey for a Canal from Sowerby Bridge to Wakefield'.[44]

When the Rochdale was more definite upon who was to make and control the new canal, and how it was to be supplied with water, they would be glad to meet them again. So the Rochdale on their own had the survey done, the result showing that it would be difficult to build a new line, and certainly a Bill could not be immediately promoted. By this time the railway had got the message: in January 1846 they offered to buy the Rochdale company and proposed to bring in an immediate Bill. Should it pass, the Calder & Hebble's position was bound to be permanently weakened. The railway then sent for the Calder & Hebble, to ask two questions difficult to answer: first, were they prepared to seek an Act to legalize the lease, as the Railway Commissioners were pressing them to do, and second, if while the Rochdale purchase Bill were passing through the Houses, Parliament should compel the railway company 'to produce their Agreement with the Calder & Hebble—are the Canal Company prepared to have their Dues revised and reduced to the Rochdale scale, and to make concessions in the amount of Rent, equal to these reductions, so as to leave the Railway Company in no worse position than they are at present'? Furthermore, Parliament might reduce the tolls still further, so 'as to render it impossible for the Railway Company to continue the arrangement'.[45]

However, in March 1847 Norris wrote to the railway that 'under any circumstances that Company* must keep out of Parliament, not that they were disposed to alter the terms of the present Agreement but will give every aid to the Manchester and Leeds Company to obtain a Confirmation of their Rochdale Canal Arrangement. If the Company* should be obliged to annul the Agreement they hoped to re-arrange one afterwards. If Parliament puts a veto altogether they would still wish to act with the Manchester and Leeds Company on the most friendly terms.'[46]

The Railway Commissioners wrote again later at the end of April, to say that they had put the leasing agreement to the Attorney General and the Solicitor General, and both had agreed it was unauthorized. They therefore asked the Calder & Hebble to cease acting on the agreement until they had applied for an Act.

The Rochdale purchase Bill was opposed by the Aire & Calder and lost in June 1847, and the Calder & Hebble had to release the railway company from their engagement, so silently that neither side minuted it nor noted when it ended. It must have been by the summer of 1847, for in September the Calder & Hebble made a different move, hardly consonant with Norris's letter: they responded to an approach by the Aire & Calder authorized at the beginning of August, offering a lease.[47] (*To continue the history of the Calder & Hebble Navigation, turn to Chapter XVII.*)

Sir John Ramsden's Canal

The 1790s saw a rapid growth in trans-Pennine road carrying, the traffic bait that during this decade was driving three canals across the hills. One such route had its canal head at Huddersfield. In April 1796, for instance, Richard Milnes was advertising 'Expeditious Conveyance of Goods to and from Manchester and Hull', with a daily sailing from Huddersfield to Wakefield to connect there with the daily Hull service.[48] He quoted freight

* The Calder & Hebble.

rates of 3s (15p) a cwt. Manchester to Hull, or 2s (10p) Huddersfield to Hull. By the end of 1797, however, he was advertising
one or more boats a day from Sowerby Bridge through to Hull,
but three or more a week from Huddersfield to Wakefield, with
a daily service beyond.[49] The quicker building progress being
made by the wide waterway Rochdale Canal than by the narrow
canal Huddersfield company, struggling with Standedge tunnel,
was already giving the Sowerby Bridge route a predominance in
canal carrying it was never to lose.

Thereafter the history of Ramsden's Canal is that of a branch
of the Calder & Hebble, sharing the increasing prosperity that
waterway brought to the area, but with a certain value added by
the access to Manchester offered by the Huddersfield Canal. That
concern, however, was not successful enough to alter Ramsden's
basic link with Yorkshire rather than Lancashire.

The negotiations that led to railway ownership, in practical
terms, of the Huddersfield Canal[50] had as a corollary the purchase
of Ramsden's also. In 1845[51] the canal was vested in the Huddersfield & Manchester Railway & Canal Co at a sale price of £46,560;
two years later that concern was vested in the London & North
Western Railway,[52] under the same conditions as the Huddersfield
Canal. (*To continue the history of Sir John Ramsden's Canal, turn to
Chapter XVII.*)

CHAPTER X

The Busy Don

++++++++++++++++++++++++++++++++++++++◆++++++++++++++++++++++++++++++++++++++

THE canal mania had a galvanic effect on the Don company, causing them to take the principal part in creating two new canals, the Dearne & Dove and the Stainforth & Keadby, and some part in launching a third, the Barnsley. They failed with a fourth, the Sheffield, though this, too, was later built, but independently.

The excitement began with a public meeting in Sheffield on 4 July 1792 to press for a navigation from Tinsley to Sheffield. The August Don shareholders' meeting not only agreed to build such a canal, perhaps with a branch towards the collieries at Eckington, but recommended another meeting to consider that were the River Dearne to be made navigable from the Don up to Barnsley, it would benefit the area round that town and would also supply the Don trade with coal from collieries then badly needing transport at a time when bigger coal supplies were wanted.

The Sheffield scheme (see Chapter XI) fell before landowners' opposition, but by September the Don had revived their old interest in a canal from Stainforth to the Trent and on 17 October launched the Stainforth & Keadby Canal (see Chapter XII) virtually under their own control. Simultaneously they did the same with the scheme that became the Dearne & Dove (see Chapter XII), agreeing with the Aire & Calder at a meeting on 20 October upon the building of both the Dearne & Dove and the Barnsley Canals and a junction between them, and then launching the company on the 22nd, also with Don shareholders in the majority. Both the Dearne & Dove and the Stainforth & Keadby companies had the Don's Richard Ellison in the chair to launch them, the Don's John Thompson, who had recently succeeded Stanley, as engineer, and their William Hoyle as law agent. The Sheffield and Eckington project was then dropped, but the other two, the Stainforth & Keadby and the Dearne & Dove, obtained their Acts in 1793 and became separate companies, though with much common shareholding, control and management.

Some trading in coal began again in 1792, though probably not for long. Company's boats are first mentioned in the minute books in the 1790s, with an order in 1797 that they were not to carry below Thorne, where at this time all coastal cargoes were transhipped, though there was an increasing amount of through working to Hull after the new century began. One gets the impression, however, that few craft were company owned, for mentions hardly ever occur in the records. But an 1802 advertisement for a new weekly service of cutters to run between London and Thorne tells us that: 'So soon as any of those Vessels arrive at Thorne, the Goods they may have in for Doncaster, Rotherham, Sheffield, Barnsley, &c will be forwarded by the utmost despatch in the River Dun Company's Boats',[1] and in 1803 four company lighters, described as having worked between Thorne and Tinsley, were advertised for sale.[2] Onward from Thorne, whether to Hull or London, carrying seems to have been by contract vessels or independent carriers.

The Don company had a strong interest in the trade beyond Thorne, and in 1798 told their committee

'to consider of the Means of promoting a competition in the Trade from Thorne to London, and that they be desired to take such Methods by advertising or otherwise as they shall think most conducive to the same'.[3]

The London trade from Thorne on the Don was then competing against those from Gainsborough on the Trent and Selby on the Aire & Calder and Ouse. One difficulty was the width of the Dutch River bridges. Another was shortage of water in dry seasons below Thorne, so that lightening vessels had to be used to take cargo from incoming craft.

In February 1800 rumbles were heard of a disagreement that was in the future to hold up necessary navigation improvements. Riparian landowners thought the river company should protect their lands from flooding, the main cause of which was the river's winding course near Barnby Dun and Fishlake, and threatened to pull down the weir at Barnby Dun.[4] The Don considered 'the Navigation Company are only liable to and have from Time to Time made good the Damages done to the Banks by the carrying on of the Navigation, and which principally if not solely arise from the use they make of the Towing Paths'.[5] The landowners wanted commissioners to meet, but almost all those named in the old Act were dead. After the committee had met the landowners, the former recommended the shareholders to seek a Bill to appoint new commissioners, and also to 'improve and amend the Navigation . . . by making several Cuts from the same as well below as above Doncaster'.[6] John Copeland, who had become the Don's engineer after Thompson's death in 1795, was asked for his suggestions, and William Jessop invited to survey the river, consider earlier surveys made by Benjamin Outram in 1795 and Robert Whitworth in 1797, and propose improvements. Meanwhile the company tactfully did some bank repairs.

By December they had agreed to seek a Bill for new cuts at Cadeby, at Doncaster, and from Kirk Sandall to the Barnby cut and thence to the Stainforth cut, changes in tolls, and the appointment of new commissioners. A notice appeared in December.[7] However, in a letter early in March 1801, Jessop advised more thought and a closer study of what was needed before a Bill was sought, especially as the Sheffield Canal scheme was again being discussed in that town.

Jessop reported[8] fully during the summer. He proposed new cuts and locks at Conisbrough and Doncaster, and brought forward a cut at Eastwood with two locks, an extension of the Rotherham cut in the direction of Aldwarke, from earlier proposals. With other smaller improvements, he costed these at £9,149. He now, however, withdrew his support for a cut from Kirk Sandall to Stainforth. He also did a preliminary study for a canal from Tinsley to Sheffield, which, he thought, needed further work done on it. His plans were circulated to shareholders, and Copeland and others did detailed surveys. After they had received Jessop's report and issued a parliamentary notice in September that included a ¾-mile extension upwards from Tinsley to Brightside,[9] the company approached the landowners for an agreement. These in turn retained William Chapman as engineering adviser, and made counter-proposals. The company were clearly willing to make some concessions on bank protection against floods in exchange for being able to make improvements without opposition, and in 1802 offered to build the landowners a drainage channel to the river at Wilsick House, or the equivalent in cash. But no agreement was reached, and in the autumn of 1802 the landowners themselves gave notice of a Bill to provide for drainage and to appoint commissioners.

This Bill seems to have got no further, but one based on Jessop's improvements reached Parliament at the end of 1803.

Though the company worked hard to get favourable petitions, it first became clear that there was no chance of getting revised tolls and then that landowners' opposition to some of the improvements would defeat them. So the Bill was withdrawn, and nothing done on the river except the rebuilding of Conisbrough lock about 1806, and negotiations with Doncaster corporation for a new cut there. By 1807 it seems that no transhipment was taking place at Thorne—presumably because the Stainforth & Keadby Canal had been opened and goods were being taken through to Hull. At this time a little traffic was coming by land from Manchester to Tinsley to be put on the river to Hull, but with the Rochdale Canal already open it cannot have been significant.

In 1807 the landowners gestured towards a compromise, and once again negotiations began. The river company got Lord Fitzwilliam's support, which was valuable enough to ask Jessop to consider whether any of his former proposals needed changing. Jessop seems to have confirmed his report, but by now the Don company had got involved in a lawsuit brought against them by Doncaster corporation over whether the latter were making illegal charges by 'fencing the Bank at Docken hill in Doncaster* for the purposes of taking Tolls contrary to the Navigation Act'.[10] The Don company eventually won, but on the matter of improvements they could not persuade their opponents, and, after they had put out a Parliamentary notice in September 1808,[11] had to give up the idea of a Bill in 1809.

In the autumn of 1813 the idea of a canal from Sheffield to the Don was revived in the town. The Don company decided not to make it themselves, and a separate company was therefore authorized in 1815. The canal was opened in 1819. The river company transferred a portion of their navigation at Tinsley to the new concern, receiving £11,000 in payment and compensation for the loss of business there. In financial terms the Don were wise to refuse, for the canal proved expensive to build and only moderately profitable. The Don's horse towing path did not extend above Rotherham, and in 1817 the Sheffield Canal company asked for one to be made to Tinsley. The Walkers objected, but it was built during 1822.

In 1809 a twice-weekly sailing packet, the *Nelson*, running be-

* Doncaster corporation had its own wharf and warehouse in Fishergate, and levied river tolls at Doncaster lock under an Act of 1772, as well as wharfage and warehousing charges. These tolls were usually let, along with the warehouse; they put many difficulties in the way of negotiations between the corporation and the Don company.

tween Hull and Thorne Waterside, was advertised as completely fitted for passengers as well as goods.[12] Then came steam, and in August 1816 the *Britannia* began to run,[13] to be followed by others. In April 1818 the owner of the *John Bull*, running three times a week between Hull and Thorne, announced a connecting coach to Doncaster,[14] which was extended to Sheffield in 1820.[15] After Goole opened in 1826, some packets from Thorne, later also from Newbridge, connected there with the steam services to Hull or up the Ouse. Others, like the *Don*, put on in 1834 and still running in 1843, went through to Hull.

At this time Thorne was the main shipbuilding centre on the Don. Thomas Steemson, who had gone bankrupt at Fishlake in 1788,[16] had started up again at Thorne, and in the 1790s built seagoing and coasting craft of up to some 400 tons, the biggest that could be got through the bridges of the Dutch River.[17] Joseph Atkinson's yard at Thorne, which was offered for sale in 1799,[18] built similar craft. In 1804 Steemson even built a 24-gun warship, the first ever to be laid down at Thorne.[19] But in 1807 Steemson moved to Paull near Hull to build bigger warships; his yard, offered for sale in 1807,[20] seems to have been taken over by Gilderdale, Pearson & Co, who ran coasting craft to London, and continued to build big ships,[21] and later river and seagoing steam packets. Smaller craft, such as keels and barges, were probably also built at these yards, as well as at Doncaster and Masborough.

In 1817 Doncaster mills, then leased to the Don company, were burned down. As their situation had obstructed the navigation, this offered a chance for re-alignment, about which the company consulted Doncaster corporation and got Rennie's advice, the corporation being advised by Chapman. This led the Don committee to prepare another improvement Bill, to include toll revisions upon which they sought the powerful Earl Fitzwilliam's clearance, and new expenditure of £70,000, including rebuilt mills.

Though the company and Doncaster corporation came to an agreement, once more it was delayed, this time by a project first conceived in 1817, to build a canal from Knottingley on the Aire down the Went valley to the Don at Went Mouth a little above Newbridge, and near the point where it entered the Dutch River, with a branch from this line at Norton to the Don at Doncaster. This scheme, the Aire & Dun, first of the forerunners of the New Junction Canal of eighty years later, was promoted by Lord

Hawke, and had as engineer William Smith the geologist,[22] who had earlier worked on the Somersetshire Coal Canal and the Sussex Ouse.[23] When the Don company were first approached by the promoters, in November 1818, a solicitor, John Carr, was accompanied by Dymoke Wells, who had worked with Smith as a contractor on the Sussex Ouse.

On 30 December 1818 Rennie, surveying for the Aire & Calder, thought little of the Dutch River. He found the bottom uneven, full of shallows and liable to silt, the banks in a bad state, the 'River . . . much contracted at the three Bridges, and consequently the current is so strong that it requires the utmost attention to pass the Barges through them in safety—I was told by an experienced Bargeman that Vessels drawing $5\frac{1}{2}$ feet Water are frequently in ordinary Neaps two Tides in getting up to Newbridge'. So he did not recommend that the Goole Canal should end in the Dutch River.

The Aire & Dun project put the Don into a quandary, whether to support it, and so by-pass their own line between Doncaster and Went Mouth, or to improve the latter. The canal promoters' object was to get traffic the Goole Canal was later to attract from the Aire & Calder's Selby Canal line, and they were therefore willing to buy the Don's support by broadly agreeing that they would pay the Don company their authorized tolls for the river section between Doncaster (Holmstile) and Fishlake upon all traffic passing the new canal from Doncaster to Went Mouth via Norton. However, in spite of Don agreement and a full subscription from the public,[24] the Aire & Dun's Bill was lost in the Commons in April 1819 without a division 'through the powerful Interest of the Aire & Calder Company, the Land owners, and others',[25] including Doncaster corporation. By now the Aire & Calder, stimulated by the Aire & Dun, were busily working out their own Knottingley & Goole canal plans, which were to be authorized in 1820.

The Don company had got no further with reviving their improvement plans than rebuilding Doncaster mills when they had a letter from Lord Hawke's agent saying that his Lordship wanted to present another Bill for a similar line to that of the Aire & Dun. This was the Went & Wakefield Canal[26] from the Barnsley Canal at Cold Hiendley to the Dutch River near Newbridge, similar to the old 1772 scheme (see p. 31). Also with William Smith as engineer, it was to have had 29 locks and a branch to near Womersley. A Parliamentary notice appeared in

November 1819,[27] but then it disappeared, overcome by the Aire & Calder's plans. Not really liking Lord Hawke's Went valley line, the Don company simultaneously planned another themselves from Sprotbrough near Doncaster parallel to the river to Wilsick House and then to Went Mouth (later Newbridge), with a branch to Womersley, of which Rennie, whom they had consulted, approved, but the Doncaster corporation emphatically did not.[28]

A shareholders' meeting in August 1819 asked Rennie for an estimate for their plan and approved Parliamentary notices to include other improvements also.[29] The engineers Leather and Thackray did the survey, Rennie approved it, and all was set for a Bill. Then two obstacles appeared: a group of landowners who objected to the line and the Aire & Calder's Bill for the Knottingley & Goole Canal, also planned by Rennie. This originally proposed to make a side connection into the Dutch River through a lock at Newbridge, but the Aire & Calder then dropped it, explaining that Rennie had recommended against it after strong opposition had developed.

The Aire & Calder got their Act. The Don thereupon revived their own scheme, estimating the main line from Doncaster to Went Mouth at some £89,000, and the branch to Womersley with a railroad extension thence to the neighbouring limestone rocks at a further £42,000. However, when they looked coldly at the branch they saw that 42,000 tons of coal a year and lime paying 1s (5p) a ton would have to pass it to pay 5 per cent on capital. As for the main line proposals and other necessary improvements, to carry them out would mean raising tolls by a third. So they dropped the branch. A railroad from the limestone near Womersley to the Don at Trumfleet near Wilsick House (Thorpe in Balne) with a capital of £15,000 was now separately promoted by a group of Rotherham and Sheffield men, supported by Lord Hawke, in opposition to the Aire & Calder's proposed Womersley branch, and with Enoch Taylor as engineer.[30] A Bill introduced in 1821 was lost on standing orders; notice of another, which included a branch to Wentbridge, was given in 1822, and of a third, now to end at Wentbridge, and to serve a different area at Womersley, in 1824. The project was then abandoned, to reappear with a different set of subscribers but the same engineer, and now to connect with the Goole Canal and not the Don, as the Heck & Wentbridge Railway[31] (see p. 166).

As for the main line, the Don decided to be less ambitious, build a cut between Doncaster and Stainforth, and make inquiries about a steam dredger 'such as is used in the Docks at Hull and in some parts of the Calder & Hebble Navigation'.[32] Their engineer, Daniel Servant, produced an estimate of £25,302; Rennie one of £32,296 for nearly the same line. In January 1821 the shareholders agreed once more to seek a Bill. They would need, they thought, to raise corn and merchandise tolls to pay for the cost.

This time, on 7 May 1821, they got their Act,[33] their first since 1740. It authorized the raising of £40,000 to build three new cuts, 473 yds long at Arksey Ings, 660 yds a little lower at Long Sandall, and 5,600 yds thence to Kirk Sandall and Barnby Dun and on to the upper end of the Stainforth cut, so providing a continuous canal from Long Sandall to Stainforth. George Leather, who had done the surveys, was to build them. The work was probably finished about the end of 1823: a year earlier Don shares had sold at £1,740.[34]

In September 1823 Walker's of Masborough were pressing for more water: they emphasized their views on one occasion by lowering the level and stopping the navigation. Out of this came a proposal to link the Sheffield Canal directly with the Tinsley cut without an intervening piece of river. Leather estimated the cost at £1,084, and the Don and Sheffield companies agreed to do it. However, Leather then pointed out that 'the diversion betwixt the entrance of the Sheff^d Canal there and Tinsley Cut should not be proceeded in by the Sheffield Canal until it is ascertained that the Sheffield Canal can be well supplied with water'[35]—this presumably because their water would now have to supply the Tinsley cut. On this the plan seems to have dropped, the Don agreeing instead to pay Walker's £260 p.a. instead of the former £90 for the water they supplied.

In 1825 the minute book records the first railway projects, from Leeds to Goole (not yet, of course, a port because the Goole Canal was still being built), and from Sheffield to Goole. A few months later George Leather put two reports to the company, proposing further improvements to the river. One at Doncaster was agreed with the corporation, another between Tinsley and Rotherham was dropped when Walker's objected, the rest went forward to a Bill. In Parliament some changes were made in the lines proposed, and the coalowners, led by Earl Fitzwilliam and Lord Milton, and supported by the Dearne & Dove and Stainforth & Keadby companies, forced the concession that a ton of coal should in future be reckoned as 25 and not 20 cwt.

A further Act[36] of 1826 authorized the raising of £64,000 to build cuts. These were to be at Eastwood for 1,220 yds to Aldwarke mill; Aldwarke, for 370 yds, to pass the mill, involving the abandonment of the Aldwarke cut; from the end of the Mexborough cut near Mexborough church to the end of the Denaby cut, where the navigation was to be continued along the old river bed as a canal, while a new 360 yd channel was to be excavated for the river and Denaby lock eliminated; from the end of Denaby cut to near the junction of the river Dearne with the Don; a short cut just beyond the Dearne; and a new cut, 440 yds long, to replace the Conisbrough cut. A new lock was also built at Sprotbrough.

At this time Priestley says of the river:[37]

'The Dun Navigation is of the utmost importance for exporting the produce of the extensive coal and iron works which abound at its western extremity; also the vast quantity of manufactured iron goods and cutlery which is annually produced in the populous town and neighbourhood of Sheffield. The trade of Rotherham, the limestone and plaster at Sprotborough, and other places in the line, together with the agricultural produce of the neighbourhood of Doncaster, constitute a considerable branch of traffic on this navigation'.

In April 1827 the committee favoured the building of a railroad north-west from Sheffield by Blackburn, Grange, Chapeltown and Mortomley to the coal-bearing areas at Wortley near Stocksbridge, and asked George Leather to estimate it. His figure was £23,500 including a basin and lock at Tinsley. However, the Duke of Norfolk, whose property was concerned, objected on the grounds that he had agreed with the coal lessees not to promote a railroad to Sheffield. So the idea fell, until later the Sheffield, Ashton-under-Lyne & Manchester Railway was built past Wortley. Meanwhile a great change took place when in 1828 Walker's agreed to sell their works at the Holmes, including the Don water at Jordan Dam and Holmes Goit, for £13,500.

The completion of the Goole Canal in 1826 greatly changed the waterway situation, for whereas the Aire & Calder now had an embryo transhipment port at Goole, the Don only had Keadby, or the almost disused Thorne. They were therefore interested in any scheme that would improve their situation. Two were considered in 1828. Firstly, Leather was asked to survey and estimate for a canal from near Stainforth on the Don to join the Goole Canal—a proposal similar to the later New Junction. Secondly, the Don committee were approached by the promoters of a

Trent & Balby Canal, an improbable scheme for a canal from
Stockwith on the Trent at the junction with the Chesterfield
Canal, by Finningley and Rossington to the Don at Balby just
above Doncaster.[38]

When Leather had produced his first figures, the Don met the
Stainforth & Keadby, who would, of course, be threatened by
the Trent & Balby scheme with the loss of the coal trade from the
Dearne & Dove to Lincolnshire and the return trade in corn.
The Stainforth & Keadby suggested that the new cut should be
made from near Hangsman Hill, just below Thorne, to the Goole
Canal, and agreed either to help make it, or pay a lock toll for
every craft passing between it and their canal. Leather produced
three estimates, varying from £38,500 to £73,000, the cheapest of
which, from Stainforth, the committee preferred. The idea then
seems to have been taken over by a group connected with the
Stainforth & Keadby company who got the Aire & Calder's
approval in principle to such a line[39] and issued Parliamentary
notices. No more was heard of it.

Meanwhile, work under the 1826 Act, which had been delayed
by the projects of the previous two years, began seriously in 1829.
The first of the new cuts, from above Eastwood lock to above
Aldwarke, was opened on 28 July 1830. Some of them, like the
one at Doncaster, bogged down in negotiations, dragged on for
many years. The Mexborough cut, for instance, was opened at the
beginning of 1844, and that to replace the Conisbrough cut was
not made at all.

In September 1830 the company learned of a proposed railway
from Sheffield by way of Rotherham, Doncaster and Thorne to
Goole. The committee thought that since 'the water Conveyance
between Sheffield and the River Ouze has recently been greatly
improved and is now improving at very considerable expence,
and will be fully equal to the transit of all sorts of Goods, Wares
and Merchandise and that at a very reasonable rate of Tonage', the
new railway was 'never likely to compensate the promoters for
anything like interest for the expenditure'.[40] They sent copies of
their resolution to the Sheffield and Dearne & Dove companies,
and agreed with the former upon a cut in grain toll between Doncaster and Sheffield just to discourage the railway promoters.
This was cut again in April 1831. However, when the Rochdale
Canal Company wrote to ask whether the Don would join them
in a general opposition to railway schemes, the latter replied
that they were opposing the Goole line, 'but they cannot think

o

they ought to enter resolution to oppose all Rail Ways generally'.[41]

By February 1831 they learned that the railway scheme had been laid aside for that session, but it had given them a useful impetus towards reaching agreement with the landowners on the lower river. In March they consented to arbitration. In June 1832 the award gave them their point, that they maintained banks and towing paths for navigation purposes only, and not as a protection against floods. They seized the opportunity now to make their peace with Doncaster corporation, by subscribing half the cost of proposed improvements to the wharves at Docken Hill.

In 1833 they complained that insufficient depth on the Dearne & Dove was threatening coal supplies, and warned that company that if it did not improve, the Don might build railways to alternative supplies round Sheffield. The company had long been accustomed to give a drawback on coal carried by sea, to offset the coastwise duties, but in 1833 they added one on coal from the Dearne & Dove going to the Witham Navigation, and also on that supplied to steam vessels. Their normal coal toll at this time was a low one: 3s 8d (18½p) per waggon of 72 cwt, or a fraction under ½d a ton/mile.

Sir George Head[42] tells us that about 1833 a new cheap passenger route was started between Manchester and London. This involved coach to Sheffield, then tide coach to Thorne, whence a daily steamer ran to Hull. Should neaps prevent the steamer coming higher than Goole, a horse-drawn passage boat* ran from Thorne to Goole. At Hull the passengers caught a steamer to London. This route was still operating in 1835, and presumably did so until the through railway connection was finished.

In 1834 the company decided to stop all towing on the waterway on Sundays. In this year also a complaint from Thorne said that the double-leaved openings of the three wooden bridges over the Dutch River were inconveniently narrow and dangerous, forty craft having been sunk by hitting the piers in the previous thirty years. The company thereupon ordered each bridge to be given a single-leaved opening of about 54 ft.

Late in 1834 the company opened negotiations for land near Holmes Goit 'for the purpose of continuing a line of Navigation to Jordan Dam',[43] and bought it soon afterwards. By August 1835

---

* 'a flat-bottomed punt, in shape like a Sunderland Keel, but furnished with a good cabin under a raised bulkhead, sufficient effectively to protect the passengers from the weather'.

the new channel was made, coal from Holmes colliery being at first allowed to pass free along it, and then for a yearly payment. The new work left the Rotherham cut to run north of the river to Jordan Dam and Tinsley, by-passing the older Bromley Sands and Ickles cuts, and providing three new locks, Ickles, Holmes and Jordan, to replace those on the old line. Downwards the Rotherham cut was extended by the Eastwood cut and two locks.

For some time the Don company had been raising the height of all river bridges to give 12 ft above the water, and in July 1835 ordered the last three on their programme, two at Rotherham and one at Kilnhurst, to be dealt with. In June 1844 the company ordered all bridges below Doncaster to be made as opening bridges, to give craft unlimited headroom: in April 1845 the first fixed-mast craft reached the town.[44]

In October 1834 the company heard of a proposed railway from Rotherham to Wortley—we remember their own scheme of 1827 —'for the purpose of supplying the River with Coal'.[45] This soon became a plan for a Sheffield–Rotherham line only, to which they pledged every possible opposition. It was thrown out in Parliament in 1835.

At the beginning of 1835, against the background of railway threatenings, Charles Bartholomew, their engineer, was asked by the committee to prepare plans for the immediate improvement of the river, though not all those authorized in 1826 had yet been finished. His proposals were approved in October: works at Sprotbrough and Doncaster, and a new 7-ft cut direct from the Don at Stainforth to run between the river and canal at Thorne and direct to near Swinefleet on the Ouse, 1½ miles below Goole, so by-passing both the Dutch River and the Stainforth & Keadby Canal for traffic to Hull or the Ouse. It was the last that caused controversy at the subsequent shareholders' meeting. Some thought that locks and a weir should be built at the mouth of the Dutch River; others that part of the Stainforth & Keadby Canal might be incorporated in the proposed cut.

George Leather, consulted, firmly turned down locks on the Dutch River, but agreed that two miles of the Stainforth & Keadby might well be utilized if that company would sell. Eventually he approved Bartholomew's line for the cut, but thought his estimate too low, whereupon the latter said he already had offers to do it at his figure. A shareholders' meeting of 9 February 1836 decided by 75 votes to 38 to support him and go ahead with a Bill, though to be on the safe side Sir John Rennie, or failing him William Walker, was to be asked to look over Bartholomew's route and estimates.

Meanwhile talks had been going on with the Stainforth & Keadby about buying 2 miles of their canal. That company, who saw themselves losing all their trade down the Trent should the new cut be built, started to oppose the Don's Bill once it got to Parliament. The result was a deal. The Don offered to drop their Bill, and to buy the Stainforth & Keadby company for £45,800 plus £700 towards their Parliamentary expenses, this sum to be paid either in cash or by allotting 19 Don shares—therefore valued at some £2,447 each—as the canal shareholders wished. Raised to £48,000 by the Don committee in the successful hope that the canal company would take cash and not shares, agreement was reached between the companies, and an authorizing Bill introduced in 1837, only to be defeated in the Lords' Committee because some of the Stainforth & Keadby's shareholders objected to the sale. So the Don lost both their own improvement Bill and the chance of controlling the existing alternative route, and were left with their old line and the Dutch River. As for the canal company's shareholders, they were to accept in 1849 a good deal less than they now refused.

By January 1836 the proposed Sheffield & Rotherham Railway were back asking for a deputation to be received. By February their Bill was in the House, they having refused to accept the Don's suggested clauses. It was passed, and the line opened on 31 October 1838. Meanwhile, in 1836 the North Midland Railway from Leeds to Derby, connecting with the Sheffield & Rotherham at Masborough, had been authorized, and in January 1837 the former Goole railway project revived as the Sheffield, North Midland & Goole, but failed to get going. The North Midland's efforts to cross the Don's property led to a lawsuit. The Don lost it, and then agreed with the railway in 1839 that the latter should pay £1,500 for the land they wanted at the Holmes, and provide a rail-canal interchange staith on the south side of Holmes New Cut. In all this activity the company had time, in May 1839, to pass plans for new offices for themselves at Rotherham wharf.

In early 1840 Charles Bartholomew reported upon the swift passenger boats used on Scottish canals and on the Lancaster[46], and the committee, thinking

'that Boats of a similar description might be established with advantage to the Company between Swinton and Doncaster, Ordered that Mr. Bartholomew procure two Boats of the same

DONCASTER AND SWINTON.

THE AQUABUS leaves SWINTON STATION for DONCASTER every Morning, Sundays excepted, on the arrival of the down train which leaves Derby at Six, Sheffield at Half-past Seven, and the up train which leaves Leeds at a Quarter-past Seven.

Again leaves the MILL BRIDGE, Doncaster, for Swinton, in the Afternoon at One o'clock, to meet the down train to Leeds, York, Hull, and Manchester, and the up train to Sheffield, Derby, &c.

Fares,—Best Cabin, 1s.—Fore Cabin, 9d.

For particulars apply at the WHITE BEAR INN, Doncaster.

N.B. POST HORSES on the shortest Notice.

Swinton, March 9, 1841.

22. The Swinton–Doncaster aquabus service in 1841

construction as those used on the above-mentioned Canals with as little delay as possible'.[47]

Two months later John Copeland resigned after 68 years with the company, and Bartholomew became manager as well as engineer.

The company seems to have bought two swift boats, built in Scotland, leasing them to J. Ashforth to operate. Called aquabuses, they ran between Swinton station on the North Midland Railway and a packet waiting-room at Doncaster; probably from 11 June 1840. A year later, only one was being regularly used, making a single round trip each day as part of a road-waterway service that also included the proprietor's coaches. On occasions like race days both boats were working. In 1843, when one was running a double trip daily, fares were 1s (5p) best cabin or 9d fore cabin against 2s (10p) inside and 1s 6d (7½p) outside on the coaches. She was then described as 'an iron-formed craft, some sixty-six feet in length; sharp built; light and corky . . . sharper in the swan-like neck, with the brass balled topping, upon which the Helmsman's eyes is fixed'.[48] The service may have continued until the railway from Swinton to Doncaster opened on 10 November 1849.

In August 1841 agreement was at last reached with Doncaster corporation over the proposed new cut there, and over buying for £1,000 their right to take certain river tolls.[49] Work on the new lock and the cut, which by-passed the whole river bend and took the navigation nearer the town, was ordered to begin in May 1842, and was opened on 2 March 1843. In 1841 also Kilnhurst lock was ordered to be rebuilt 'to the dimensions of the most improved Locks on the Navigation'.[50] It was opened in October 1843.

In January 1843 Parker, Shore & Co, the company's bankers in Sheffield, failed, owing the company £4,001. The Shores had been shareholders and committeemen of the company since its inception. Some dividends for which money had been set aside at the bank had to be paid a second time, and the Sheffield Banking Co were appointed bankers in future.

Since 1841, when the company had asked the Stainforth & Keadby whether they intended to build their authorized cut at Hangsman Hill, they had had improvement of the lower river in mind. Now, in June 1844, they offered to lease the Stainforth & Keadby on condition that they could make the cut, so improving the Trent–Ouse link. That tiresome company agreed, only to go back on their agreement (see Chapter XII).

Meanwhile, in July 1844, the Don concern made a first move towards greater involvement with the coming railways with an agreement for transfer of traffic to and from the Sheffield & Rotherham Railway. In October they were ready to negotiate with the 'Manchester Railway Company for carrying goods between Manchester and the Dun Navigation and the Navigation and the Railway',[51] and seem also to have had in mind a possible short extension upwards of the navigation and then a communication, perhaps by railway, with Lord Effingham's coalfield in the Blackburn valley.

Many railway schemes were in the air. By early 1845 the company had decided that the worst threats were a proposed railway from Doncaster to Goole, and schemes for a line to the Barnsley coalfield. They moved quickly to counter the latter. By May they had agreed to buy the Barnsley Canal (see Chapter VIII) and then told Aire & Calder representatives that they had done so to prevent it passing into railway hands and to secure Barnsley coal to the Don and Aire & Calder companies. They went on to offer to transfer the Barnsley to the Aire & Calder, and themselves to buy the Dearne & Dove, so forming 'two entire lines of Navigation from the Barnsley Coalfield to Goole to be worked, as far as may be, to mutual advantage'.[52] However, the Aire & Calder only agreed to buy the Barnsley if the Bill that would be necessary to authorize it were not altered in Parliament to remove any of their privileges under earlier Acts, upon which the Don said that they could not wait, and broke off negotiations. This may have been a pretext, for by now they had realized that if they joined forces with a promising railway, they would have considerable influence on the combined transport lines that would result, whereas if they opposed all schemes, they might lose much of what they had. They therefore agreed to amalagamate with the promoters of the South Yorkshire Coal Railway, a concern which had Charles Bartholomew as engineer and, the Aire & Calder considered, had been encouraged into existence by the Don company to build a line up the Blackburn valley to Barnsley and the coalfield, and to join other railways planned or building. The object being to extend the market for Barnsley coal while safeguarding its access to the Don itself.

By the time of their shareholders' meeting the Don company had agreed to take over the Dearne & Dove from the end of the year, were making friendly noises in the direction of the Sheffield Canal Company, and had made their agreement with the Barnsley. This was an attractive proposition to any group of railway promoters, and those of the South Yorkshire agreed to a share exchange into the new amalgamated company that would secure for ever the Don's current dividend of £120 p.a. on their 150 shares,* and that mortgage and other debts should be transferred to the new company. Dearne & Dove and Barnsley Canal shareholders were to be given an opportunity of subscribing for railway shares.

The South Yorkshire Bill ran into heavy opposition in Parlia-

---

* The final arrangement was £3,000 of railway stock for each Don share, on which 4 per cent would be guaranteed to the opening of the railway. After that, shareholders could choose to continue with a guaranteed 4 per cent, or take their chance with the annual railway dividends.

ment, and was lost against Aire & Calder opposition. The South Yorkshire then strengthened their position by amalgamating with the Goole, Doncaster, Sheffield & Manchester Junction Railway promoters, while the Don seem to have thought it wise to placate the powerful Aire & Calder by backing out of their agreement with the Barnsley. That done, and the Barnsley free to move into the Aire & Calder's orbit, the Don and the South Yorkshire (now the South Yorkshire, Doncaster & Goole) were free to try again for a Bill.

In September 1846 the Don company, hearing that the Sheffield & Lincolnshire Railway had agreed to buy the Sheffield Canal, themselves started to buy land for an independent access to Sheffield. This threat, which went as far as a Bill, coupled with the Sheffield town council's support for the Don and opposition to railway control, sufficed to persuade the Manchester, Sheffield & Lincolnshire Railway, who had succeeded to the Sheffield & Lincolnshire at the beginning of 1847, to part with the Sheffield Canal to the Don. Control passed to the Don in July 1848, the authorizing Act following a year later.

On 22 July 1847 the South Yorkshire, Doncaster & Goole Railway's Act received the royal assent.[53] It provided that the amalgamation with the Don should not take place until half the railway's capital had been raised and expended. This took place by certificate of the Railway Commissioners on 19 April 1850.

In April 1847 representatives of the Don and the South Yorkshire had met the Stainforth & Keadby and agreed upon a lease. But yet again that elusive company had backed out. When, a year later, another meeting took place, the Don was in no mood for conciliation. The Stainforth & Keadby, offered considerable worse terms than before, or the prospect of the Don going ahead with improvements that would be damaging to their trade, chose the former (see Chapter XII), and the canal was transferred from 1 January 1849.

In April 1848 a historic name appeared in the company's books, when they leased Rotherham Forge Works for 14 years at £360 p.a. to 'Messrs John Brown the Elder, Geo: Brown and John Brown the younger from the first of Novr last'.[54]

The navigation's takings and dividends rose only slowly in the ten years to 1803. The opening of the Dearne & Dove Canal in 1804, however, with its increasingly heavy shipments of Barnsley and other coals, made a great difference, soon to be reflected in dividends. The payment of £8,347·50 for that year had become

£11,970 by 1810. Thereafter the dividend payments figure remained steady at from £11,000 to £12,600 until 1826 saw a rise to £15,000. The Don's programme of modernization, combined with the industrial growth of the towns along its banks and those of the canals connected with it, caused payments to reach £18,000, representing £120 p.a. per £349 share, at which figure it was kept until amalgamation. Indeed, even at that dividend level, Don surpluses enabled South Yorkshire Railway shareholders to get dividends while their line was being built, an unusual situation for any company.

Here are averaged figures:

Years	Toll revenue £	Dividend payments £	Payment per £349 share £ s d		
1794–98		8,397	55	17	7
1799–1803		8,611	57	8	10
1804–08		9,010·50	58	1	5
1809–13		11,351·50	75	16	2
1814–18		12,127·50	80	17	0
1819–23		12,600	84	0	0
1824–28		14,040	93	12	0
1829–33	25,599*	15,000	100	0	0
1834–38	27,707	15,395	102	10	0
1839–43	28,986	17,775	118	10	0
1844–48	33,234	18,000	120	0	0

* Years 1831 to 1833 only.

(*To continue the history of the Don Navigation, turn to Chapter XVIII.*)

Greasbrough (Park Gate) Canal

At the end of 1793 John Stephenson & Son announced that they had 'completed a new Winning of the Old Park Gate Coal of the best quality, which will be delivered on board at 12s per waggon'.[55]

At some time after the canal was built, a branch was made from the main line not far from the Don for some ½ mile to Newbiggin, whence colliery tramroads ran to pits at Swallow Wood and Rawmarsh.[56] In 1834, 10,452 tons of coal from Earl Fitzwilliam's Park Gate colliery passed on to the Sheffield Canal.[57] This coal was loaded into containers at the pit, which were then transferred to boats. Each boat carried 30 tons, and these were worked three in a train by one horse.[58]

In 1836 the Sheffield & Rotherham Railway Act empowered that company to build a branch to the Greasbrough Canal for a 'better supply of Coal from the Coal Mines of Greasbrough and Rawmarsh', though power was given to the North Midland Company to make the branch instead should their line be authorized in the same session.[59] The railway was cheaper than the Sheffield Canal line, and much traffic transferred to it.

By 1840 the tramroads leading to the upper part of the canal had become disused as traffic had transferred to rail. This section therefore became disused, part being converted to a road, and only the bottom ⅝ mile and the Newbiggin branch remained in use. (*To continue the history of the Greasbrough Canal, turn to Chapter XVIII.*)

Thorne and Hatfield Moors Peat Canals

The Stainforth & Keadby Canal and its accompanying land drains eliminated the Thorne boating dyke, while the cheap transport of coal it offered led to a decline in the peat trade, a movement accelerated by the drainage and enlosure of areas of peat moor. In 1815 the Hatfield, Thorne and Fishlake Enclosure Commissioners authorized a new drain, about 2 miles long, to be cut along the edge of Thorne Waste. This was probably navigable, along with about 4 miles of other drain, until the waterborne trade which had been attracting fewer boats, probably almost died out after the 1830s. The craft used were clinker-built, about 28 ft × 6 ft, and able to work in either direction without having to be turned.[60] (*To continue the history of the Thorne and Hatfield Moors Peat Canals, turn to Chapter XVIII.*)

NOTES

Notes to Chapter I

1. For the early history of the Aire & Calder see W. N. Slatcher, 'The Aire and Calder Navigation', a M.Sc. thesis of Manchester University, 1967, which is most useful for the first 75 years of the navigation's history. I am grateful to Dr Slatcher for making it available to me, and for much detailed help; see also R. W. Unwin, 'The Aire and Calder Navigation', Parts I and II, *The Bradford Antiquary*, November 1964 and September 1967.
2. 10 & 11 Will III *c*. 19.
3. For the trade of Hull at this time, see Ralph Davis, 'The Trade and Shipping of Hull, 1500–1700', *East Yorkshire Local History Society*, No. 17, 1964.
4. For Pickering, see Slatcher, op. cit., p. 20.
5. J.H.C., 12 January 1698, NS, 11 January 1669, NS.
6. Ed. J. J. Cartwright, *The Travels through England of Dr. Richard Pococke*. Camden Society, 1888–9, Vol. I, p. 171.
7. John Hadley was associated with George Sorocold, who in 1694 and 1695 had built waterworks at Leeds. See Slatcher, op. cit., pp. 23ff.
8. J. Hunter, ed., *Diary of Ralph Thoresby, F.R.S.*, 1830, Vol. II, p. 442, quo. Unwin, 'Aire & Calder', op. cit.
9. J. Priestley, *Historical Account of the Navigable Rivers, Canals*, etc., 1831
10. Seemingly Isaac Newton was also consulted by the Lords. See Slatcher, 'The Aire and Calder Navigation', op. cit., pp. 38ff.
11. B.T.H.R., ACN 3/19.
12. For a detailed account of these quarrels, see Unwin, 'Aire and Calder', Part II, op. cit.
13. For detailed accounts of the early finances, see Slatcher and Unwin, op. cit.
14. Aire & Calder Navigation Undertakers' Minute Book, 29 May 1729.
15. Unwin, 'Aire & Calder', Part II, op. cit.
16. West Riding Registry of Deeds, book C, p. 1, entry 1, and book C, p. 4, entry 2, lease and release 23 and 24 September 1705, registered 27 September 1705.
17. Daniel Defoe, *A Tour through England and Wales*, Vol. II, p. 208 (Everyman ed).
18. Ibid.
19. *Leeds Mercury*, 23 October 1744.
20. Aire & Calder Navigation Undertakers' Minute Book, 25 June 1731.
21. See Unwin, 'Aire & Calder Navigation', Part II, op. cit., and the beginning of Chapter II.
22. See Slatcher, op. cit., for a full account.
23. For the years after 1750, see Slatcher, op. cit., and R. G. Wilson, 'The Aire & Calder Navigation', Part III, 'The Navigation in the Second Half of the Eighteenth Century', *The Bradford Antiquary*, July 1969.
24. *Leeds Intelligencer*, 18 July 1758, quo. Slatcher, op. cit.
25. This and the previous paragraph are based on the evidence given to the House of Commons committee in February 1773 on the first Leeds & Selby Canal Bill.
26. J.H.C., 22 February 1774.
27. *York Courant*, 28 August 1764.
28. For the Leeds & Liverpool Canal, see Charles Hadfield and Gordon Biddle, *The Canals of North West England*, 1970.

29. J.H.C., XXVI, 56.
30. *Leeds Mercury*, 21 February 1769.
31. *Reports of the late John Smeaton*, 1812, Vol. II, p. 131, report of 28 December 1771.
32. Ibid.
33. *Letter of Sir George Savile, Bart, on an attempt made to interfere with the Aire & Calder Navigation, in the year 1772.* 1828 (Goldsmith's Library).
34. Plan, Royal Society's Smeaton's *Designs*, VI, fo. 81.
35. Plan, Aire & Calder Records.
36. *The Brotherton Cutt*, East Riding Record Office, DDX 42/2.
37. J.H.C., 28 February 1772.
38. *York Courant*, 4 February 1772.
39. *The Report of John Smith, Engineer, Pointing out the method of making a Navigable Canal from Wakefield to the Don*, 1772 (South Yorkshire Industrial Museum, Cusworth Hall, Doncaster).
40. *Reports of the late John Smeaton*, 1812, Vol. II, p. 151. B.T.H.R., ACN 3/8.
41. J.H.C., 17 January 1774.
42. *Prescott's Manchester Journal*, 31 July 1773. See also a broadsheet issued in August 1773, *Considerations on the Utility and Advantages of a Navigable Canal from Leeds to Selby*, B.T.H.R., HRP 6/46/15.
43. 14 Geo III, *c*. 96.
44. Aire & Calder Navigation Undertakers' Minute Book, 4 July 1774.
45. *York Courant*, 12 May 1778.
46. Ibid., 12 January 1791.
47. *Wheeler's Manchester Chronicle*, 6 March 1784.
48. Aire & Calder Navigation Undertakers' Minute Book, 5 July 1779.
49. Ibid., 6 July 1778.
50. Ibid., 1 July 1782.
51. Aire & Calder Navigation Undertakers' Minute Book, 8 October 1787.
52. See especially Baron F. Duckham, 'Selby and the Aire & Calder Navigation 1774–1826', *Journal of Transport History*, November 1965.
53. J. Mountain, *Selby, Ancient and Modern*, 1800, p. 159.
54. Aire & Calder Navigation Undertakers' Minute Book, 15 January 1783.
55. Ibid., 31 May 1784.
56. Ibid., 4 January 1787.
57. *York Courant*, 15 December 1789.
58. Aire & Calder Navigation Undertakers' Minute Book, 31 January 1793.
59. Ibid., 25 July 1795.
60. Ibid., 9 February 1792.
61. Aire & Calder Navigation Undertakers' Minute Book, 27 August 1792.
62. Printed report of shareholders' meeting, 20 September 1792 (South Yorkshire Industrial Museum, Cusworth Hall, Doncaster).
63. Barnsley Canal Proprietors' Minute Book, 29 October 1792.
64. See Charles Hadfield and Gordon Biddle, *The Canals of North West England*, 1970, p. 323.
65. I have used the summaries in R. G. Wilson, op. cit., Part III.

Notes to Chapter II

1. J.H.C., 3 March 1735 (NS).
2. R. W. Unwin, 'The Aire and Calder Navigation: Part II: The Navigation in the pre-canal Age', *The Bradford Antiquary*, September 1967. This article describes the road schemes in some detail.
3. J.H.C., 9 December 1740.
4. J.H.C., 21 January 1741 (NS).
5. For Thomas Steers, see Charles Hadfield and Gordon Biddle, *The Canals of

North West England, 1970. He had played an important part in promoting the Mersey & Irwell and the Douglas Navigations. John Eyes' map and his and Steers' canal plan are in the Aire & Calder records.

6. Calder & Hebble Navigation Minute Book, 22 July 1757.
7. Plan in Aire & Calder records, B.T.H.R., ACN 3/7.
8. Ibid., 27 August 1757.
9. Ed. J. J. Cartwright, *The Travels through England of Dr. Richard Pococke,* Camden Society, 1888–9, Vol. I, p. 50.
10. J.H.C., 21 January 1740.
11. J.H.C., 14 March 1758.
12. Calder & Hebble Navigation Minute Book, 27 August 1757.
13. John Smeaton, *Reports,* Vol. I, facing p. 7 and pp. 20–1. Also *A Plan of the River Calder from Wakefield to Brooksmouth and from thence to Salterhebble Bridge.* From a survey in October and November 1757. By John Smeaton (Manchester P.L., ff. 386. C9).
14. J.H.C., 14 March 1758.
15. Calder & Hebble Navigation Minute Book, 23 November 1757.
16. J.H.C., 8 February 1758.
17. Calder & Hebble Navigation Minute Book, 14 January 1758.
18. 31 Geo II *c.* 72.
19. J.H.C., 19, 20 April, 24 May 1758.
20. See Charles Hadfield, *The Canals of South & South East England,* 1969, pp. 296–7.
21. See Charles Hadfield & Gordon Biddle, *The Canals of North West England,* 1970, p. 263.
22. Calder & Hebble Navigation Minute Book, 18 June 1761.
23. Ibid., 6 December 1764.
24. Ibid., 11 April 1765.
25. *Williamson's Advertiser & Mercantile Gazette* (Liverpool), 29 March 1765.
26. Calder & Hebble Navigation Minute Book, 3 July 1765.
27. See Charles Hadfield & Gordon Biddle, *The Canals of North West England,* 1970, Chapter X.
28. Ibid., Chapter I.
29. See Charles Hadfield, *The Canals of the West Midlands,* 2nd ed., 1969.
30. See preamble to 1769 Act.
31. Halifax P.L., SH:2: R. & W. Longbotham's receipt is dated 26 May 1768. His estimate for the canal was only £3,242.
32. Smeaton, *Reports,* II, p. 125.
33. Petition of creditors, J.H.C., 13 December 1768.
34. 9 Geo III *c.* 71.
35. *Letter of Sir George Savile, Bart . . .* 1828 (Goldsmiths Library, I 2.828).
36. *York Courant,* 8 August 1769
37. *Leeds Intelligencer,* 2 October 1770.
38. Smeaton, *Reports,* II, pp. 128–30. Calder & Hebble Navigation Committee Minute Book, 23 January 1771.
39. Longbotham was at the time pushing forward the Leeds & Liverpool Canal, authorized in May 1770. Bradford was then connected to it, rather than to the Calder & Hebble, under the Bradford Canal Act of 1771. See Charles Hadfield & Gordon Biddle, *The Canals of North West England,* 1970, Chapter III.
40. John Rennie, *Notebooks,* 10 November 1791 (Rochdale Canal).
41. Calder & Hebble Navigation Committee Minute Book, 20 May 1772.
42. John F. Goodchild, 'An Eighteenth Century Railway Tunnel', *Journal of the Railway & Canal Historical Society,* May 1959.
43. Calder & Hebble Navigation Committee Minute Book, 15 February 1775.
44. Ibid., Proprietors' Minute Book, 30 March 1774.
45. Ibid., Committee Minute Book, 17 February 1773.
46. Ibid., 7 December 1775.
47. Ibid., 2 April 1776.
48. *Prescott's Manchester Journal,* 10 April 1779.

49. Calder & Hebble Navigation Committee Minute Book, 23 March 1785.
50. *Manchester Mercury*, January, February 1788.
51. *York Courant*, 4 April 1786.
52. For the Rochdale Canal, see Charles Hadfield & Gordon Biddle, *The Canals of North West England*, 1970, Chapter X.
53. Charles Hadfield & Gordon Biddle, *The Canals of North West England*, 1970, pp. 247, 265.
54. For the Huddersfield Canal, see Charles Hadfield & Gordon Biddle, *The Canals of North West England*, 1970, Chapter XII.
55. Calder & Hebble Navigation Committee Minute Book, 23 February 1793.
56. For Luke Holt, see the article by J. H. Goodchild on the Ossett Mill Co., in *Textile History*, Vol. I. He also later worked on the first Hull dock under Berry.
57. J.H.C., 26 January 1774.
58. Evidence before the Lords Committee, 24 February 1774.
59. 14 Geo III *c.* 13.
60. *A Plan of the intended Navigable Canal from Cooper Bridge to Huddersfield* . . . 6 November 1773 (Manchester P.L., ff. 386. C.9.).
61. B.T.H.R., ACN 4/36.
62. W. B. Stocks, *Pennine Journey*, 1958.
63. J. Hewitt, *The History and Topography of the Parish of Wakefield*, 1862–64, p. 290.
64. *York Courant*, 5 February 1788
65. John F. Goodchild, 'Emmet's Canal: An Industrial Canal of the West Riding', *Journal of the Railway & Canal Historical Society*, September 1959.

Notes to Chapter III

1. *Calendar of Patent Rolls*, Edw. III (1343–5), p. 91, 20 May 1343.
2. *The Fabric Rolls of York Minster*, Surtees Society, XXXV, p. 21 (*c.* 1400), p. 34 (*c.* 1415), p. 101 (November 1527 to November 1528).
3. L. E. Harris, *Vermuyden and the Fens*, 1953. S. Smiles, *Lives of the Engineers*, Vol. I.
4. J. Priestley, *Navigable Rivers, Canals*, etc., 1831.
5. *A Case in relation to making the River Dun Navigable*, N.D. (*c.* 1731), Sheffield P.L.
6. For the period to 1750, see Professor T. S. Willan's *The Early History of the Don Navigation*, 1965
7. For the Idle and Trent navigations, see my *The Canals of the East Midlands*, 2nd ed., 1970.
8. Doncaster Corporation records, 2 November 1691, Cal. IV, p. 155.
9. Ralph Thoresby writes in 1703 of 'assisting Mr Kirk and Mr Arthington in taking a level for the new canal that is now making from the water engine . . . to the corn-mill (at Sprotbrough), whence he (Sir Godfrey Copley) can go by water to Coningsbury Castle on one hand, or Doncaster on the other'. J. Hunter ed., *Diary of Ralph Thoresby, F.R.S.*, 1830, Vol. I, pp. 412–13, but I know of no evidence that this mill canal was ever used for navigation.
10. Doncaster Corporation records, 18 November 1703 (Cal. IV, p. 161), 12 October 1704 (Cal. IV, p. 162), 30 October 1704 (Cal. IV, p. 163).
11. W. N. Slatcher, 'The Aire & Calder Navigation', Manchester University M.Sc. thesis, 1967, pp. 25ff.
12. Doncaster Corporation records, 22 December 1721 (Cal. IV, p. 187).
13. For the Mersey & Irwell, see Charles Hadfield & Gordon Biddle, *The Canals of North West England*, 1970.
14. Aire & Calder Navigation Minute Book, 5 January, 16 February 1722.
15. Palmer was a surveyor from York, who was later to be concerned with the navigation of the Ouse: Atkinson was the son of George Atkinson, who had helped to build the Aire & Calder, as had Joshua Mitchel, who had also been an undertaker on the Derwent.

16. *A Survey of the River Dunn*, by Will. Palmer & Partners, 1722. (Courtesy of Mr J. E. Day.)
17. Doncaster Corporation records, 7 January 1724 NS (Cal. IV, p. 193).
18. Doncaster Corporation records, 3 December 1724 (Cal. IV, pp. 194–5).
19. 12 Geo I *c.* 38.
20. The letters between John Smith and his wife while the Bill was in Parliament, 25 February to 7 May 1726, are in the Leader Collection, Sheffield P.L.
21. Don Navigation Account Book, B.T.H.R., DUN 4/1.
22. Alan Goodfellow, 'Sheffield's Waterway to the Sea' (*Trans. Hunter Arch. Soc.*), Vol. 5, 1937–43, p. 246.
23. Doncaster Corporation records, 23 December 1726 (Cal. IV, p. 199).
24. 13 Geo I *c.* 20.
25. The Sheffield group has issued shares for £95 each: the Doncaster group's at September 1721 were £85, so they called another £10 to equalize them at £95. Between this date and that of application for the Act, another £20 was called on both sets of shares, giving them the value of £115 quoted in the 1733 Act.
26. *A Case in relation to making the River Dun Navigable*, ND (*c.* 1731) (Sheffield P.L.).
27. Don Navigation Minute Book, 25 May 1731.
28. 6 Geo II *c.* 9.
29. J.H.C. xxii, 526, 547, 562.
30. J.H.C., 31 January 1740 NS.
31. 13 Geo II, *c.* 11.
32. J.H.C., 14, 19 February 1740 NS.
33. Don Navigation Minute Book, 10 August 1749.
34. Ibid.
35. Wedgwood papers.
36. *Yorkshire Journal*, 5 September 1789.
37. *York Courant*, 19 November 1771.
38. Ibid., 7 August 1764.
39. Don Navigation Minute Book, 9 August 1750.
40. Ibid., 22 March 1759.
41. Ibid., 14 August 1760.
42. For the Walkers, see T. S. Ashton, *Iron and Steel in the Industrial Revolution*, 2nd ed., 1951, pp. 46–8, John Guest, *Historic Notices of Rotherham*, 1879, pp. 485 et seq., and A. H. John, ed., *The Walker Family*, 1951.
43. Plan of this canal and surroundings, A. H. John, ed., *The Walker Family*, 1951, between pp. 8 and 9.
44. Don Navigation Minute Book, 11 August 1763.
45. Ibid., 14 August 1760.
46. Ibid., 24 June 1762.
47. Ibid., 11 August 1763.
48. Ibid., 25 October 1770.
49. For the dangers of the tide at Goole bridge, see William Jessop's report on the proposed Selby bridge, *York Courant*, 16 February 1790.
50. Survey done by John Needham, B.T.H.R., SYD 4/9.
51. Don Navigation Minute Book, 12 May 1769.
52. See Charles Hadfield, *The Canals of the East Midlands*, 2nd ed., 1970, p. 34.
53. *York Courant*, 4 August 1772. Plan in Sheffield P.L., and references in the catalogue there of the Rockingham letters.
54. Information from Mr J. E. Day.
55. *York Courant*, 14 September 1773.
56. Holland, *Tour of the Don*, II, pp. 325–6 (17 September 1836); Carlisle Canal Minute Book, 25 August 1837.
57. Don Navigation Minute Book, 8 August 1782.
58. Don Navigation Minute Book, 14 August 1783.
59. Ibid., 9 August 1787.
60. Wentworth Woodhouse MSS., MP 47. (Sheffield P.L.)
61. William Fairbank, *A Plan of a Navigable Canal made in the Township of Greas-*

borough by the late Marquis of Rockingham, 1783. (South Yorkshire Industrial Museum, Cusworth Hall, Doncaster.)
62. P. Rodgers, *Greasborough Ings . . . A Poem*, 1831. I am grateful to Mr. John Goodchild for this extract.
63. All the material for my account of these canals has been made available to me from the researches of Mr John Goodchild of the South Yorkshire Industrial Museum, Cusworth Hall, Doncaster, to whom I am greatly indebted.

Notes to Chapter IV

1. For most of the information in these paragraphs about the Hull River, I am indebted to Dr Michael Lewis.
2. Charles Frost, *Notices relative to the early History of the Town and Port of Hull*, 1827, pp. 128–9.
3. Henry Best, *Rural Economy in Yorkshire in 1641*, Surtees Society, Vol. 33, 1857, pp. 111–12.
4. George Poulson, *The History and Antiquities of the Seigneury of Holderness*, 1840, Vol. II, pp. 306–7.
5. For the drainage, see June A. Sheppard, 'The Draining of the Hull Valley', *East Yorkshire Local History Society*, 1958.
6. For the Beck generally, see K. A. Macmahon, 'Beverley and its Beck: Borough Finance and a Town Navigation, 1700–1835', *Transport History*, July 1971.
7. T. S. Willan, *River Navigation in England, 1600–1750*, 1936, p. 71.
8. 13 Geo I c. 4.
9. Willan, *River Navigation*, op. cit., p. 126.
10. J.H.C., 31 January, 8 February 1744.
11. 18 Geo II c. 13.
12. Beverley Corporation Minute Book, 4 May 1752.
13. Willan, *River Navigation*, op. cit., p. 5.
14. I am indebted to Baron F. Duckham for this suggestion.
15. *Reports of the late John Smeaton*, 1812, Vol. I, pp. 207–8. The cut was to leave the river at 'Townsend near Skerne', and alternative estimates for lines with and without a lock were given.
16. East Riding Record Office, DDSY 68/85. Most of the navigation's records are held by this office.
17. Preamble to Act of 1767.
18. 7 Geo. III c. 97.
19. *York Courant*, 21 November 1769.
20. Ibid., 1 May 1770.
21. Driffield Old Navigation Minute Book, 11 May 1769.
22. DDSY 68/141 (E.R.R.O.).
23. Driffield Old Navigation Minute Book, 1 July 1783.
24. For the background, see June A. Sheppard, 'The Draining of the Marshlands of South Holderness and the Vale of York' *East Yorkshire Local History Society*, 1966.
25. *York Courant*, 15 October 1765. *Reports of the Late John Smeaton*, 1812, Vol. I, pp. 234–5.
26. *York Courant*, 4 August 1767
27. Ibid., 23 April 1771.
28. 12 Geo II c. 37.
29. Joseph Priestley, *Navigable Rivers, Canals*, etc., 1831, p. 443.
30. Market Weighton Canal Commissioners' Minute Book, 3 September 1772. Minute books are held by the Market Weighton Drainage Board at Pocklington, some account books by Doncaster Museum, and other papers at the East Riding Record Office, Beverley.

31. *The Report of John Grundy, Esq: respecting the Drainage and Navigation proposed for Walling Fenns, &c.* 1772, East Riding Record office, DDCC 143/103.
32. *York Courant*, 10 November 1772
33. Market Weighton Canal Trustees' Minute Book, 3 July 1778.
34. Ed. Caine, *Strother's Journal*, 1784–5.
35. Market Weighton Canal Trustees' Minute Book, 2 June 1784.
36. *York Courant*, 29 September 1789.
37. E. Baines, *History, Directory & Gazetteer of the County of York*, Vol. 2.
38. DDMW/3 (E.R.R.O.).

Notes to Chapter V

1. This brief account of the Ouse is based, with his kind permission, upon Baron F. Duckham's excellent book *The Yorkshire Ouse*, 1967, which is a full account of the navigation's history.
2. Charter of the Lord Protector, 26 June 1657.
3. quo. Duckham, *Yorkshire Ouse*, p. 54.
4. 13 Geo I *c* 33.
5. 5 Geo II *c*. 15.
6. Duckham, *Yorkshire Ouse*, p. 66.
7. *York Courant*, 16 February 1790.
8. Ibid.
9. My account of the Derwent Navigation owes much to Baron F. Duckham, 'The Fitzwilliams and the Navigation of the Yorkshire Derwent', *Northern History*, 1967.
10. R. W. Unwin, 'The Aire and Calder Navigation. Part I: The Beginning of the Navigation', *The Bradford Antiquary*, November 1964. Appendix. I have punctuated the quotation.
11. W. N. Slatcher, 'The Aire and Calder Navigation', Manchester University M.Sc. thesis, 1967, pp. 22ff. See also F. Williamson, 'George Sorocold of Derby', *Journal Derbyshire Arch. & Nat. Hist. Soc.*, 1936 and F. Williamson & W. B. Crump, 'Sorocold's Water Works at Leeds', *Publications of the Thoresby Society*, 37, 1941, pp. 166–82.
12. 1 Anne *c*. 14.
13. ZCG IX 1–2, North Riding Record Office.
14. Ibid.
15. So Joseph Atkinson, one of the Aire & Calder lessees, says in a letter of 31 January 1744 (Slatcher, op. cit., pp. 126–7).
16. ZCG IX 1–2, North Riding Record Office.
17. *York Courrant*, 1 September 1772.
18. Rough MS minutes of meeting at Yedingham, 15 September 1772 (East Riding Record Office, DDSY/11).
19. *York Courant*, 22 September 1772.
20. For the Springs branch, see Charles Hadfield and Gordon Biddle, *The Canals of North West England*, 1970.
21. Duckham, op. cit. See also *A Register of Vessels in the North Riding*, made under the 1795 Act (North Riding Record Office), and B.T.H.R., DER 4/5.
22. Aire & Calder Navigation Undertakers' Minute Book, 20 September 1792.
23. R. W. Unwin, 'The Aire & Calder Navigation, Part I. The Beginning of the Navigation, *The Bradford Antiquary*, November 1964, appendix. I have punctuated the extract.
24. *Manchester Mercury*, 22 May 1753.
25. J.H.C., 14 March 1758.
26. Inf. from John Goodchild, from Pontefract Quarter Sessions Records, April 1756.
27. *Leeds Intelligencer*, 27 July 1762.

P

28. *York Courant*, 14 September 1762.
29. Ibid., 23 August 1763.
30. Ibid., 28 February 1764.
31. Ibid., 9 February 1773.
32. Graham S. Hudson, *The Aberford Railway and the History of the Garforth Collieries*, 1971, pp. 40–2. In spite of the cartouche of Dixon's survey, it is more likely that, like George Dixon's Cockfield Fell project (see p.114), this was for tub-boats and not for keels.
33. Aire & Calder Navigation Undertakers' Minute Book, 9 April 1779.
34. J.H.C., 12 February 1698 NS.
35. J.H.C., 15 February 1698 NS.
36. B.T.H.R., ACN 4/35.
37. J.H.C., 26 January, 4, 13 February 1736; York Corporation Minute Books, Vol. 42, pp. 218, 225.
38. York Corporation Minute Books, Vol. 43, p. 87.
39. *York Courant*, 16, 30 September 1766.
40. Ibid., 9 December 1766.
41. John Smeaton, *Plan of the River Ure* (North Riding C.R.O.).
42. William Grainger, *The Vale of Mowbray*, 1859, p. 80.
43. J.H.C., 26 January, 2 March 1767.
44. Ouse Navigation Trustees' Minute Book, 15 April 1767 (York P.L.).
45. 7 Geo III *c*. 96.
46. *A Survey of the River Swale*, 1767 (North Riding C.R.O.).
47. *York Courant*, 15 August 1769.
48. Ibid., 13 August 1771.
49. Market Weighton Canal Commissioners' Minute Book, 16 July 1772.
50. Jackson's report, 21 May 1768, Swale and Bedale Beck papers, Linton Lock Commissioners' records.
51. Ibid., 15 June 1768.
52. Ibid., 25 January 1769.
53. *York Courant*, 18 July 1780.
54. Ibid., 28 November 1769.
55. Ibid., 26 December 1769.
56. 10 Geo III *c*. 111.
57. *York Courant*, 10 September 1771.
58. Ibid., 7 September 1773.
59. Ibid., 4 September 1781.
60. Inf. from Mr J. G. Goodchild.
61. *York Courant*, 28 March 1775.
62. Ibid., 17 February 1778.
63. Ibid., 23 October 1781.
64. Ouse Navigation Trustees' Minute Book, 1 December 1787.
65. John Tuke, *A Map of the Rivers Ure & Ouse*, 1794 (North Riding C.R.O.).
66. 7 Geo III *c*. 95.
67. J.H.C., 2 March 1767.
68. Copy of undated plan (North Riding C.R.O.).
69. *London Chronicle*, 2–4 June 1767, quo. E. Thompson, *My Book of Thirsk*, 1947.
70. For the work at Thirsk, see Jennifer Tann, 'A Survey of Thirsk, Yorkshire', *Industrial Archaeology*, 1967, p. 246.
71. This was later taken down and converted into a bridge. W. Grainger, *The Vale of Mowbray*, 1859.
72. *York Courant*, 9 May 1769.
73. Ibid., 10 July 1770.
74. Ibid., 16 February 1779.
75. 7 Geo III *c*. 93.
76. Under an Act of 1692. See William Albert, 'The Justices' Rates for Land Carriage 1784–1827, Reconsidered', *Transport History*, I, 2 July 1968.
77. As stated in the 1820 Act.

78. *York Courant*, 28 April 1772.
79. Ibid., 16 February 1773.
80. *York Chronicle*, 11 April 1777.
81. *York Courant*, 20 November 1781.
82. I am indebted to Mr John Goodchild for these figures.
83. T. S. Turner, *History of Aldborough and Boroughbridge*, 1853.
84. Aire & Calder Navigation Undertakers' Minute Book, 6 July 1789.
85. Ibid., 27 August, 19 November 1792.
86. *York Courant*, 24 October 1769.
87. Ibid., 17 November, 22 December 1772
88. John Weatherill, 'Rievaulx Abbey', *Yorkshire Archaeological Journal*, Vol. XXXVIII.
89. North Riding Record Office, Strickland archive (ZCG).
90. I am indebted to Mr Percy Burnett of Whitby for this information.
91. North Riding Record Office, ZCG IV 5/1/1–4.
92. Inf. from Mr M. Wyatt Wheeler; see also J. Backhouse, *Lead Mining in Swaledale* (MS), p. 27 (Leeds P.L., MSQ 622.344 B12Y).
93. John Bailey, *General View of the Agriculture of the County of Durham*, 1810, p. 275.
94. Ibid., pp. 278–9.
95. *York Courant*, 20 October 1767.
96. Ibid., 8 December 1767.
97. E. Thompson, *My Book of Thirsk*, 1947.
98. This account is based on Tomlinson, *The North Eastern Railway*, 1914, Bailey, *A General View of the Agriculture of the County of Durham*, 1810, and the plan signed by Robert Whitworth in the August 1772 issue of the *Gentleman's Magazine*.
99. 3 Geo I.
100. 13 Geo I *c*. 6.
101. *A Plan of the River Wear from Newbridge to Sunderland Barr*, by Burleigh and Thompson (Manchester P.L. ff. 386 C9).
102. 20 Geo II *c*. 18.
103. J.H.C., 14 March 1759.
104. Letter 29 March 1759. Journal of the Court of Common Council, Vol. 62, fol. 2b (City of London Record Office). I am grateful to Mr J. H. Boyes for this reference.
105. 32 Geo II *c*. 64.
106. *A Plan of the River Wear from Biddick Ford to the City of Durham, with a Projection of a Navigation thereon*, by J. Smeaton. This has been shown to me by Mr J. H. Boyes. See also *Reports of the late John Smeaton*, 1812, Vol. I, pp. 18–20.
107. Jona. Thompson, *Observations*, Newcastle, 1795.
108. J.H.C., 20, 27 February 1710, NS.
109. *Reports of the late John Smeaton*, 1812, Vol. II, pp. 238–9.

Notes to Chapter VI

1. Aire & Calder Navigation Undertakers' Minute Book, 1 July 1793.
2. *Doncaster Gazette*, 3 August 1798.
3. For keels, see John Frank, 'Humber Keels', *Mariners' Mirror*, November 1955 and August 1958, and F. C. G. Carr, *Sailing Barges*, 1951, Ch. IX.
4. *Doncaster Gazette*, 30 April 1796.
5. Aire & Calder Navigation Undertakers' Minute Book, 7 May 1795.
6. Ibid., 7 August 1797.
7. *Hull Advertiser*, 16 August 1806.
8. *Doncaster Gazette*, 14 June 1811.
9. *Yorkshire Gazette*, 14 March 1795.
10. *Doncaster Gazette*, 2 April 1796.

11. Aire & Calder Navigation Undertakers' Minute Book, 16 April 1796.
12. Aire & Calder Navigation Committee Minute Book, 16 August 1798.
13. Aire & Calder Navigation Undertakers' Minute Book, 1 September 1799.
14. Ibid., 15 November 1804.
15. Ibid., 6 July 1807.
16. Ibid.
17. *Doncaster Gazette*, 8 July 1803.
18. Ibid., 20 January 1804.
19. Aire & Calder Navigation Undertakers' Minute Book, 6 July 1807.
20. Ibid., 6 August 1807.
21. Ibid., 2 April 1818.
22. *York Courant*, 6 July 1818.
23. Wilson, op. cit., Part III.
24. *Doncaster Gazette*, 2 July 1813; date from John Mayhall, *The Annals of Yorkshire*.
25. Ibid., 30 July 1813.
26. *Doncaster Gazette*, 11 September 1818.
27. Aire & Calder Navigation Report for July–June 1817–18 read 6 July 1818.
28. George Leather, *A Further Report . . . on the Stockton & Auckland Canal*, 1818, p. 12n. (Darlington P.L.).
29. John Rennie's report of 3 March 1820.
30. George Leather's report of 23 January 1822.
31. *Hull Advertiser*, 11 May 1816.
32. Ibid., 23 April 1819.
33. Calder & Hebble Navigation Directors' Minute Book, 9 June 1821.
34. Aire & Calder Navigation Undertakers' Minute Book, 7 July 1817.
35. 1 Geo IV *c.* 39.
36. Aire & Calder Navigation Directors' Minute Book, 21 July 1821.
37. Ibid., 7 February 1822.
38. Aire & Calder Navigation Report for 1828–9, read August 1829.
39. Ibid., 1823–4, read 2 August 1824.
40. *Hull Advertiser*, 20 September 1822.
41. Ibid., 29 March 1822.
42. Ibid., 25 June 1819.
43. Ibid., 20 June 1823.
44. Ibid., 1 July 1825.
45. Ibid., 20 May 1825.
46. Aire & Calder Navigation Directors' Minute Book, 10 March 1821.
47. *Hull Advertiser*, 15 June 1821, supported by Priestley's Report for 1820–1.
48. Aire & Calder Navigation Report for 1822–3, read 4 August 1823.
49. Thomas Baines, *Yorkshire Past and Present*, 1873.
50. Aire & Calder Navigation Report for 1823–4, read 2 August 1824.
51. Haxby MSS (South Yorkshire Industrial Museum, Cusworth Hall, Doncaster).
52. E. Baines, *History & Directory of Yorkshire*, I, 1822.
53. C. Forrest, *History & Antiquities of Knottingley*, 1871.
54. T. Langdale, *Topographical Dictionary of Yorkshire*, 2nd ed., 1822; *Doncaster Gazette*, 13 April 1827; W. White, *History & Directory of the West Riding*, II, 1838.
55. *Hull Advertiser*, 3 September 1824.
56. Ibid., 7 January 1825.
57. *The Times*, 2 August 1825.
58. For Goole generally, see Baron F. Duckham, *The Yorkshire Ouse*, 1967, and 'The Founding of Goole', *Industrial Archaeology*, 1967, pp. 19–28; also J. D. Porteous, *The Company Town of Goole*, University of Hull Occasional Papers in Geography No. 12, 1969.
59. *Hull Advertiser*, 21 July 1826.
60. Ibid., 14 July 1826.
61. Aire & Calder Navigation Minute Book, 7 August 1826.

62. *Hull Advertiser*, 4 August 1826.
63. Aire & Calder Navigation Directors' Minute Book, 31 December 1826.
64. John Marshall, *The Lancashire & Yorkshire Railway*, 1969, Vol. I, p. 201.
65. *Doncaster Gazette*, 5 September 1828.

Notes to Chapter VII

 1. Aire & Calder Navigation Report for 1827, read 4 August 1828.
 2. G. C. Dickinson, 'Stage-Coach Services in the West Riding of Yorkshire be-
    tween 1830 and 1840'. *Journal of Transport History*, May 1959.
 3. W. W. Morrell, *The History and Antiquities of Selby*, 1867.
 4. Leather's report of 31 July 1824.
 5. Aire & Calder Navigation Directors' Minute Book, 8 January 1825.
 6. Ibid., 5 December 1826.
 7. Plan in Fairbank papers, ECa 545 Sheffield P.L.
 8. *Prospectus of an intended Canal, from Wakefield to Ferrybridge* (South Yorkshire
    Industrial Museum, Cusworth Hall, Doncaster).
 9. Aire & Calder Navigation Directors' Minute Book, 5 December 1826.
10. Telford's report, B.T.H.R., ACN 1/28, 17 July 1827, and the deposited plan at
    Wakefield.
11. *The Times*, 6 February 1828, letter from 'A Subscriber for Ten Shares'.
12. Ibid., 15 February 1828, letter from 'Once a Subscriber for Ten Shares'.
13. 9 Geo IV *c*. 98.
14. Aire & Calder Navigation Report for 1829, read 2 August 1830.
15. Ibid., 1836, read 7 August 1837
16. Ibid., 1834, read 3 August 1835.
17. Ibid., 1832, read 5 August 1833.
18. Sir George Head, *A Home Tour through the Manufacturing Districts of England in
    the Summer of 1835*, 1836, pp. 234–5.
19. Aire & Calder Navigation Report for 1839, read 3 August 1840.
20. Thomas Moore papers 1835, Lancashire C.R.O.
21. Aire & Calder Navigation Report for 1839, read 3 August 1840.
22. Head, *A Home Tour*, op. cit., p. 227.
23. East Riding C.R.O., DDX 58/2.
24. Head, *A Home Tour*, op. cit., pp. 210ff., gives an account of being stranded
    between Selby and Goole.
25. For the promotion of the Leeds, Selby and Hull lines, see K. A. MacMahon,
    'The Beginnings of the East Yorkshire Railways', *East Yorkshire Local History
    Society*, 1953.
26. Aire & Calder Navigation Directors' Minute Book, 27 December 1830.
27. Ibid , 14 April 1834.
28. Ibid·, 28 January 1833.
29. *Doncaster Gazette*, 22 October 1830.
30. Head, *A Home Tour*, op. cit., pp. 231–2.
31. *Doncaster Gazette*, 30 October 1835.
32. Aire & Calder Navigation Report for 1834, read 3 August 1835.
33. *Accounts & Papers*, 1819 session.
34. Aire & Calder Navigation Report for 1824, read 1 August 1825.
35. *Hull Advertiser*, 7 July 1826.
36. Aire & Calder Navigation Report for 1833, read 4 August 1834.
37. Ibid., 1846, read 2 August 1847.
38. *Accounts & Papers*, 1837–8, Vol. X.
39. Generally, see W. L. Norman, 'The Wakefield Soke Mills to 1853', *Industrial
    Archaeology*, May 1970.
40. See Charles Hadfield and Gordon Biddle, *The Canals of North West England*,
    1970, pp. 172–3. For the prospectus, see B.T.H.R., PROS 2/1 (8).

41. Aire & Calder Navigation Report for 1845, read 3 August 1846.
42. Manchester & Leeds Railway Minute Book, 18 January 1836.
43. Ibid., 11 April 1836.
44. Aire & Calder Navigation Report for 1835, read 1 August 1836.
45. Manchester & Leeds Railway Minute Book, 3 May 1841.
46. Ibid., 26 August 1841.
47. Aire & Calder Navigation Report for 1837, read 6 August 1838.
48. Manchester & Leeds Railway Minute Book, 23 November 1840.
49. Aire & Calder Navigation Report for 1840, read 2 August 1841.
50. Ibid.
51. Aire & Calder Navigation Directors' Minute Book, 3 October 1842.
52. For the Calder & Hebble's story, see Chapter IX; for the Rochdale's, Charles Hadfield and Gordon Biddle, *The Canals of North West England*, 1970, Chapter X.
53. Aire & Calder Navigation Report for 1844, read 4 August 1845.
54. York & North Midland Railway Minute Book, 24 December 1844.
55. 7 Geo IV *c*. 46.
56. For this railway, see B. Baxter, *Stone Blocks and Iron Rails*, 1966, p. 167; *The Railway Magazine*, November 1937, pp. 375–7 and March 1938, p. 204 and pp. 224–5, and papers SCR 274–293 in Sheffield P.L.
57. 8 Geo IV *c*. 20.
58. Aire & Calder Navigation Directors' Minute Book, 20 October 1828.
59. Ibid., 9 July 1829.
60. *Doncaster Gazette*, 24 October 1828.
61. Ibid., 28 January 1831.
62. Barnsley Canal Committee Minute Book, 14 January 1833.
63. Aire & Calder Navigation Directors' Minute Book, 6 August 1832.

Notes to Chapter VIII

1. Aire & Calder Navigation Undertakers' Minute Book, 20 September 1792.
2. Aire & Calder Undertakers' Committee Minute Book, 2 July 1792.
3. Aire & Calder Navigation Undertakers' Minute Book, 27 August 1792.
4. Ibid., 6 September 1792.
5. Ibid., 20 September 1792.
6. Barnsley Canal Proprietors' Minute Book, 15 October 1792.
7. Elmhirst papers, EM 1714, Sheffield P.L.
8. For Stanhope, see W. N. Slatcher, 'The Barnsley Canal: its first twenty years', *Transport History*, March 1968.
9. Printed Barnsley Canal report of 8 July 1797 (South Yorkshire Industrial Museum, Cusworth Hall, Doncaster).
10. This line is shown on the map accompanying J. Hodskinson's report of 10 April 1793 *To the Committee . . . in opposition to the intended Warmfield cum Heath and Barnsley Canal* (South Yorkshire Industrial Museum, Cusworth Hall, Doncaster). For material about Beaumont's opposition, see the Bretton Hall MSS 116, Yorkshire Archaeological Society Library, Leeds.
11. *Reasons for opposing the two Bills for making Canals from . . . Heath to Barnsley . . . and Barnsley to Swinton . . .*, N.D. (Elmhirst papers, EM 1717, Sheffield P.L.)
12. J. Hodskinson's report of 10 April 1793.
13. Ibid.
14. 33 Geo III *c*. 110.
15. *Derby Mercury*, 10 October 1793.
16. *Doncaster Journal*, 5 October 1793.
17. *Doncaster Gazette*, 14 June 1799.
18. Ibid., 15 March 1805.
19. Printed committee report, 29 August 1807 (South Yorkshire Industrial Museum, Cusworth Hall, Doncaster).

20. J.H.C., LXIII, 1808, pp. 6, 38, 44, 215, quo. Slatcher, 'Barnsley Canal', op. cit.
21. Barnsley Canal Committee Minute Book, 29 August 1807.
22. 48 Geo III *c.* 13.
23. Don Navigation Minute Book, 15 November 1808.
24. For the tramroads, see B. Baxter, *Stone Blocks and Iron Rails*, 1966, pp. 170–1.
25. Barnsley Canal Proprietors' Minute Book, 14 September 1813.
26. Don Navigation Minute Book, 17 February 1803.
27. Barnsley Canal Minute Book, 21 September 1821.
28. Baxter, *Stone Blocks & Iron Rails*, op. cit., pp. 169–70.
29. Barnsley Canal Committee Minute Book, 20 November 1823.
30. Barnsley Canal Proprietors' Minute Book, 5 July 1826.
31. Ibid., 2 July 1828.
32. *Doncaster Gazette*, 8 January 1830.
33. Barnsley Canal Committee Minute Book, 24 September 1831.
34. Don Navigation Minute Book, 21 October 1831.
35. Ibid., 6 January 1832.
36. Barnsley Canal Committee Minute Book, 30 June 1838.
37. Ibid., 18 March 1842.
38. Barnsley Canal Proprietors' Minute Book, 6 July 1842.
39. Barnsley Canal Committee Minute Book, 30 December 1842.
40. Aire & Calder Navigation Directors' Minute Book, 23 May 1845.
41. Aire & Calder Navigation Report for 1845, dated 3 August 1846.
42. Don Navigation Minute Book, 24 January 1846. Barnsley Canal Committee Minute Book, 13 February 1846.
43. Aire & Calder Navigation Proprietors' Minute Book, 20 April 1846.

Notes to Chapter IX

1. Calder & Hebble Navigation Committee Minute Book, 24 February 1798.
2. Ibid., 23 December 1799.
3. Ibid., 13 October 1810.
4. Ibid., 5 March 1810.
5. Calder & Hebble Navigation Proprietors' Minute Book, midsummer 1819.
6. Ibid., 19 June 1823.
7. Ibid., 2 June 1825.
8. For the Bridgewater Canal, see Charles Hadfield & Gordon Biddle, *The Canals of North West England*, 1970.
9. Calder & Hebble Proprietors' Minute Book, midsummer 1816.
10. Calder & Hebble Navigation Committee Minute Book, 9 June 1821.
11. 6 Geo IV *c.* 17.
12. Calder & Hebble Navigation Committee Minute Book, 10 February 1827.
13. Ibid., 26 January 1828.
14. Sir George Head, *A Home Tour through the Manufacturing Districts of England in the Summer of 1835*, 1836, rept. 1968, pp. 126–7.
15. H. R. de Salis, *A Chronology of Inland Navigation*, 1897, p. 64.
16. Huddersfield Canal Minute Book, 24 June 1830.
17. Diary of Miss Anne Lister of Shibden Hall (MS), 14 April, 13 November 1829 (Halifax P.L.).
18. Calder & Hebble Navigation Committee Minute Book, 12 April 1828.
19. Memorandum of the Will of James Lister, Halifax P. L., SH:3:R&W 11.
20. Calder & Hebble Navigation Committee Minute Book, 12 December 1829.
21. Ibid., 5 June 1830.
22. Ibid., 20 November 1830.
23. Ibid., 22 January 1831.
24. Ibid., 2 April 1831.
25. Ibid., 3 December 1831.

26. Ibid., 15 March 1833.
27. Ibid., 15 November 1833.
28. Ibid., 13 February 1834.
29. 4 Will IV *c.* 12.
30. A MS copy is in Halifax P.L., SH:R&W 12.
31. Huddersfield Canal Minute Book, 25 April 1834.
32. Calder & Hebble Navigation Proprietors' Minute Book, 2 January 1836.
33. Calder & Hebble Navigation Committee Minute Book, 10 October 1835.
34. Ibid., 13 January 1836.
35. Manchester & Leeds Railway Minute Book, 22 January, 14 February 1838.
36. Calder & Hebble Navigation Proprietors' Minute Book, 21 June 1838.
37. *Derby Mercury*, 30 November 1842.
38. Calder & Hebble Navigation Committee Minute Book, 10 January 1843.
39. This letter is quoted in Charles Hadfield & Gordon Biddle, *The Canals of North West England*, 1970, p. 290. The account of the Rochdale Canal in this book should be read together with that given here.
40. Calder & Hebble Navigation Committee Minute Book, 2 March 1843.
41. Ibid., 13 March 1843.
42. Ibid., 20 March 1843.
43. Manchester & Leeds Railway Minute Book, LY 1/12, 27 March 1843.
44. Aire & Calder Navigation Directors' Minute Book, 24 September 1845.
45. Calder & Hebble Navigation Committee Minute Book, 21 January 1847.
46. Manchester & Leeds Railway Minute Book, 5 March 1847.
47. Aire & Calder Navigation Directors' Minute Book, 2 August 1847.
48. *Hull Advertiser*, 9 April 1796.
49. Ibid., 16 December 1797.
50. For these, see Charles Hadfield & Gordon Biddle, *The Canals of North West England*, 1970.
51. 8 & 9 Vic. *c.* 105.
52. 10 & 11 Vic *c.* 159.

Notes to Chapter X

1. *Doncaster Gazette*, 12 February 1802.
2. Ibid., 25 November 1803.
3. Don Navigation Minute Book, 24 October 1798.
4. *Doncaster Gazette*, 11 July 1800.
5. Don Navigation Minute Book, 21 February 1800.
6. Ibid., 10 September 1800.
7. *Doncaster Gazette*, 26 December 1800.
8. Sheffield Public Library. His first report is dated 11 February 1801. It mainly supports the Kirk Sandall to Stainforth cut, a new cut and lock at Doncaster, and works to increase depth across shallows. The second is undated, and much fuller.
9. *Doncaster Gazette*, 11 September 1801.
10. Don Navigation Minute Book, 16 August 1808.
11. *Doncaster Gazette*, 16 September 1801.
12. Ibid., 27 January 1809, *Hull Advertiser*, 10 March 1810.
13. Ibid., 9 August 1816.
14. *Hull Advertiser*, 4 April 1818.
15. *Doncaster Gazette*, 22 December 1820, 2 February 1821.
16. *Yorkshire Journal*, 26 January 1788, 12 December 1789.
17. *Doncaster Gazette*, 20 January 1797, 22 November 1799.
18. Ibid., 27 December 1799.
19. Ibid., 9 November 1804.
20. Ibid., 30 January 1807.

21. Ibid., 18 October 1811, 15 July 1814.
22. Joan M. Eyles, 'William Smith: Some Aspects of his Life and Work', *Towards a History of Geology* (M.I.T.), 1969.
23. For the Somersetshire Coal Canal and the Sussex Ouse, see Charles Hadfield, *The Canals of South & South East England*, 1969.
24. *York Courant*, 11 January 1819.
25. Don Navigation Minute Book, 5 May 1819.
26. Goole Public Library, Garside Collection.
27. *Doncaster Gazette*, 19 November 1819.
28. Doncaster Corporation records, 28 October 1819 (Cal IV, p. 286).
29. *Doncaster Gazette*, 10 September 1819, J.H.C., 9 December 1819.
30. Goole Public Library, Garside Collection.
31. Don Navigation Minute Book, 10 November 1820, 5 January 1821: Aire & Calder Navigation Directors' Minute Book, 26 January and 14 November 1821, 16 December 1822: *Doncaster Gazette*, 15 September, 8, 29 December 1820, 19 January, 2 February, 16 March, 6 April, 4 May, 13 September 1822, 1 October 1824.
32. Don Navigation Minute Book, 18 August 1820.
33. 2 Geo IV *c*. 46.
34. *Doncaster Gazette*, 26 July 1822.
35. Don Navigation Minute Book, 25 February 1824.
36. 7 Geo IV *c*. 97.
37. J. Priestley, *Navigable Rivers, Canals, etc.*, 1831.
38. See *Doncaster Gazette*, 28 December 1827.
39. Aire & Calder Navigation Minute Book, 27 November 1828.
40. Don Navigation Minute Book, 10 September 1830.
41. Ibid., 26 November 1830.
42. *A Home Tour through the Manufacturing Districts of England in the Summer of 1835*, p. 215.
43. Don Navigation Minute Book, 20 November 1834.
44. *Doncaster Gazette*, 11 April 1845.
45. Don Navigation Minute Book, 3 October 1834.
46. For these, see Jean Lindsay, *The Canals of Scotland*, 1968, and Charles Hadfield and Gordon Biddle, *The Canals of North West England*, 1970.
47. Don Navigation Minute Book, 4 February 1840.
48. *Doncaster Gazette*, 26 May 1843.
49. In 1833 they were let for £250 p.a. See *Doncaster Gazette*, 20 December 1833, report of evidence given before the Municipal Corporation Commission.
50. Ibid., 23 February 1841.
51. Don Navigation Minute Book, 4 October 1844.
52. Aire & Calder Navigation Committee Minute Book, 23 May 1845.
53. For a history of the South Yorkshire company on the railway side, see George Dow, *Great Central*, 1959, I, Chapter XVI.
54. Don Navigation Minute Book, 14 April 1848.
55. *Doncaster Journal*, 7 December 1793.
56. The branch canal and tramroads are shown on a map of 1835–6 showing the proposed Sheffield & Rotherham Railway (Sheffield P.L., SP 60). The 'Canal at the New Beggin', is referred to in an advertisement for the sale of a sloop, *Doncaster Gazette*, 29 November 1833.
57. SP 59, Sheffield Public Library.
58. SP 60, Sheffield Public Library.
59. 6 & 7 William IV *c*. 109
60. Information from Mr. John Goodchild.

INDEX TO VOLUME I

The principal references to canals and river navigations are indicated in bold type